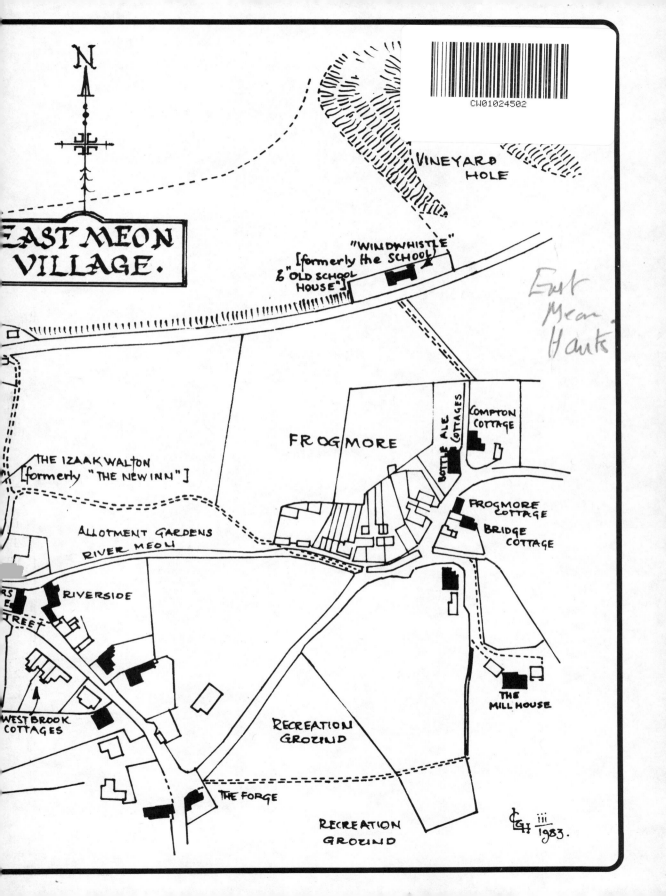

EAST MEON VILLAGE.

N

VINEYARD HOLE

"WINDWHISTLE"
[formerly the SCHOOL
& "OLD SCHOOL
HOUSE"]

East
Meon.
Hants

FROGMORE

BOTTLE ALE COTTAGES

COMPTON COTTAGE

THE IZAAK WALTON
[formerly "THE NEW INN"]

FROGMORE COTTAGE

BRIDGE COTTAGE

ALLOTMENT GARDENS
RIVER MEON

RIVERSIDE

RS
STREET

WEST BROOK COTTAGES

THE MILL HOUSE

RECREATION GROUND

THE FORGE

RECREATION GROUND

CGH iii 1983.

A HISTORY OF
EAST MEON

Frontispiece: All Saints' Church (Photo: Stan Smith)

A History of
EAST MEON

F. G. Standfield

Phillimore

1984
Published by
PHILLIMORE & CO. LTD.
Shopwyke Hall, Chichester, Sussex

ISBN 0 85033 495 0

Printed and bound in Great Britain by
BILLING & SONS LTD
Worcester, England

To the people of East Meon

CONTENTS

LIST OF PLATES
(between pages 44 and 45)

LIST OF TEXT ILLUSTRATIONS

ACKNOWLEDGEMENTS

When a lawyer has the temerity to write an historical work he depends heavily upon the expertise and good nature of professionals, as I soon discovered after embarking on this venture four years ago. They must be a kindly race, for, without exception, every enquiry has elicited a tolerant and patient response, besides yielding invaluable information. Space alone prevents my naming the many authors, lecturers, librarians, archivists and museum curators to whom I owe immense gratitude; though I am particularly indebted to Dr. Peter Reynolds (director of the Butser Ancient Farm Research Project) for reading and constructively criticising Chapter 1, to archivist Elspeth Griffiths who has spent many hours translating and transcribing early manorial and pipe rolls, and to the staff of the Hampshire Record Office whom I have badgered times out of number.

Bill Whiteman, neighbouring Steep's historian, generously put at my disposal much of his material (for East Meon and Steep were formerly within the same hundred), and has thrown light on otherwise obscure Anglo-Saxon charters; Arthur Gill helpfully loaned me a copy of the late Carol Rosen's extensive historical notes; cartographer Leslie Holden, a perfectionist, took great pains over preparation of village and parochial maps; and Irene Hewitt (possessing the specialist skill of deciphering my handwriting) cheerfully typed, re-typed and again re-typed my tortuous drafts.

As for pictures, I thank the following for permission to reproduce photographs: the Trustees of the British Museum for nos. 3 and 4, the Fleet Photographic Unit for no. 45 and the many residents, past and present, of East Meon who have loaned numerous old and treasured photographs of people, places and events. Contemporary pictures, other than those mentioned above, are the work of two highly skilled photographers, my good friends Guy Gravett (nos. 1, 2, 19, 20, 22, 24, 26, 28, 36, 52-6, 58-61, 63, 64 and 66) and Stan Smith (nos. 51, 57, 62, 65, 67 and 68), the latter having also expended much time copying countless old, faded and damaged picture postcards and other photographs from which those used have been selected.

Finally, my sincere thanks are due to dozens of parishioners, former parishioners and their descendants, many elderly (including a prolific correspondent in Australia) who have endured my probing cross-examination. Without their help and the ever available guidance of Phillimore & Co. Ltd. nothing would have been possible. The shortcomings are of course entirely my own responsibility.

F.G.S.

Forge Cottage,
East Meon.

1984

EDITORIAL METHOD

In quoting from numerous documents spaced over 2,000 years, some degree of editing has been desirable, mainly to render quotations more readable and intelligible. Original spellings, however eccentric or inconsistent, have been retained, but use of capital letters has been adjusted to conform with modern usage, and punctuation, or its lack, similarly updated (though generally unchanged in wills and other legal documents, which have always been, and still are, usually devoid of punctuation). The initial 'ff' has been reproduced as a capital letter, 'ye' as 'the' and numerals and the ampersand as written, subject only to Roman numerals being converted to Arabic.

Abbreviations and contractions have been extended, and the words 'Imprimis' and 'Item', both constantly used in wills and inventories, have been omitted. Monetary references are always to pre-decimalisation terms—usually pounds, shillings and pence, except where (especially in wills and inventories) there is specific mention of sovereigns, marks, angels, crowns or groats. As for dates, the year of each early pipe roll (or rent roll) of the Bishopric of Winchester normally ran from Michaelmas to Michaelmas, and as Lord Beveridge has dated these rolls according to each opening Michaelmas, that system has been followed. Other dates have been reproduced as in the text of documents quoted— i.e. with the civil and legal calendar year, prior to 1752, beginning on 25 March.

The only exception to what has been said above arises in relation to the copy will, inventory and copy surrender (on pages 28, 30 and 38 respectively), where the transcripts on the facing pages or below are virtually facsimile.

ABBREVIATIONS

H.M.S.O.	Her Majesty's Stationery Office
H.R.O.	Hampshire Record Office, Winchester
Parl. R.	Parliamentary Reports
P.R.O.	Public Record Office, London
V.C.H.	Victoria County History of England

INTRODUCTION

Waking to the clang of a nearby anvil and the persistent, pleasantly monotonous bleating of sheep on surrounding hills is no bad beginning to the day. Twenty odd years ago these timeless sounds roused me, a newcomer to East Meon, as they had greeted others for 1,000 years and more. The village's antiquity was obvious—Georgian and Tudor houses, a medieval Court Hall, Norman church, and nearby Roman villas, an Iron Age hill-fort, 'Celtic' fields and many a Bronze Age burial mound. Enquiry showed that Meone (formerly embracing East and West Meon) belonged to King Alfred, who willed it to his younger son in 899; and thereafter, for nearly 800 years, East Meon was part of the huge estates of successive bishops of Winchester—southern England's biggest landowners. Surely, it seemed, there could be a story waiting to be told.

After fruitful research, and faced with an embarrassment of riches, ruthless selectivity was needed; for compilation of an encyclopaedic tome crammed with the minutiae of countless past generations might constitute a challenging academic exercise, but who would read it? Accordingly, much fact and rather less comment has been jettisoned, with the optimistic aim of producing a narrative that is neither superficial, unduly disjointed nor pretentiously erudite. Again, though local history has ceased to be the Cinderella among historical studies, its appeal remains limited; so I have tried to broaden parochial horizons by occasionally weaving East Meon's history into the vastly wider saga of our nation, believing the happenings of an ancient village are, in microcosm, the happenings of England; and, as an old downland village had, and still has its own characteristics, those qualities must be shared by hundreds of other such villages.

This brings me to 'the golden hoof', an expression possibly sounding reminiscent of Greek mythology, but in fact reflecting the vital link between sheep husbandry and man's evolution over many millenia. Sheep had been domesticated in South-West Asia around 9000 B.C., and by 1000 B.C. wool production was well established in Babylonia. In the dim days of our own prehistory, long before Julius Caesar's arrival in 55 B.C., sheep's wool clothed homo sapiens, sheep's milk nourished him and sheep's dung fertilised the soil he tilled. As Professor Barry Cunliffe has written, 'the symbiosis between sheep and fertile arable land cannot be over-stressed . . . without large flocks, grain production on its Iron Age level would have been impossible to maintain'.

Roman Britain was more than the granary of the north, exporting woollen products, probably manufactured at Winchester; whilst later, Saxon dairying was based on sheep and goats, and both wool and manufactured garments were exported. Thus, in the distant past, the economic importance of sheep depended mainly on their wool and milk production, their land fertilisation, and, to a far lesser extent, their meat.

As for Middle Age farmers, Jean Gimpel, in *The Medieval Machine*, says 'manure was highly prized . . . a rare and precious product, none of which must be wasted. The most blessed of all the animals was the sheep. They were led ceremoniously to fertilise the fallow land and a sheep's hoof was known, justifiably, as the golden hoof'. The educational boom of the 12th century created an increased demand for parchment (sheep's skins); and by the 14th century wool, England's main raw material, was exported on a huge scale —35,000 sacks per annum. Then, between the mid-14th and 15th centuries, manufacture of cloth expanded dramatically, and a hundred years later an estimated 160,000 broadcloths, as well as 250,000 kersies were being produced annually. Sheep are believed to have outnumbered humans by three to one, and, on the debit side, widespread enclosures and depopulation in rural areas caused unemployment and much misery among landless labourers.

An agrarian revolution had occurred, English wool was reputed the best in Europe, and we became the leading textile manufacturing nation, with resulting national wealth, prosperity and power. At local level, cloth production in Petersfield, the small market town five miles from East Meon, allegedly employed 1,000 people in James I's reign, many of whom must have been recruited from surrounding villages.

The following pages will show how, in the 16th and 17th centuries, sheep became tantamount to a form of currency, many a death-bed testator finding it natural to bequeath legacies to the Church, to faithful servants and to his family and godchildren in the form of sheep or lambs; and after Acts of 1667 and 1668, burial in wool was obligatory—even corpses could not escape the affinity that first burgeoned thousands of years earlier.

Today, largely due to E.E.C. subsidies, East Meon's pastures (and Britain's) are more thickly dotted with sheep than for decades. In spite of man-made fibres and artificial fertilisers, sheep farming still plays a tremendously important part in the nation's largest primary industry—agriculture. The hoof remains golden.

Chapter One

EARLIEST DAYS

MEDIEVAL EAST MEON was always an important place—the settlement, the manor, the church, the hundred, and finally the parish. Although it emerged from the mists of antiquity only after the post-Roman Anglo-Saxon invasions, the history of even earlier periods is an inseparable part of any account of the region.

Man had first arrived in Britain, then part of the European Continent, between ice ages or during a warmer period of an ice age. At Portchester, on the downland slopes overlooking Portsmouth, flint tools and horse bones estimated to be 120,000 years old have been excavated; and on the fringe of East Meon parish, near the summit of Butser Hill, a Palaeolithic hand-axe approaching that age was found. Thereafter, the last ice age precluded human existence till its final retreat about 10,000 B.C., whereupon man returned. The climate grew warmer, producing tundra-like vegetation at first, and dense forests later. About 6000 B.C. geological changes resulted in the North Sea and English Channel coming into existence, and, for the first time, Britain became a group of islands.

The climate continued to improve during the succeeding Late Mesolithic Period (very approximately 6000–3200 B.C.), oak, alder, elm and lime predominated in the forests, and deer, wild cattle and boar were hunted. Flint tools and weapons of this period have been recovered at Old Winchester Hill, Butser Hill and Salt Hill, probably evidencing seasonal hunting camps, for men were still leading a semi-nomadic rather than a settled existence. There were flint-working sites on Butser Hill and Windmill Hill, Chalton.

The great pedestrian highway leading from Dover and Beachy Head to Salisbury Plain, then the centre of civilisation in England, was already in use.[1] The section known as the South Hampshire Ridgeway traversed (and still traverses) the southern part of what is now East Meon parish, passing from Butser Hill over Tegdown, Hyden Hill and Long Down before leaving the parish and continuing over Teglease crossroads and Old Winchester Hill and thence westwards.

Part of this ancient track, extending for 80 miles from Beachy Head to Buriton, near Petersfield, is still used, having become the splendid long-distance public footpath called the South Downs Way. The whole highway has been trodden by invaders, colonisers, traders and others pushing west from mainland Europe for thousands of years, certainly well before part of it became the route linking the chain of Iron Age forts referred to below. It may even have existed before the sea separated Britain from the rest of Europe. So, whilst there were no known 'permanent residents' in and around East Meon, still less anything resembling a village, the area was used by the so-called 'hunter-gatherers', and innumerable travellers passed through.

The Neolithic Age (roughly 3200–2000 B.C.), saw the gradual introduction of farming into Britain. The cultivation of cereals and other crops and the domestication of animals had begun in the Middle East soon after 8000 B.C. Very gradually, westward migration reached our shores, bringing new ideas and techniques. As Sir Arthur Bryant has written:[2]

> The earliest of all were traders in tin and copper from the Mediterranean . . . Such pioneers brought with them a knowledge of agriculture; of grain growing and domestic animals, of the hoe, spade and grinding-stone; of weaving clothes and fashioning pots of clay.

Southern England's downland was readily accessible to colonists, and moreover the vegetation of bushes and scrub lent itself to slow clearance by generations of goats, sheep and pigs, aided by man's simple implements. Small settlements were created consisting of groups of huts which, together with tillage and pasturage, laid the foundations of a settled life. Cereals such as emmer, einkorn and six-row barley were introduced, but corn-growing for long remained subsidiary to pastoral and semi-nomadic farming. Population size is unknown, the greatest problem in forming an estimate being the continual discovery of more and more sites.

The visible evidence of these distant transitional times consists of henge monuments, causewayed enclosures and long barrows. Such barrows were elongated mounds, many having contained a burial structure. East Meon's long barrow, officially described as being 'of Wessex type with flanking ditches, orientated NE–SW', lies on Salt Hill, half a mile north of the Ridgeway. Its existence, coupled with that of a Neolithic site on Oxenbourne Down, thought to have been an implement factory; the finding there (in 1919) of a polished Neolithic axe; discovery nearby of re-chipped axes and leaf-shaped arrowheads; and the finding (in 1934) of a flint knife in Hen Wood collectively add to our scant knowledge of the period.

The succeeding Bronze Age extended, very approximately, from about 2000–700 B.C., the main significance of the period being introduction of new ideas and techniques by fresh waves of immigrants—probably colonists rather than invaders, for there is no evidence of warfare. These men, believed by some to have originated in Portugal and by others to have moved from eastern Europe via the Low Countries, arrived in Dorset from Brittany, established themselves in Wessex, were absorbed by the natives, and dominated southern Britain for 1,000 years. With their knowledge of metal working they built up a remarkable 'Wessex Culture', with wide-flung trade connections. Farmers as well as warriors, they exploited the existing agricultural beginnings, though pasturing their flocks may no longer have taken precedence over corn growing; and old trackways were developed into a system of prehistoric communications.

At first, burials took place singly in the well-known round barrows, each accompanied by a beaker and other grave goods—hence the title of 'Beaker Folk'. Later, burials in flat graves became customary. Barrows were usually sited on high ground, particularly downland ridges or 'false crests', and frequently close to tradeways. East Meon parish and its immediate vicinity have a wealth of these barrows, especially near the line of the Ridgeway. They can be seen on Butser Hill, at Hyden Hill, Hyden Cross, Hyden Wood, Long Down, Teglease Down, Old Winchester Hill, War Hill, Dollys Firs, Tigwell Farm, Lower Bordean, near Drayton House, and (of course) on Barrow Hill. Even that list is far from exhaustive.

As well as barrows, there are Bronze Age (or slightly later) earthworks, called 'cross ridge dykes', on Butser Hill and Hyden Hill, the latter including a series of two banks and three ditches astride the Ridgeway and extending for half a mile. The precise purpose of these earthworks is uncertain, but according to Professor Barry Cunliffe:[3]

Probably between 1500 and 500 B.C. communal centres, comprising large tracts of hill plateaux defined by banks and ditches cutting off the adjacent spurs came into existence. One is known on Butser Hill. It may be suggested that such enclosures provided places of assembly for the tribe at certain times of the year.

Evidence of actual Bronze Age occupation sites is comparatively scarce, though mention must be made of the garden of Westbury Cottage, which actually abuts on to East Meon's western parish boundary. There in 1971 the occupier, schoolmaster George Walker, discovered the base of a large pottery vessel, which prompted further archaeological examination of the fruit garden, leading to dramatic results. For a time horticulture was abandoned, and Walker and Elizabeth Lewis (now curator of Winchester City Museum) stripped a considerable area to the natural chalk.

After patient and skilful work their finds included a quantity of Middle Bronze Age pottery, fragments of Sussex ironstone querns, fragments of sandstone whetstones, a flint tanged arrowhead and other artefacts of flint and bone as well as numerous bones of horses, oxen, sheep, goats and pigs. The conclusions are that a circular hut having a diameter of 12–15 feet stood on a levelled chalk floor during the Middle Bronze Age, perhaps about 1200 B.C., and that the flint arrowhead and a beaker sherd could be evidence of far earlier occupation.[4] It only remains to add that this small cottage garden has also yielded scattered finds of Iron Age, Roman and medieval date, thereby raising the possibility of more or less continuous site occupation for 3,000–4,000 years.

Other finds in East Meon parish include an Early Bronze Age, or possibly Late Neolithic hollow-based flint arrowhead (on Park Farm), a Middle Bronze Age spear tip (at Hilhampton Bottom), and a Late Bronze Age urn (at Coombe); whilst just beyond the parish, a bronze knife and chisel were excavated from a Froxfield burial mound in 1888, Bronze Age pottery has been recovered from the demonstration area and research sites of the Butser Ancient Farm, and yet another Bronze Age site existed at Chalton, just south-east of East Meon, in the late second millennium B.C.

The Iron Age succeeded the Bronze Age, and extended from approximately 700 B.C. until the Roman Conquest that began in A.D. 43. The transition from one period to the other was gradual, extended over many years, and it was formerly assumed that waves of warlike Celtic Continental invaders brought the new ideas and techniques as they overran the indigenous people. More recent thought accepts the possibility of changes resulting either from trading contacts (which were undoubtedly extensive), non-hostile colonisation, or sporadic raiders who, to quote Julius Caesar, 'came to raid and stayed to till'. The truth may well lie in a combination of each of these theories.

By far the most impressive local legacy of the Iron Age is Old Winchester Hill, a downland hill-fort 650 feet above sea level, sited half a mile beyond the parish's western boundary. The single ditch and bank, still measuring 18 to 23 feet vertically from crest to ditch, enclose, within an almost regular oval, an area of approximately 14 acres. Openings at the east and west parts of the perimeter, guarded by inturned ends to the bank, allow the South Hampshire Ridgeway to pass straight through. 'Celtic fields' run almost up to the ramparts.[5]

The primary purpose of this hill-fort and tribal centre, one of a chain of five stretching from St Catherine's Hill, near Winchester, to Cissbury Ring in the east, was to defend local tribes against enemies, whether from overseas or nearer. Old Winchester Hill juts into and commands the Meon Valley 400 feet below, and in times of actual or anticipated attack, families from the surrounding area, together with their livestock, would doubtless have taken refuge within the fort until the enemy had passed on or been repelled.

Most hill-forts were inhabited to some extent on a permanent basis, though it is unknown whether residents merely represented lookout men, maintenance workers and the nucleus of a garrison, or whether each hill-fort represented a 'hill-town', a sort of service industrial complex, as distinct from the farms which represented a production industry. Lack of ready access to water would have presented problems, yet it seems unlikely that after the tremendous united effort required to construct such massive defence works with simple tools—shoulder blades of cattle for shovels, deer antlers for picks, and baskets for transport, the fort would have been left unguarded and unmaintained. A group of three round Bronze Age barrows sited within the perimeter, are prima facie evidence of the enormous respect shown for religious monuments by a people who lived hundreds of years later. There is a possibility that the fort might date back to the Late Bronze Age, though the more widely held view puts it at about 250 B.C.

Today, Old Winchester Hill and adjacent downland totalling 150 acres, is a National Nature Reserve, accessible to the public. Turf that has never known artificial fertilisers or chemical sprays is grazed by rabbits, assisted by sheep. Myriad wild flowers, including cowslips, violets, harebells, scabious, thyme, and 14 species of orchid, bloom between spring and autumn, insects and butterflies abound, and, notwithstanding human disturbance, birds and wild mammals use the natural and varied habitat. It is a lovely place.

Less spectacular than Old Winchester Hill are the innumerable fields and field systems scattered over the parish's higher ground. The first Bronze Age plots for cultivation of cereals were small and irregular in shape, followed by Iron Age 'Celtic fields' of more regular rectangular shape, the typical area of each being half to one and a half acres. Such fields, sometimes called 'contour lynchets' where they gradually became more or less levelled out from gentle slopes, exist just north of Hyden Cross, on the western sides of Salt Hill and Hen Wood, and north of War Hill.

The name of Salt Hill is a reminder that salt was an important product, being a condiment; used in leather production; and, perhaps most important, as a preservative for meat and fish. Iron Age saltern sites existed in Chichester and Portsmouth harbours, on Hayling Island, and the Isle of Wight; and Salt Hill and adjoining Salt Lane (the latter ancient track running north from the Ridgeway to Coombe Cross) may well have derived their name from a packhorse route by which the precious commodity was brought inland for many hundreds of years.

After over 2,000 years, 'Celtic fields' are readily visible, even to the inexpert eye, standing out particularly clearly when the low-angled sun shines on bare winter landscapes. Equally surprising, the extent of Iron Age downland cultivation is believed to have comprised two-thirds of that cultivated today. Moreover, Celtic farmers, with their ox-drawn 'ploughs' (strictly speaking, *ards,* which broke up and stirred the soil rather than inverting it) were strikingly successful in spite of their obvious limitations. Cattle, goats, pigs and, increasingly, sheep were reared, whilst wheat, barley and oats were grown, the livestock fertilising arable ground prior to ploughing and sowing. Sheep had the special merit of being least dependent on a regular supply of drinking water, and were relatively easy to maintain during autumn and winter. Dr. Peter Reynolds, director of the Butser Experimental Iron Age Farm, estimates that the grain yield obtained by Late Iron Age farmers could have reached two tons per acre, comparable to that of the present day.[6] Corn and leather were exported to the Continent in exchange for commodities unavailable here, and wool spun into yarn and woven into cloth, probably on a 'cottage industry' basis, judging by the widespread evidence of clay and stone loom-weights.

In the two centuries preceding the Roman Conquest, further incursions by warlike bands from north-western Gaul contributed to a time of turmoil. About the same time, coins appeared, coming from France and Belgium through trade or invasion, and before long copies derived from these were minted in Britain. The recently excavated Hayling Island Iron Age temple (which preceded the Roman temple on the same site) has yielded a vast number of coins and other objects that tell us much of contemporary civilisation.[7]

The temple is thought to have been erected in the second half of the first century B.C. when the area was probably occupied by or under the sway of the Belgic tribe of the Atrebates. Objects recovered include bronze spiral finger rings, bracelets and tweezers; bracelets of shale and glass; decorated glass beads; fragments of hand mirrors; horse and vehicle trappings, including a three-link bridle-bit of cast bronze; and iron currency bars. As for Celtic coins, 92 were found in the first three seasonal excavations, covering the period from about 50 B.C.–A.D. 40, many having originated in Britain, and others in Continental Gaul.

Let us pause to summarise what is known of life in and around the present East Meon parish just over 2,000 years ago. Agriculture was the basic occupation, certainly extending over the downland's gentler slopes, and involving virtually everyone in the area, possibly excepting a warrior elite. We know from the writings of Pytheas, a Greek trader who visited Britain in the fourth century B.C., that corn was collected in sheaves and threshed in barns. The bottom of the river valley may have been too badly drained and choked with dense vegetation to be cultivated, but this is by no means certain, for other river valleys, including those of the Thames, Severn and Avon, are known to have been densely occupied. As for houses, Iron Age dwellings were round with thatched roofs, some of substantial size, but beyond that a degree of speculation is necessary. Nevertheless, evidence largely based upon post-holes, has led to the construction at the Butser Experimental Farm of conjectural versions of such houses, which would have provided shelter and warmth at scattered farmsteads. Villages in valley sites were not to originate until five or six hundred years later; for, with farms possibly well under a mile apart, villages, or even hamlets, would not have been needed, especially if a local 'town'—e.g. the fort on Old Winchester Hill, were not far away.

We are not discussing wild, half-naked savages, but a race of people who, as warriors, impressed Caesar in 55 and 54 B.C.,[8] and whose artisans included highly skilled carpenters, blacksmiths, silversmiths and goldsmiths. As for agricultural efficiency, Reynolds says there is a greater gap between the agriculture of today and 30 years ago than 30 years ago and 300 B.C.!

In the spring of A.D. 43 the Roman invasion of Britain, launched from Boulogne with a force of 40,000 men, achieved victory at the first battle of the Medway, and within weeks south-eastern England was under Roman control. Factors contributing towards triggering off the invasion could have included the desire of Emperor Claudius for glory, and the need to improve his image; support from some British tribes for rebellions in Gaul; and the fabled wealth of Britain, with its corn, wool, tin, oysters and pearls, some of which was already being exported.

Part of the native *Atrebatic* territory, stretching from Beachy Head to the River Meon, was occupied by people known as the *Regni*, whose capital, *Noviomagus*, was at Chichester. Before the invasion they were pro-Roman, and almost immediately after, a client king, Tiberius Claudius Cogidubnus, appeared on the scene. It is uncertain whether he was selected by the Romans from the local ruling household after their arrival, or, more probably, was previously living in exile and brought over with the Roman army. He faithfully supported Rome into the 70s and 80s, was styled 'King and legate to the emperor in Britain',[9] and the palace, the finest outside Italy, built at Fishbourne, near Chichester, about 30 years after the invasion, may have been constructed for him.

The spread of Roman occupation to north and west Britain took many years, and was never complete, yet central southern England was under Roman control for 367 years, longer than the period from the English Civil War till today; so consequential changes were of a gradual and progressive nature. The most striking change was that men ceased to live in fear of foreign invasion or violence and bloodshed caused by internal tribal rivalry. No longer was it necessary to maintain Old Winchester Hill as a fort guarding the district against seaborne and other attacks. The next most important change was an increase in the extent of cultivated land. Downland farming continued much as before, though with a tendency for fields to be laid out with greater regimentation, and for many small square fields to be replaced by larger rectangular ones; but better organisation, greater efficiency, and, probably an expanding population, led to cultivation of additional rich but heavier valley soil.

At least 40 'villas'—farmhouses varying considerably in size and importance—are known within the *Regni* territory. Concentrated in good farming country, as time passed they were built by Romanised Britons in Roman style. Stone foundations supported timber-framed walls infilled with wattle and daub; and Tudor farmhouses of 1,000 years later were similarly constructed, though lacking the refinements of tessellated floors, hypocaust underfloor heating, and bath suites. Grouped round the villas were barns, cattle sheds, threshing floors, grain-drying kilns and labourers' cottages; and for every villa there were numerous native farmsteads. In time many of the army of occupation married British girls, and others, on retirement, settled permanently in special veterans' colonies as part of a systematic policy of Romanisation. Thus, the distinction between natives and occupation forces became blurred, especially in areas where hostility had never existed.

Improved agricultural output led to Britain being called the granary of the north, there being sufficient food and clothing for the natives and for the army of occupation numbering 55,000–65,000 men, and even a surplus of grain, cattle hides and woollen products for export to Europe. Other exports included slaves, hunting dogs, pearls, basket-work and minerals. In A.D. 301 the administrative genius, Emperor Diocletian, froze all prices, wages and salaries throughout the Empire; British products caught up by this edict being the 'Birrus Britannicus', a waterproof cloak, and the 'Tapete Britannicum', a woollen rug.

Gradually a change of farming emphasis occurred, with more sheep producing more wool, this, in turn, leading to depopulation of some rural areas, and expansion of towns. Though spinning and weaving of woollen cloth had for long been widespread, in the fourth century the government set up weaving mills and dye-works to produce cloth for the army and civil service. One such weaving factory was established at 'Venta', perhaps *Venta Belgarum* (Winchester) though there were two other Ventas.[10] Imports helping to increase the comfort and sophistication of life included wine and oil from the Mediterranean, perfumes, mosaics, silver tableware, glass, bronze ornaments, and red-glazed crockery from Gaul. Poultry, geese and pheasants had been introduced, as well as pears, cherries, peaches, damsons, figs and mulberries. A probable consequence of freedom from warfare, coupled with improved food, clothing and housing, was an increase in Britain's population, though its size is bound to be a matter of speculation. However, a price had to be paid for these widespread advantages, in the shape of taxation, sometimes consisting of a tithe, or tenth, of all wheat production.

Specific Romano-British evidence in and around East Meon is inevitably limited. The Stroud villa is sited just south of the A272 road, 200–300 yards east of the 19th-century parish boundary, but well within the former boundaries of Steep, which, in turn, was within the *parochia,* or mother parish, of East Meon. The villa, excavated in 1907–8, was typical of the period of 150 years immunity from barbarian raids commencing about A.D. 211, 'a period in which the Romanization of native Britain reached its culminating point'.[11] Within an enclosing yard wall, groups of buildings comprised a nine-room dwelling of unpretentious character, a substantial barn, and other structures that could have been cattle-stalls, a wagon shed and storage space. An uncharacteristically large and elaborate group of bath-houses may point to their use by travellers, or the existence of other dwellings nearby.

At 225 feet above sea-level, the site of this villa establishment, in a lush meadow beside a tiny, sparkling spring-fed brook, is now marked by semi-permanent concrete posts. The fertile valley of clay and loam soil lies between Butser Hill (at 888 feet, the highest point in Hampshire) less than two miles south, and the 700-foot Froxfield escarpment a mile north. The position and nature of the villa suggests it could have been the hub of a farm covering at least several hundreds of acres not known to have been previously cultivated, and it may have been the centre of a locally important administrative or economic unit.

The upper valley of the Meon, which rises two miles away, was probably likewise farmed, for neither the soil's nature nor clearance and drainage would have presented insurmountable problems. Confirmatory evidence resulted from the chance discovery in December 1976 of a site at Old Down Farm, East Meon, by a mechanical excavator operator engaged in back-filling a disused chalk quarry. The spot is a mile east of Westbury Cottage, and, predictably, Walker was soon on the scene. Over the following two months, in atrocious weather and ground conditions, he undertook investigations which salvaged quantities of pottery, two cremation burials, grave goods, iron nails, roof- and box-tile fragments, and pieces of quern-stone. Ditches and a group of postholes were also revealed:

> The features . . . are a representative fraction of a much larger Romano-British rural farm complex. Indeed, the quantities of roof- and box-tile fragments seem to indicate a building of some substance in the vicinity.[12]

This site is dated to the second century A.D., as is part of a limestone statue accidentally discovered in 1937 at Redwood Cottage, near the north-western extremity of the parish and not far from Old Down Farm and Westbury Cottage. The poultry-farming brothers, Edward and Geoffrey Jennings, were replacing an outbuilding's decayed wooden upright when they encountered an unusual 'lump of rock', which, after washing, proved to be the representation of a woman's head. This is now housed in the British Museum.

The face, less than lifesize, is largely destroyed, but the sides and back of the head are still in fairly good condition, with ears and hair. The latter, rendered in flat grooving and running to a small knot behind, still bears some of the original paint, now grey-black. Serrated chisel-tooling is visible in the neck below the ears, whilst the hairdressing style suggests a date in the second half of the second century.[13]

Roman coins, one dated to the third century and of *antoninianus* denomination, have turned up periodically on what is now the site of a recently-built house in Halnaker Lane, Drayton, literally a stone's throw from the river, whilst Roman pottery fragments came to light when a swimming pool was dug at Westbury House in 1967. Reference has already been made to scattered Roman finds at Westbury Cottage, so, whether or not by coincidence, all known evidence of occupation within the present parish is concentrated into a comparatively small area in its north-west corner.

Future chance discoveries or archaeological investigation must surely show that the remainder of this large parish was not devoid of Romano-British occupation, especially as there was a building on the Froxfield ridge (overlooking the Stroud villa, though probably of earlier date); a villa at Lippen Wood, West Meon; another building hidden in Holt Down Plantation, Queen Elizabeth Country Park (just beyond East Meon's south-western boundary); and Romano-British fields at Windmill Hill, Chalton, which obliterated earlier Late Iron Age settlements.

So, in the belief that the East Meon area was extensively occupied and farmed, perhaps for hundreds of years, during the Roman occupation of Britain, it can be assumed that by the third century the more prosperous natives, mainly farmers, were leading secure lives of considerable comfort, with families well-clothed and fed. Winchester and Chichester were but 20 miles distant (in opposite directions) and occasional visits to these urban centres, with their markets and shops, would have provided glimpses of a world undreamed-of before the Conquest. Even the 'working class' natives shared the benefits of peace and prosperity, though to a lesser extent.

Notwithstanding the generalisation that the Romans brought and maintained peace in southern England there was, in fact, a decisive battle fought at Woolmer Common, near Liss (about nine miles north-east of East Meon) in A.D. 296. Two successive usurping British emperors had been in power for the previous 10 years, defying Roman rule. When Constantius Chlorus, already nominated as Caesar of the West, defeated and killed the usurping emperor Allectus at Woolmer Common, thereby recapturing the colony, Britons enthusiastically welcomed the returning Roman army.

Yet history shows all empires are destined to crumble sooner or later, and by the end of the fourth century the huge and highly organised Roman empire was disintegrating. In A.D. 407 the last of the legions were recalled to defend Italy, and by 410 Roman rule had ended and the Britons, protected for so long that they had almost forgotten how to defend themselves, were open to attack. For 30 years or so Romano-British civilisation survived with the help of German mercenaries, but in 442 the mercenaries claimed they had been underpaid, broke out of their treaty territories, and overran the country. The writing was on the wall. 'Britain, long troubled by various happenings and disasters passed under the authority of the Saxons' says a 442 entry in the *Gallic Chronicle*.

Wave after wave of Anglo-Saxon invaders from the eastern shores of the North Sea arrived, fought and settled until, following a British defeat at Strathclyde in 603, yet another conquest was virtually complete. The newcomers were hard working and efficient farmers, and with their large ploughs drawn by four or even eight oxen, cultivated increasing areas of heavy clay land previously shunned. Professor W. G. Hoskins, in *The Making of the English Landscape,* states that:

> The Anglo-Saxon settlement was spread over some twenty generations between about 450 and 1066. During this time England became a land of villages . . . along the river-valleys for the most part, which earlier village-dwellers had ignored—selected by the Old English the Danes and the Norwegians . . .

Among the newcomers were the Jutes, who colonised Kent, the Isle of Wight and parts of Hampshire. There is a widely-held, but not universal belief, that it was they who settled in the Meon Valley, where they became known as the *Meonwara* until absorbed in Wessex. So let us consider the evidence in favour of the belief, and, if acceptable, speculate how far up the valley the colonisation extended. Prior to 735, the Venerable Bede, who died in that year, wrote:

> From the Jutes are descended the *Cantuarii* and the *Victuarii,* that is, the people which holds the Isle of Wight and that which to this day is called the *Jutarum natio* in the province of the West Saxons set opposite the Isle of Wight.

But 'opposite the Isle of Wight' applies equally well to the New Forest, undoubtedly an area of Jutish settlement. Bede also describes the Isle of Wight as 'opposite the frontier between the South Saxons and the *Gewissae',* he having regarded *Gewissae* as another name for the West Saxons, though they may originally have been a distinct tribal group. Finally, Bede says the 'River Hamble runs through the land of the Jutes, which belong to the *Gewissae.* The rivers Hamble and Meon trace more or less parallel lines three or four miles apart as they approach the sea, so if the Hamble ran *through* Jutish territory, as distinct from bounding it, there must be a likelihood that the nearby Meon Valley was also Jutish.

Bede's opinion, though entitled to respect, is not conclusive. However, I propose for the moment to accept it at face value, and to assume the *Meonwara* were in fact Jutes, though unsure whether they came from Jutland as their name implies, or from Friesland or the Rhineland. We do know that the *Meonwara,* evangelised by St Wilfrid of York between 681 and 686, were among the last people in England to become Christians. They were probably well settled by that time, in which case their arrival could have dated to the sixth century, and they may originally have formed a 'buffer state' between powerful Wessex on their west and Sussex to the east.

What was the extent of Jutish penetration up the valley? Should we accept the view that, as the *Meonwara* advanced from the sea, pushing the Romanised British before them, West Meon represented the limit of their colonisation? Sheep Bridge, half a mile downstream from West Meon, is locally pronounced 'Ship Bridge' and can be interpreted as the highest point up the Meon river to which Jutish boats could voyage. If this reasoning is sound, the people of West and East Meon had different and antipathetic blood in their veins, and, to support this theory, coolness has ever since seemed to exist between the villages. Perhaps, after 1,300 or 1,400 years this is fanciful, but even today there are clearly recognisable temperamental differences between the two communities only four miles apart, social intercourse is very limited, and the rivalry of inter-cricket and football matches is spiced with a little extra 'edge'.

Yet evidence exists pointing to Jutish presence four miles north-east of Sheep Bridge— right on, or extremely close to, East Meon's parish boundary on the A272 road near the

Privett turning. The first clue is the former name of Roundabout Copse, situate 50 yards south of the road, which was called 'Eathins' on the 1636 Riplington Tithing map, and 'Eadens' in the 1851 Tithe Terrier. The name may well be the same as 'Ytedene' mentioned in the bishops' pipe rolls in 1263 and 1301, a word almost certainly meaning 'valley of the Jutes'.[14] The second clue relates to a chance discovery by one Richard Ford, who lived at Turnpike House, Bramsdean, between 1840 and 1845. Described by his family as a yeoman, he was a versatile man, including among his occupations those of road surveyor and member of the local turnpike trust, and he apparently also 'farmed' three or four turnpike gates. In about 1842 the section of the present main road from the *West Meon Hut* towards Petersfield was reconstructed to turnpike standards under Richard Ford's supervision. The line of the road followed, and still follows, the course of the gently winding shallow valley running barely half a mile south of Privett village; and a track had probably followed that line for 1,000 years or more, constituting the northern boundary of East Meon parish (and of Riplington Tithing) west of Dolly's Firs.

When the road-making gang were working a quarter of a mile east of what is now the tunnel under the great disused railway embankment, a rectangular man-made, decorative, brooch-like object measuring 1in. by 1.4in. was disinterred and came into the superintendent's possession. Living as he did close to the Civil War battlefield at Cheriton, Ford understandably assumed the object to be a 'Cromwellian relic'. At any rate, he kept the interesting curiosity, and many years later gave it to his 16-year-old grandson, Frank Ford, telling him where it had been found, 'at a place where a small cutting was made'. Frank cared for grandad's gift, keeping it for 50 years in a writing desk's secret compartment. Then, about 1936, nearly 100 years after its discovery, Frank sent it to the British Museum for identification; whereupon it was recognised as a Jutish buckle-plate, made of gilt-bronze, with an animal pattern surrounding a garnet setting. The museum's experts considered it was probably of Kentish manufacture, and dated to the sixth century.[15] The story had a satisfactory ending, as this important, handsome and rare object ended up in the Winchester City Museum: Its place of discovery is not of course proof of Jutish occupation there, but if it were intentionally buried in a Jutish grave, then the likelihood becomes stronger; and, when coupled with nearby 'Eadens', the circumstantial evidence gathers weight.

Nevertheless, it is worth remembering the German mercenaries who rebelled and broke out of their treaty territories in 442. Cunliffe refers to strong evidence of a German detachment of mercenaries at Portchester from about A.D. 370; and one of his maps shows mercenary-held land extending from the Meon estuary to a point north of Hayling Island, and stretching inland to East Meon and Rowlands Castle.[16] Therefore these people could have been the settlers. This idea is attractive because the picture one gets of early Saxon incursions into Hampshire is of attacks by war bands, not of migration of a colonising tribe capable of settling in an area extending from the south coast as far inland as East Meon. So where does the truth lie? Perhaps we shall never know, though continuing archaeological discoveries may eventually contribute towards a convincing answer. Meanwhile it is unnecessary to reject the Jutish or the German mercenary theory, since the two peoples may have been of similar blood and compatible; and the possibility must be faced that both combined—not necessarily at the same time—to take over the valley and acquire the name of *Meonwara*.

In the eighth century when churches were increasingly being built in England, and the earliest books and manuscripts were being written and painted by monks, we encounter the apparent first written mention of 'Meon'. In 790 King Beotric of the West Saxons granted land in *Hissaburn* (Hurstbourne) to Prince Hemele in exchange for land on the River *Meones,* which he had bought from King Kinewulf. Thereafter, Viking raids, at first on a small scale, casual and for plunder, increased until involving fleets of a hundred or more vessels. Landing at many points on the south and east coasts, 'They burned and destroyed everywhere, especially churches, monastries and convents'.[17] Christianity was almost extinguished, and England cringed. A national leader was desperately needed, and he emerged in 871 in the person of Alfred, who became the first King of all England. Following English victory over the Vikings in the great battle of Ethandune, the Treaty of Wedmore (or Chippenham) partitioned England between the English in the south-west and the Danes in the north-east—the Danelaw.

Winchester having emerged as a centre of the Kingdom of Wessex, Alfred made Wolvesey Palace there his principal home. His policy was to create a country in which people of many races could live in peace, harmony and common allegiance, putting former hatreds behind them. A learned scholar as well as a fearless warrior, he restored education, justice and religion and thereby rebuilt the life of nation and church. When the great king died in 899 he willed land that included East Meon to his younger son.

Though his successors, Edward the Elder and Athelstan, respectively his son and grandson, were also great kings, they were too occupied resisting fresh Danish invasions, and re-establishing rule over the Danelaw to be educationalists. The power of Wessex increased, Edward became overlord of the North, and completed the minster at Winchester started by Alfred. At this time ordinary country folk were living in rough shacks, with wattle and daub walls, thatched roofs and earthen floors. But the rule of law and the feudal system were both developing, and by the 10th century the boundaries of English shires were established and many parishes had taken shape. Saxon land charters of this period, particularly informative regarding estate boundaries and ownership, lack any description of what lay within the bounds. The charters were written in Old English, and in the absence of maps or plans, necessarily referred in detail to innumerable physical features, of which many are now difficult or impossible to identify, and some ceased to exist 1,000 years ago.

Dr. G. B. Grundy, a leading authority, translated and interpreted five royal charters of the ninth, 10th and 11th centuries affecting East Meon Hundred, though even he described their elucidation as the most formidable task in the counties of Hants, Berks and Wilts.[18] He explained that most modern parish boundaries are very ancient, each parish representing a single land-unit of early times, because in the greater part of the three counties land was settled and cultivated at an early date; and in such cases when the church came to set up the ecclesiastical unit of the parish, it found the pre-existing land-units of a size suitable for its purpose, and adopted them without modification.

Grundy added that regions of early settlement are those in which arable agriculture could be started with least difficulty, especially where woodland clearance was unnecessary. In such regions the land-unit was usually 10 hides, a secular unit which, in respect to area and population, was large enough to form the later ecclesiastical unit of the parish. But settlement of wild woodland regions came later, and evidently took a different form. Individuals and families seem either to have cleared parts of the forest or to have settled in isolated open spaces, thereby creating secular units too small to be adopted as ecclesiastical parishes.

Accordingly, these smaller units were combined with others for church purposes, though each retained its former identity as a 'tithing'. The land comprised in the 'Meon Charters' falls within this category of former small units grouped together, and follows boundaries which are in many cases those of tithings, and only in parts those of parishes also. Grundy says that a complex situation is made even more so by much of the text of these charters being 'very corrupt', suggesting that extant copies are of post-Conquest date, made by persons not fully versed in the Anglo-Saxon language.

The earliest of the charters, reputedly dated 824, records a grant of 22 hides by Egbert, King of the West Saxons, to the prefect Wulfgeard, of land *Aet Meone*. It includes the whole of the parish of Froxfield except the tithing of Oakshott, and the tithings of Peak and Westbury (and possibly Bereleigh), but it is 'the most difficult of the . . . Meon charters', due to corruption of the text. So, rather than wrestle with the detailed survey, I propose to turn to the next charter, that granted to his thegn, Eadric, by King Eadwig (or Edwy), whose short reign lasted only from 956–958. Its precise date is unknown, but the land comprised 50 hides, and included Steep, Langrish, Oakshott tithing in Froxfield, and Oxenbourne tithing in East Meon, all of which was collectively labelled 'Meone'.

The boundaries, defined by tracks, streams, hills, fords and even flimsy buildings and individual trees, make colourful and fascinating reading. The draftsman commences on the south-west boundary: *'Aerest of Citwara Beca on Hremnes Beorh'*—meaning 'First from the Watercourse of the People of Chidden to Raven's Barrow'. The probable watercourse has long since been a dry valley running about a furlong east of Hyden Farm, though 'Raven's Barrow' may be the tumulus on Wether Down, East Meon.

Proceeding in a clockwise direction (i.e. northwards initially), the boundary runs 'by the Fir-tree' to a particular thorn tree, then 'along the track to Luh's Ford', which may have been the ford at South Mill. Still going north, we pass 'along the Dean out to the Old Clearing', then 'Ofer Bord (Beorh) Dene on Wunces Hyl'. Grundy's translation gives 'Barrow Dene' for Beorh Dene—i.e. today's place-name Bordean, derived from Barrow Dene. We next veer north-eastwards 'On Rythaeres Heafod',—to Rother Head. Rythaeres was probably the old name of the stream running down the combe called Rothercombe, Langrish, and the Heafod was at the junction of the parishes of Steep, Langrish and Froxfield. Then, through the steep hills of the Wealden scarp, via 'the House of Bark' to 'the Promontory of the Shady Quarry' and 'Outside Burdock Hollow', before arriving 'Outside Oakshott Ford', at the north-east corner of Froxfield parish.

Soon bearing southwards, the boundary runs to Princes Bridge, Liss, 'Along the Bright Stream to Hwethel's Hollow' (where the Ashford stream enters the River Rother), along Loud Bourne, from the Ford of the Loud Bourne up to the Cattlepen (probably the site of the *Harrow Inn* at Steep), thence 'by the Hillfoot out to Wothbine Brook' (the hillfoot was the bottom of the hill where Steep village stands), 'along Wothbine Brook outside Tile Lea' (Tilmore), and 'Outside the Stream of the Wood' (the tiny brook at Stroud where the Roman establishment stood 600 years earlier).

The line then continues southwards to 'Cirscumbe Stream' (translated by Grundy as 'Cherrycombe', but possibly meaning, in Old English, 'Gravelly narrow valley'), then 'to the House on the Boundary' and 'up to Bright's Hillslope' (the north slope of Butser Hill which derives its name from the Anglo-Saxon *'Bryttes'*), 'To the Moderate Slope in a downward direction' (the south slope of Butser), thence westwards 'along Long Lea, to Finchs Pole, along the wood to the Gate of the Farmsteading of the Ashtree, along the Wood to the Boundary (or Balk) of the people of Chidden', and, finally, back to the starting point, 'Chidden Watercourse'. A perambulation of the estate's bounds would exceed 20 miles.

The next charter, probably dated about 960 and also entitled *'Aet Meone'*, comprised even more land than the last, 65 hides, and was granted by King Edgar (reigned 959–975) to his grandmother, Queen Eadgifu (Edith), replacing a charter she gave him for safe keeping and which he lost. The estate comprised the whole of Froxfield, Steep and Langrish, part of Privett, and the tithings of Coombe, Riplington, Bereleigh and Church in East Meon, estimated by Grundy to exceed 19,000 acres.

The description commences on the west: 'First to Seol's Bourne' (the stream rising south of Whitewool Farm), and, heading north, passes via 'Hengest's Trench' (on the slope south of Hen Wood) along the ridgeway and over the comb of the ridge on which Westbury Park stands, the ridgeway being a northwards continuation of Salt Lane. But the next sentence is particularly interesting: 'Obliquely over the Meon river to the Street'.

Accepting Grundy's opinion that 'the Street' followed the line of the present-day long, straight public footpath running a mile north-north-east from near the river crossing to Peak Farm, and continuing beyond on that line a further half mile, have we evidence of a former minor Roman road? Certainly, the Old English word 'street' means a Roman road (though admittedly sometimes used to describe non-Roman tracks) and the route's straightness is typically Roman. We know of Romano-British occupation in this particular area, which must have involved construction of normally straight minor connecting roads. So we may be discussing a boundary line that originated some 1,800 years ago, still existed in the 10th century, continued as a tithing boundary in 1636, and is now a public footpath.

However, returning to the charter, its boundary, after leaving the Street, leads to 'Flax Steading' (about three-quarters of a mile south-west of Privett village), by the Highway round Writel's Thorntree, then *'Andlang thaes Grenan Weges to Wud Huw on butan th' hit cymth hut aet Beorhtulfes Treowe'*, which, translated, means 'Along the Green Way to the Ridge-end of the Wood winding round till it comes out at Beortulf's Tree', the latter possibly just west of Farnfield Farm. Next, we pass 'Pluta's Pond, Churls' Gate, the Hollow of the Thatched House, the Willow Pond, and the Promontory of the Shady Quarry'. Having by this stage taken in Froxfield parish, the boundary of the earlier charter is rejoined, and thereafter followed most of the way to its starting point at Seol's Bourne.

In 967 King Edgar made another grant of eight hides 'aet Meone and to Fearnfelda' to the noble matron Winfled. The land include Westbury tithing south of the Meon, whilst north of the river Peak and Privett seem to be included, though the bounds are uncertain. The name 'Fearnfelda', meaning 'fern moorland', survives in that of Farnfield Farm, east of Privett church.

The first specific reference to East Meon (as distinct from *'Meone'*, which *included* part or all of East Meon) is found when Alwyn, Bishop of Winchester from 1032–1047, granted East and West Meon to 'the monks of Winchester', retaining the management in his own hands, thereby in effect allocating the income for their benefit. The bishop, or his predecessors, had apparently acquired 'ownership' of the two Meons by charters, perhaps a whole series, presumably after the estates had reverted to the Crown. Certainly King Hardacanute, in 1042, granted the bishops a comparatively small area, one hide, extending very approximately from Whitewool to the South Hampshire Ridgeway, and including the hamlet and part or all of Coombe tithing. It follows that there must have been one or more other charters comprising far more land.

Before passing from the Saxon to the Norman period, I propose briefly to refer to an earthwork and a church, unconnected, except that each is relevant to pre-Conquest East Meon. The earthwork, running east and west, extends with breaks for a mile in West Meon parish and continues for half a mile in East Meon parish. The latter section runs slightly east of Heathfield Lane, in a strip of wood and beside a farm road, to Peak Farm. This work, being defensive and facing north, might have marked the northern boundary of *Meonwara* territory, though the position of *'Eadens'* and the site of discovery of the buckle-plate do not readily fit in with that view. The excellent local history of West Meon, by John Hurst and Frances Collins, describes the ditch and double bank as 'the most interesting Saxon relic in the parish'. If and when further knowledge is acquired those words may be echoed in respect of East Meon parish.

East Meon's Norman church, All Saints, built between 1075 and 1150 (approximately) will be described in the next chapter, but was it preceded by a Saxon church? No physical trace is known of such an earlier church, either beneath the site of the Norman church or elsewhere. Yet Warnford, a few miles down the Meon Valley, has a church reputedly founded by St Wilfred in 782, and nearby Corhampton's church is also Saxon. Indeed, Warnford claims to have been the saint's local headquarters, set up as a subordinate bishopstool to his see at Selsey: and legend has it that he preached under a tree in West Meon, thereafter known as 'St Wilfred's yew'. Irrespective of the reliability of these details, there can be little doubt that Wilfred preached at all the valley's population centres up to and including West Meon, and possibly beyond; and he would almost certainly have built at least temporary mud and wattle churches in the villages.

It is unbelievable that East Meon would have been without a church for over 400 years—from St Wilfred's time until after the Conquest. However, mere supposition can be carried further. First, by a charter dated 963, King Edgar granted the manor of Ambersham, comprising eight hides, to the 'Church of St Andrew the Apostle at Meon'.[19] As kings did not give whole manors to 'field churches', St Andrew's church must have been an important one in the 10th century.[20] It is therefore probable that this was East Meon's Saxon church, subsequently replaced by the Normans, who changed its dedication to their popular choice—'All Saints'. Incidentally, the Ambersham land, over 12 miles distant from East Meon, was a small 'island' of Hampshire, and of East Meon Hundred, well within Sussex, until the last century. It was also part of the parish of Steep until 1916, and as late as 1842 an Ambersham resident was buried at Steep, and two others were married there in 1856.

Finally, although chronologically the Domesday Survey of 1086 also falls within the scope of the next chapter, it does record that Bishop Walkelin was then holding in East Meon six hides and one virgate *with the church* and a mill;[21] which is surely conclusive as to the existence of an earlier church.

Chapter Two

THE FEUDAL VILLAGE

BY THE BEGINNING of the 11th century the hierarchal feudal system, with the king at its head, was well developed. All land belonged to the king and it was in return for his grants of huge estates that powerful nobles pledged allegiance to the monarch and undertook to provide armed forces for his support in time of war or rebellion. These nobles, in turn, granted what would now be called sub-leases of parts of their territories to knights—one rung down the ladder of power—again in return for military support consisting of bands of fighting men. Finally, still lower in the hierarchy were the vast majority of people, manorial tenants of varying status, and, at the very bottom, slaves. In exchange for theoretical protection, the peasant masses (themselves sub-divided into strict categories) had to pay homage and swear allegiance to their manorial lord; to make defined payments in cash or kind (loosely called 'fines') to the lord; except for the minority of 'free tenants', to provide specified gratuitous manual labour or transport for the lord's benefit; to attend all sittings of the manorial court; to pay to have their corn ground at the lord's mill; and even to drive their sheep into the lord's fold overnight that their dung would benefit the lord's land. The relationship was very one-sided.

This simplified summary of a complex system must be qualified by noting the steadily increasing status and power of the Church, a power which eventually grew until it rivalled that of the king. One-tenth of produce, of smallholdings and gardens, as well as of farms, went to the Church, plus a 'mortuary' on death. Other voluntary gifts to the Church, especially by will, were prompted by piety, sometimes in the belief that a passport to Heaven could be bought by benevolence on earth.

By 1066 a third of Hampshire was in episcopal or other religious hands,[1] including the overlordship of East Meon Hundred, which still rightfully belonged to Winchester bishopric; though, following the pre-1047 grant by Bishop Alwyn, the bishops were mere managers, passing the income to 'the monks of Winchester'—St Swithun's Priory, otherwise the Old Minster. This was, subject to the bishops' beneficial retention of the church, six and a quarter hides of land and a mill, representing in area roughly a twelfth of the Hundred, and almost certainly corresponding with what became known as Meon Church Manor and Tithing.

Alwyn's successor, Bishop Stigand, former chaplain to King Canute, wrongfully retained the Winchester bishopric and the whole East Meon overlordship when uncanonically appointed Archbishop of Canterbury after 14 September 1052. The appointment led to his excommunication by five successive popes, though his primacy continued long enough for participation in William's coronation. But in 1070 the king deprived him of his offices and clapped him in prison, yet failed to appropriate the overlordship, possibly believing Stigand's entitlement, as distinct from his bishopric, extended for life. However, on Stigand's death in 1072, the king seized the Hundred—except the church, six and a quarter hides and the mill—not merely as overlord, but beneficially as well!

15

With six years' delay from the Conquest till the overlordship change the catastrophic events of 1066 may initially have had a minimal impact on East Meon. Most great landed estates were soon confiscated from their Saxon owners and granted by the king to his Norman followers, thereby substituting stern, foreign overlords and their henchmen for the old nobility. Feudal inequality, harshness and unfairness were perpetuated, and even hardened. Yet, for those first years East Meon experienced a continuation of the old order, under familiar masters, and even thereafter the minor but important area previously held by the bishops beneficially, remained theirs.

Which leads to the Domesday Survey, 'unmatched in Europe for many centuries, the product of a sophisticated and experienced English administration, fully exploited by the Conqueror's commanding energy'.[2] According to the *Saxon Chronicle,* in 1085 'at Gloucester at midwinter . . . the King had deep speech with his counsellors . . . and sent men all over England to each shire . . . to find out . . . what or how much each landowner held . . . in land and livestock, and what it was worth'. Within a year (the Survey is dated 1086) it was completed by commissioners who took evidence on oath 'from the Sheriff; from all the barons and their Frenchmen; and from the whole Hundred, the priests, the reeves and six villagers from each village'. Ownership and values 'before 1066', as well as in 1086, were specified, providing a valuable link between old and new regimes. Though the Survey's primary object was to record all *geldable*—i.e. taxable land, by reference to the land units called hides, an important secondary purpose was the compilation of an official register of individual ownerships, so that 'every man should know his right and not usurp another's'.

East Meon Hundred occupies two separate entries, seemingly a duplication, though not really so. First, under the heading 'Hantescire' (Hampshire), and sub-heading 'Land of the King: in (East) MEON Hundred':

> (East) MEON. Archbishop Stigand held it before 1066 for the use of the monks; later he had it for his life-time. Then there were 72 hides; it paid tax for 35 hides and 1 virgate. Land for 64 ploughs. In lordship 8 ploughs; 70 villagers and 32 smallholders with 56 ploughs. 15 slaves; 6 mills at 40s; meadow, 8 acres; woodland at 200 pigs from pasturage; from grazing 7s. 6d. Value before 1066 £60; later £40; now £60; however, it pays £100 by weight in revenue but it cannot bear it. Bishop Walkelin holds 6 hides and 1 virgate of this manor's land with a church. These hides of the Bishop paid tax; now [for] 3 hides and 1 virgate; the others did not pay tax.

The Commissioners intended to emphasise that the property described in the last three lines quoted was *not* held by the king, that part of the Hundred reappearing under the separate sub-heading 'Land of the Bishop of Winchester: In (East) MEON Hundred'

> The Bishop himself holds 6 hides and 1 virgate with the church in (East) MEON. Land for 4 ploughs. In lordship 1½ ploughs; 11 villagers and 8 smallholders with 3 ploughs. 2 slaves; 1 mill at 30d; meadow, 4 acres. Value before 1066 and later £4; now 100s.

Before leaving Domesday, its figures can be used to form a rough estimate of the Hundred's population. Taking the total male adults—138 villagers, smallholders and slaves, assuming an equal number of female adults, and adding one child for every two adults, we arrive at 414 souls; reasonably rounded off at 425 by including manorial administrators, the vicar and several curates.

Adverting to the Hundred's 'ownership', the greater part remained with the Crown until Stephen, nephew of Henry I, and grandson of the Conqueror, became king in 1135.

His younger brother, Henry of Blois, Abbot of Glastonbury and also Bishop of Winchester, was a man of power, and played a crucial part in helping Stephen to the throne. Accordingly a strong likelihood arises of brotherly persuasion for the new king to restore the major part of the Hundred to its rightful owners after a lapse of 63 years, coupled with the suggestion that this would benefit the king's soul. Certainly an 1137 bull of Pope Innocent II confirmed to the bishop the manors of Meones and Weregrave 'which were taken from the Church by King William and lately restored by Stephen'; so Stephen made the restoration within two years of his accession. Confirmatory charters granted by each of the next three kings, Henry II, Richard I, and John, may reflect caution by successive bishops to avoid doubt as to the permanence of the restoration; or the greed of royal advisers extracting fees for each charter.

Meanwhile, the village had witnessed great events, probably at the initiative of Walkelin. Stigand's immediate successor as Bishop of Winchester, who, in 1086, held the minor part of the Hundred. Walkelin, the Conqueror's cousin, a great ecclesiastic, educationalist and architect, began the rebuilding of Winchester Cathedral, and rebuilding or remodelling churches in his Hampshire manors. Architectural evidence dates East Meon's cruciform Norman church at 1075-1150, and the elegance of its tower and other Norman work, recalling that of the cathedral, could point to Walkelin having at least commenced its rebuilding. On his death in 1098 the structure was probably incomplete, for with limited skilled labour available, and much building in progress, construction of so large a church would inevitably take many years. Indeed, the ornamentation of the tower, more profuse than that of the chancel arches, emphasises the point.

About 1230, the Lady Chapel was built, and the south aisle added to the nave. The spire, described by purists as an incongruous addition to the Norman tower, may also have been erected about 1230, possibly somewhat later. Nevertheless, the church's general appearance, whether viewed at close quarters or from afar, pleases most eyes, nestling under Park Hill's precipitous downland slope. Much-travelled William Cobbett was greatly impressed (though wrongly describing the tower as 'Saxon'!), and Pevsner called it 'one of the most thrilling village churches in Hampshire'. It was the mother church of Froxfield and Steep, each served by chaplains appointed by East Meon's vicar, and, before the Conquest, Hambledon and other districts may have fallen within the aegis of the earlier church.[3]

A magnificent font, made by the famous Tournai sculptors from a single block of black marble, is an outstanding feature. About 1150 it was brought 500 miles down the Scheldt, across the North Sea and English Channel, up the Itchen, and then laboriously overland. Carving on its four sides depicts, first, the flat Earth supported on pillars (upheld by God) and on it, composite creatures—fish, reptile, bird and animal, all in one; then the creation of Adam and Eve, followed by the offer and eating of the forbidden fruit. A third shows the Gate of Paradise, barred by the Angel with his sword, Adam being taught to dig, and Eve to spin; whilst on the last side the flat Earth on its pillars is again seen with fierce dogs chasing doves, thereby representing the faithful's persecution by the wicked in a fallen world. Seven Tournai fonts are in England, the four Hampshire specimens—including one in Winchester cathedral—probably being gifts from Henry of Blois.

Whether Wakelin built a residence in East Meon, perhaps also serving as an administrative centre for his estate of about 750 acres, is conjectural. Likewise, the tradition that King John (1199-1216) was married in East Meon and had his wedding reception in 'the Bishop's Palace' there, lacks proof, and seems unlikely. The Court House, including a fine medieval hall, stands almost opposite the church, is dated to the mid or late 14th century, and was preceded by an earlier building, most likely on the same site. By 1137 at the latest the bishop's estate had increased in size, perhaps twelvefold—a huge area justifying the large manorial court hall and administrative buildings, with tiled roofs and the luxury of glass windows which existed at the beginning of the 13th century, perhaps much earlier. As will be seen, the living accommodation was considered fit to house an archbishop on his visitation; and the adjacent deer park provided a ready supply of venison for the lord's table. Indeed, in 1279 a commission of oyer and terminer was granted to Robert Fulconis and William de Brayboef, touching the persons who broke the parks of Nicholas, Bishop of Winchester, at East Meon, hunted therein, and carried away deer.[4]

During the 13th, 14th and 15th centuries most of East Meon's written history falls into two categories: first, the *pipe rolls,* an enrolment of the annual accounts rendered by the bishopric's local officers (bailiff and reeves) of receipts, 'issues' and stock of the manors. All farming activities, including sale and purchase of stock, maintenance of buildings and equipment, payment of wages (in money and in kind) and rent collections were covered by these lengthy rolls, as well as lists of fines paid on transfers of copyhold property *inter vivos,* as *heriots* on death, *merchets,* or punishments for a variety of misdemeanours and shortcomings. Even tithes (originally received in kind) were recorded. The affairs of the main manor—headed *'Menes Manerium',* or just *'Menes',* and of the smaller Meon church, or *'Estmunes Ecclesia',* were separately covered by each roll, as were those of the 20 other Hampshire manors. The second category of documents comprises the *manorial rolls,* which are more of the nature of public records, covering the proceedings of the Manor Court, and which, like the pipe rolls, are written in Latin.

The Manor Court was presided over by the lord's steward, who travelled around the various manors rather like a minor circuit judge, the bailiff deputising when necessary. The Court's jurisdiction depended upon whether it was sitting as a three-weekly Court Baron or as a bi-annual Court Leet. The former was part of the lord's property (his domanial jurisdiction) and, in addition to appointing the reeve, beadle, hayward and certain other officials, swore in the Homage or Jury—the assembled tenants—and proceeded with its business. That included enforcement of manorial customs, transfers of copyholds (by surrender and admission), escheats for want of heirs or due to felony, use of common fields and wastes, and disputes between lord and tenants.

The Court Leet, though also held in the lord's hall, presided over by his steward and attended by the tenants, was the lord's franchisal jurisdiction, a public court, even having authority over the lord himself. It approximated to a cross between a modern County Court and a Magistrates' Court. Having elected the constable, ale taster and pinder, it handled civil claims for debt, trespass, defamation, unjust hue and cry, petty criminal offences such as theft, assault and breaches of the Assizes of Bread and Ale, and miscellaneous other matters including complaints of highway disrepair. Both courts imposed countless fines, and their decisions were recorded in the court rolls. As available pipe rolls span more than 500 years, and court rolls extend over six centuries, only tiny samples of their contents can be quoted.

The earliest surviving pipe roll covers Michaelmas 1207 to Michaelmas 1208[5]—the latter year marked by Pope Innocent III laying England under an interdict, following King John's quarrel with the papacy over a new archbishop of Canterbury, which resulted in five years of church closures. Richard and Thomas (no surnames) were the reeves, and Geoffrey and Audelinus the 'servants' or clerks of Menes Manor. Farm produce exemplifies the vital interdependence of sheep husbandry and cereal growing which had been a feature of the Iron Age and succeeding Romano-British economies, and, to a varying extent, has continued ever since. Corn sold included 110½ quarters of wheat (£14 10s. 4d.), 33 quarters of barley (67s.), and small quantities of rye and oats. But, as payment was made for *threshing* 451 quarters of corn, the balance was presumably despatched to St Swithun's Priory or consumed locally. Wool sales brought £10 13s. 4d., and pells from 95 sheep, 82 hoggets and 262 lambs that all died, 35s. Milk from 412 ewes was 'farmed' for £4 2s. 6d.—i.e. leased to an unnamed individual to exploit for his own benefit, whilst an unusual item was six quarters of nuts sold for 10s., and perhaps an even more unusual product, four tuns of wine (£4 2s. 0d.).

A tun of wine represented 252 gallons, so over 1,000 gallons—equivalent to 6,000 bottles—were sold, representing (by present standards) the average output of a two-acre vineyard. Could this represent a link with today's landscape feature, the huge hollow indented in the side of Park Hill, a furlong east of the Court Hall called 'Vineyard Hole'? Gouged by nature out of the steep, chalky hillside, facing due south and completely protected from northerly winds, an ideal site for vini-culture, its name must be derived from past use, though no one knows when it ceased.

Manorial expenses incurred were varied:

> Ironwork for two ploughs [and] 17 draught animals 7s. 6½d.
> Often repairing the ploughs, harrows and carts 3s. 6d.
> Repairing the new fish-pond 2s. 6d.
> Planting a new orchard and ditching around 18s. 10d.
> One millstone bought [almost certainly imported from abroad, via Southampton] 13s. 4d.
> Boards and nails for the same mill and in making from new the mill-house and repairing the pond of the same mill 23s.
> Pay of one carter, one hayward, 3 ploughmen per annum 15s. 4d.
> Drink and food for the great boon reaping and 16 other harvest services 35s. 9d.
> Corrody of 4 reeves in the autumn 8s. 8d.

The prevailing cash wage for non-specialist manual workers (about 1½d a day) illustrates the substantial size of the new orchard (almost certainly of apple trees), the great cost of a millstone—over half the expense of rebuilding the mill and mill-house—and the meagreness of 15s. 4d. for five men for a year. Several explanations could have applied to this last point: part-time employees; benefits in kind—especially food and drink whilst employed, and a grain allowance after harvest; remission of rent; extra grazing rights; and finally, all copyholders apart from the free tenants were customarily obliged to render unpaid services to the lord. Regarding *four* reeves, these were temporary foremen or 'reepreeves' assisting Geoffrey and Audelinus when nearly 500 acres of corn were harvested by a veritable army of part-timers.

The mill had apparently been 'farmed', the roll reading: 'In default of the mill of the chapel taken into demesne 10s.'. Since South Mill was a stone's throw from the chapel of ease, St Mary's in the Field (assuming it then existed) that was doubtless the mill 'made from new', provided with a fresh millstone, and taken into the lord's possession— the expenditure soon recouped, as revenue received within the year was 37s. 9d.

Examples of fines were 6d. to 3s. for merchets, 12d. imposed upon Stephen Blakeman 'because he has not ploughed', 6d. upon Richard Grede 'for ale sold contrary to the assize', 6d. upon William Carter for false hue and cry, and the same amount upon several others for 'affray'.

Turning to Meon church, a twelfth the size of Menes Manor, corn sales were far greater, totalling 386 quarters. An obvious possible explanation is that all produce surplus to local requirements could be sold; and perhaps a higher proportion of its land was in demesne—a theory consistent with its *three* full-time reeves (Robert, Thomas and Patrick), since nearly all bishopric manors had but one. Wool sales, realising £6 16s. 4d., were sizeable, but less than those of Menes. Expenses included purchase of axes, twibills, spades and shovels, wages of a carter, ox-man, hayward and dairyman for the year, and four carters in the autumn, and 11s. 8d. for re-roofing (probably *repairing*) the granges of Menes, Froxfield, Stepe (Steep) and Hameldon (Hambledon). The first three were within the same Hundred, and Hambledon had previously been described as an 'appendage' of East Meon. Another repair, 're-roofing the hall and chamber 4s. 7d.', is the first clear written reference to the original Court Hall.

Among disbursements in kind were 38 quarters of grain (probably barley), for one carter for the year and seven carters in autumn, 10 quarters for the reeves, 42 quarters for 'corrody of 7 horses through autumn and six guardians'—the horses at any rate preferring oats—six quarters for 'autumn ale', and three and a half quarters for 'feeding the pigs'.

The inventory of stock in hand at the year's end ranged from oxen to hens, and cider to salt, including 36 oxen, 162 lambs, 45 ganders and 12 piglets, all except the oxen having been received as tithe, plus 32 hens *de cheriset*—that is, church scot or churchetts, a payment to the bishop, representing the church, usually made in grain or poultry. Examples of commodities in hand are 119 little cheeses, received as tithe and expended in autumn (probably at the boon reaping), one tun of cider and four sesters of salt. The cider stock had started the year at seven tuns, been increased by a fresh tun and then depleted by a half tun 'spoiled', another half tun 'gone acid' and six tuns used as 'expenses of the Lord Bishop at Menes and Waltham' (Bishops Waltham, one of his residences). Wine and cider were the extraordinary and ordinary drink of the household and official class, and both were produced in quantity at the Meon manors. Bitterne was the main supply centre for salt, but four sesters brought into stock came from Hambledon, perhaps pointing to that adjoining manor being a sub-depot, or, alternatively, simply over-stocked.

The ratio of oxen to horses is interesting, 36 of the former and only seven (temporary) horses. If such numbers are typical, the transition from one to the other, taking hundreds of years, was at an early stage. Oxen moved at only two-thirds of a horse's speed, but were cheaper to keep, needing far less oats than horses, and, as contemporary agronomist Walter of Henley observed, a worn-out horse had nothing of value but his skin, whilst an old ox could be fattened for selling or killing with 10d. of grass!

The next available pipe roll, for 1210,[6] tells of personal violence in Menes, with eight fines for affray; and of the assart of a new meadow (fine 2s. 3d.), later mowed for 3s. 6d., showing farming expansion. In Meon church 18d. was paid for 'timber cut down to roof the cider press', 12d. for a new cider cask, and 6d. for cider-making. A new building, requiring 3,000 slates costing 6s. 3d., was made 'in the Court'—labour 5s. 8d. Either unusual activity or an organisational breakdown could explain 'expenses of the Bishop's bakers at Menes for 4 weeks and their helpers 10s. 7d.'. But the most remarkable entry concerns fish: '3 lasts of herrings bought at Porthesmouth and delivered to Thomas, servant of Fereham 78s. 2d.'. As a last was a load, generally weighing about 4,000 lbs., over five tons of herrings were acquired and promptly shipped to nearby Fareham, another of the bishopric manors, where Thomas supervised their salting down for winter consumption, especially in Lent. Fareham was probably a combined depot and staging post, since the ox-drawn transport of fresh fish from Portsmouth to East Meon would have been too slow for the cargo to arrive in condition; which helps to build a picture of the bishopric's vast property-owning, farming and financial empire, where each manor was an independent cog in the machine, but the officials having overall supervision of affairs ensured a degree of co-operation and mutual assistance between manors.

During the remainder of the 13th and for almost the first half of the 14th centuries life in East Meon, according to the pipe rolls, continued much as before. In 1285[7] the hall and chamber were re-roofed, probably only partially, with 3,000 slates bought for 3s. (less than half their cost 70-odd years before), 100 lathes for 5d., and 500 nails, also for 5d., labour costing 6s. 'The grange of the tithing' (Meon Church) was completely re-roofed, doubtless with straw, for 8s. 2½d. It may have been the tithe barn. The next year, in Menes Manor Robert Stoyere was fined 6d. 'for his sheep in the wheat', Walter Lekuhl the same amount 'for taking corn from the grange', and Adam Ray 3d. 'for bad custody of his sheep'.[8]

Over the next decade there were numerous repairs to buildings, bridges and boundary hedges and ditches, roofs, in particular, needing constant attention. Labour for re-roofing the Bishop's chamber with shingles came to 2s. 10d. and the nails cost 6d., whilst boards sawn for flooring the bailiff's chamber cost 2s. and the nails 13½d.[9] Furniture, even in the village's most important building, was rudimentary in 1289:

> Sawing 3 tables in the hall at the lord's dais and one bench in the hall and a serving board, with the wages of the carpenter . . . 2s. 6d.[10]

At about the same time boards for 're-carpentering and remaking the dovecote', with nails and wages, totalled 7s. 5½d. Apparently this was a wooden structure, but nevertheless it housed a vital source of fresh meat in winter; and a few years later 'one man [was] hired to catch the birds destroying the dovecote—12d.' and a cord rope for its window was bought for 1d.[11]

In one year fines of 6d. were imposed on Henry Pomel 'for contumelious words against Adam Ray', on W. Gileberd for beating Walter Eliot's boy and on Robert Hus for hitting Philip le Hayward. But Thomas de Scheregrey's punishment 'for false measure', regarded more seriously than assault and battery, was a 2s. fine.[12] In 1296 fines were particularly numerous—perhaps the manorial authorities were making a drive to restore discipline.[13] Breaches of the Assize of Ale occurred 39 times in Meon Church and 123 times in Menes Manor; Edith Coleville and Walter Hugh were fined for bad custody of the lord's sheep, Richard atte Burghe for breaking the pound, Thomas de Cartare and Gilbert de Pipercombe for not performing the office of beadle, and John Coleville because he married Margaret Nel without licence.

Two other events deserve attention: first, 1305 was a noteworthy year, marked by the archbishop's visit and overnight stay at the Court House, when 18d. was laid out for nine quarters of charcoal,[14] sufficient to roast an ox (so perhaps charcoal grills are nothing new); and secondly, during the following year[15] three men were paid 18d. 'to help the gardener dig in the garden for planting vines there', and later, 'weeding the vines sometimes', cost 12d. Whether these expenses were for a new vineyard or for replanting or extending an existing one is uncertain, but the work was clearly more than the regular gardener could manage alone.

The financial and other burdens borne by the great majority of people as already described were of a local, manorial nature. Yet national taxation, having existed since the danegeld of Saxon times, had by 1327 evolved into 'lay subsidies'—periodic grants to the Crown authorised by parliament and so-called because they applied to laymen as opposed to clergy, who were separately assessed. In rural areas assessments represented a fifteenth of the theoretical value of a person's moveables, including growing crops, and the 1327[16] roll of payments due from East Meon Hundred groups taxpayers under their respective *villata* or tithings, giving another slant on monetary affairs. East Meon villata's 14 assessable individuals yielded 22s. 8d., Mark de Ponte's 3s. 0d. being the largest payment. Wealthier Ramsdean villata's total tax, from 13 assessments, was 37s. 6d., and its highest payers, at 5s. 0d. each, were William atte Strode, James de Holewey and Henry atte Hacche. Though a few other individuals within the hundred also paid 5s. 0d., no liability was higher, as though the assessors had tacitly agreed that capital wealth, represented by chattels and crops, should never exceed £3 15s. 0d. Other taxpayers' surnames, most comparatively newly acquired and with a Norman flavour, are evocative: Adam de Parkir, Philip le Bakere and Richard Cordewainir (occupational); William de Draytone, Roger de Coumbe, Henry de Pipercumbe and John in the Lane (relating to past or present homes, the first three place-names still surviving locally); Nicholes le Bule and Robert le Cok (probably nicknames), and John de Palmere who, or whose father or grandfather, may have visited the Holy Land.

Moving on to 1344,[17] when William de Overton was bailiff of Meon Manor, with a salary of £10 p.a.—roughly equivalent to the value of 200 sheep or 25 oxen—livestock sales were impressive: £29 18s. 2d. received from 679 sheep, rams and lambs all sold after shearing; £13 6s. 10d. from 54 cows, bullocks, calves and a bull; and £7 14s. 10d. from 98 pigs and piglets. Preponderance of sheep is underlined by wool sales—coarse wool from 1,503 sheep, rams, ewes and hoggets; and lambs' wool from 514 lambs, plus the pells of over 100 that had died. This large-scale sheep farming involved expenses of 18s. 4d. for tar (for treating feet), 10s. 7d. for ointment, 10d. for red dye (for the rams), 16d. for 80 hurdles, 'for making the fold', 18s. 6d. for building materials—mainly straw, and 12d. for making a crib. Other expenditure included castrating and ringing pigs, carrying venison to Farnham (3d.), mending a mill spindle, and labour for threshing and winnowing corn. Still in 1344, Meon Church spent 2s. 6d. on labour 'roofing the grange for hay broken by a great wind', and there were numerous other roofing items, perhaps also due to the 'great wind'. Surprisingly, the sale of 10 doves fetched 3s. 4d., doves and lambs having a similar value!

By August 1348, approaching 300 years after the Conquest, England's population had reached, perhaps passed, a peak of about four million, possibly even five million. Resulting land scarcity had been relieved by assarting and also bringing into cultivation poor, thin soil—nowadays called 'marginal land'. Feudalism still held the vast majority of ordinary folk in subjection, though commutation of service obligations into monetary payments had begun as early as the 12th century, and made tentative progress in the 13th, often at the lord's instigation, sometimes on a temporary basis only.

Suddenly, without warning, there began the most awful human calamity to befall these islands, when bubonic (and, to a far less extent, pneumonic) plague arrived, and, within 14 months, wiped out a fraction of the population variously estimated at a quarter to a half. Thousands upon thousands of whole families succumbed, sometimes complete villages. Neither antidote nor cure were known, for the good reason that then, *and for the next 550 years,* the disease (certainly the bubonic form) was wrongly thought to be transmitted by air-borne germs. In fact, the vectors were fleas carried by infected black rats, and, perhaps on a lesser scale, human fleas.

Then, and until the late 17th century, the black rat was the commensal rat in Britain and on the Continent. Without doubt the Plague, or the Great Pestilence as it was widely called ('Black Death' was a 16th-century term), arrived here through the unintended importation of these rodents aboard ships. In turn, native rats became infected, while fleas, forsaking their dead hosts, transferred themselves to humans. One species of rat flea, having ingested plague bacilli, suffered from a blocked organ at the entrance to its stomach (the *proventriculus*), so that, on attempting to take a meal of human blood, it succeeded only in regurgitating blood under the human skin, carring with it plague bacilli.[18] Some species of rat flea, and also human fleas, have no proventriculus, yet they can still transmit bacilli via their proboscis, though less efficiently.

The bubonic form of plague is characteristically a warm-weather disease, reaching its peak in this country around August and September, the common early symptom being a bubo or painful swelling of one or more of the lymphatic glands. Sometimes blood poisoning (septicaemic plague) ensues, death following within a day, though more usually 'the plague toxins may give rise to high fever, coma, heart-failure, inflammation of the spleen or kidneys and sometimes . . . internal haemorrhage'.[19] Untreated by modern drugs, 60–80 per cent. of victims die within five days. Pneumonic plague, highly infectious and caused by the same bacillus, is not dependent on warm weather, being directly transmitted between humans from infected droplets expelled from the lungs. Case rate fatality is even higher than that of the bubonic form, and likely to occur within a day of first symptoms appearing. Predictably, the poor, mostly living in squalor, were more susceptible than the affluent minority; and consequently, when a household became infected, there was a high risk of all members suffering the same fate.

If East Meon's population at Domesday was about 425, and if subsequent expansion was typical of the countrywide trend, there may have been 850 inhabitants when plague first struck. For strike it did, the pipe rolls leavng no doubt as to its severity. The 1348 roll,[20] covering Michaelmas 1348–Michaelmas 1349, and sub-headed 'Default through plague', lists many properties in the lord's hands owing to lack of tenants—probably pointing not only to deaths of former tenants, but of heirs too. Within this category were John Glast, John Curtonn and John de Hoo, all of Oxenbourne, and Adam de Poundere, Richard de Poundere and Margaret Coleville of Meon. Money heriots were payable on 78 deaths.

Notwithstanding the problem of estimating the number of local plague deaths, an attempt can be made, assisted by some guesswork. So, assuming that, say, 90 heriots in all fell due in the year (for not *all* heriots would have been commuted), and further assuming about 10 tenants died from non-plague causes, we are left with 80 plague deaths of copyhold tenants. Probably a few were widows or spinsters, but, disregarding that minor complexity, it would seem fair to multiply the figure of 80 by three to account for wives and children, thereby reaching the horrible overall total of 240—over 28 per cent. of the estimated population.

The pipe rolls recorded numerous tenancy changes during the following three years, though often the preceding deaths had clearly occurred in 1348; which is not surprising, since a national land shortage had suddenly become a surplus, and lords had difficulty in finding sufficient tenants. So fundamental a change in the laws of supply and demand meant that when the country picked up the threads of normal life, realisation dawned that labour had become more precious than land. Marginal land ceased to be cultivated, often reverting to sheepwalks or waste, labourers' wages rose, and commutation of service obligations into monetary payments progressed until by the mid-15th century villeinage had largely died out.

So much for generalisations. 'Ecclesiastical bodies enjoyed a corporate experience denied to private landowners',[21] and the Bishop of Winchester's profits actually increased for two years following the plague, due to the receipt of heriots and fines from incoming tenants, and inevitable changes came about more slowly in bishopric manors than most places.

Thus, when East Meon's manorial court sat, 'in the 11th year of Bishop William of Wykeham' (1377),[22] the rolls showed little departure from the old ways. *Essoins*—excuses for non-attendance—were made and accepted on behalf of 20 male adults, who included William Stygant, whose surname will reappear on the village scene 350 years later. Having disposed of 'apologies for absence', the Homage 'presented' that all was well—meaning no disputes or other problems, in the tithings of Coombe, Oxenbourne, Ramsdean, Bordene and Menes Manor. Then, after fining three non-attenders a few pence each 'for default', the Court gave preliminary consideration to 30 civil disputes, mostly debt claims, with several complaints of detention of cattle or goods. Some plaintiffs were fined 2d., 3d. or 4d. each, 'in mercy' for failing to appear, or as punishment for false claims, and others 2d. to 6d. for the lord's licence to sue.

A year later, in October 1378,[23] the Court imposed 29 fines for 'brewing and breaking assize'. Isobel atte Wode, one of the seven female culprits, was let off with the minimum 2d. fine, but Thomas Colpays had to pay the maximum 18d. for seven brewings. Conclusions are that beer brewing for sale, as distinct from home consumption, was virtually a 'cottage industry'; that many women were brewers; and that those who 'presented' these wrongdoers must have decided, like their predecessors back in 1296, to instigate a campaign against a general and flagrant breach of the law.

Others fined for wrongdoing included Alice Michel and Henry Lynche 'for unjust hue and cry', and John atte Strode and John Southover, both millers, for taking tolls contrary to the assize (John Southover three fines for breaches in three different tithings). Adam atte Berghe, John Dymayn and William Boghyere were all 'in mercy' for marrying their respective daughters within the demesne without the lord's licence. Non-imposition of fines was probably because the bridegrooms lived 'within the demesne', since a fourth father, Thomas atte Hulmette, was fined 2s. for his daughter's marriage outside the demesne.

This particular Court ordered escheat of the goods and chattels of Thomas Andreu of Bordene, a 'felon fugitive'. The nature of the felony is unknown, but Andrew was a smallish farmer, for the price inventory of his possessions included 13 quarters of grain (sold for 46s. 8d.), two horses, two cows, two calves, 32 ewes, 28 lambs, 7 cwts. of wool, a rick of straw, a half cartload of hay, five small cheeses, a barrel, an empty pipe, a sieve, a riddle, two brass bowls, a stoup, a broken tripod and three broken coffers. The wretched Thomas's wife and children (if any) must have been left completely destitute.

In 1399 the Manor Court was still, on the surface, functioning as before,[24] but, 50 years after the plague's arrival, monetary punishments seem less frequent. Richard Raghoud was in trouble, and severely fined—20s.—for issuing a writ without licence 'in Court of the Lord King' versus three manorial officials, Robert Boughiere, Richard Cousday and Simon Courtenay, 'against the ancient custom of the Manor, in prejudice to the lord and his Church and to great damage to Robert, Richard and Simon'. However, no tenants were presented for breaking the assize of ale, for wrongfully taking tolls, marrying off daughters or raising a hue and cry. Indeed, apart from some debt claims, the business of the Court was largely confined to the jury's reports of animals that had died 'in the murrain and not from any lack of care', and to complaints that the king's highway in both manors, and specifically at Stenybrygge, Blakeman's and Brandeslane was foundrous. Repairs were ordered.

During the preceding half century—between c. 1350–1400—the Court Hall and contemporary two-storey wing as they now exist were massively rebuilt with five-foot-thick walls of flint and stone rubble and dressings of stone—probably quarried at Langrish. The hall, three bays long, rising to 50 feet, its crown-post roof timbers showing smoke blackening from the original central hearth. Massive tie-beams, supported by braces, rest on corbels carved with the heads of four kings and four bishops, the hall lit by square-headed mullioned and transomed windows, each with two quatrefoil lights. The two-storey north wing, at right-angles to the hall, probably first comprised a pantry and buttery at ground level. Above, the Great Chamber, still with its original fireplace and roof of similar construction to that of the hall, accommodated important visitors, whose comfort was completed by a *garderobe* (latrine), with a chute opening through the north outer wall. As William of Wykeham's episcopacy extended from 1366–1404, he may have had a hand in the rebuilding, and in his will he showed a special interest in East Meon's church, bequeathing to it a breviary and chalice.

Having illustrated the lives of ordinary people by reference to pipe and manorial rolls and other written sources, another chapter entitled 'Tudor Times' looms up, 1485 being the arbitrary dividing line. Of course no sudden and dramatic changes overtook the locality in that year; for even the momentous events of A.D. 43 and 1066 failed to revolutionise everyday life overnight. Nevertheless, the gradual easing of manorial servitude, to a varying extent speeded by the plague, and steadily progressing over the succeeding century, once led to near-anarchy in the village.

In August 1461, when Edward IV went on progress in Hampshire, the tenants of the manor of East Meon and elsewhere 'in grete multitude and nombre' petitioned the king for relief from certain services, customs, and dues which Bishop Waynflete and his agents were attempting to exact, particularly 'churchetts', pannage and payment of tithing-pence. They also complained that the court of the bishop was being held within the site of the parsonage of East Meon, not within the site of the manor of East Meon, and asserted that tenants within the lordship of East Meon were freeholders and not copyholders. Diplomatically, Edward declined to give a decision, pointing out that the aggrieved tenants could bring a civil action against the bishop in the House of Lords. This they did in the following December, when judgment was given against them on all points, the king 'gevying his good and gracious assent to the same'.[25]

Chapter Three

TUDOR TIMES, 1485–1603

AS HISTORY UNFOLDS, available documentary evidence increases. Wills, especially when accompanied by detailed priced inventories, are especially useful, revealing minute information about the lives, families, worldly possessions and even thoughts and hopes of men and women who lived and died hundreds of years ago. Although uncommon before the mid–16th century, wills have been known since Anglo-Saxon times, and their probate—that is, proof of authenticity—had always fallen within the jurisdiction of a Church Court, usually the court of the archdeaconry where the testator died. Notable exceptions to this rule were 'peculiars'—parishes or groups of parishes exempt from archdeaconry authority, and where the bishop or a local incumbent usually held the court. East Meon, including Steep and Froxfield, was a peculiar—the bishop's.

Certain generalisations apply to East Meon's 16th-century wills: first, testators almost invariably deferred will-making till they were seriously ill, frequently dying shortly after; secondly, almost all wills were 'professionally' prepared, in the sense of being drafted with skill and clarity by persons practised in the art. (Indeed, in many respects the wording, style and layout of some wills was strikingly similar to those prepared by today's lawyers.) The draftsmen were probably local clergy, since few laymen were literate, and the parish priest or a curate was likely to be in touch with gravely ill parishioners.

Most testators commenced by bequeathing their souls to God, followed by small legacies to the parish church, and often to the 'mother church'—Winchester Cathedral. One or more executors were appointed to carry out the testator's wishes, and if he had young children, guardians (often called 'governors') might be named. Appointment of 'overseers', as well as executors, was customary, especially where a farming or other business was involved. Varying in number from one to six, they, like executors and guardians, were usually relatives or friends of the testator, their function being purely advisory, and they usually received a modest legacy.

A priced inventory of a deceased person's possessions (excluding freeholds and copyholds, fixtures thereto, and goods to which the deceased was entitled in right of his wife) became a necessary part of the process of obtaining probate about the middle of the 16th century. Prepared on oath by, or in the presence of, executors or neighbours who were qualified to assess values, inventories have limitations. Not only were appraisers often illiterate, but they commonly priced the contents of an entire room *en bloc,* and groups of items such as clothing, pewter and brass throughout the house were often lumped together. Criticism that some values appeared unduly low should be treated with reserve, as appraisers would have hesitated before falsifying a document made on oath.

An early local will is that of the vicar, William Edwards, dated 6 June 1522,[1] pre-Reformation, and the year Pope Leo X conferred on Henry VIII the title *'fidei defensor'*. As the contemporary probate copy of this document and its transcription are reproduced below, it calls for no comment beyond its typically specific reference to a bed and bedding, and the direction to the executor to 'fynd a prest syngyng and prayng for my soule . . . on hole yere . . .'. This last provision probably involved a priest, who could have been a secular Roman Catholic Mass-Priest, saying or singing a daily Mass for the dead in the parish church.

Women's wills were particularly uncommon because, if married, all their property belonged to their husbands until they were widowed. Elizabeth Godwyn, a farmer's widow with three sons, probably a daughter, and grandchildren, made her will in 1538[2] when Henry had just completed his breach with Rome. Notwithstanding the religious upheavals, she followed the custom of bequeathing her soul to God, our Lady and the Holy Company of Heaven, directing her body to be buried in the Church 'lytte' of East Meon, giving 2d. to the Mother Church, a sheep to the High Altar of East Meon, and two sheep to the local 'Guild off Jesus'. Then followed family provisions—a cow, 10 sheep and four bushels of wheat for son Rychard, 3s. 4d. for his daughter Elizabet and one sheep for each of Rychard's children. Marget Hamon, almost certainly the testatrix's daughter, received '10 sheep & a fetherbedde and bolster and a pere off shetes a brasse pott a cuborde & a bullok off 12 monyth olde'. Another son, Phylyppe, had a 'cow & all the shepe in hys kepyng above 30', and each of his and Marget's children were to have a sheep, and each godchild 2d. The will concluded by appointing Phylyppe overseer, with a blanket and sheet for his labour, and giving the residue of the estate to the third son, Ralf.

Rychard Lomer of Westbury, whose surname was probably derived from the lost medieval village a mile or two south-west, was a substantial farmer, making his will in 1548,[3] 'in the second yere of the raygne of Kyng Edwarde the Syxth by the grace of God Kyng of England Fraunce & Ireland defender of the fayth and of the Churche of England & also of Ireland the supreme hedd'. Describing the sickly boy-king as 'Kyng of Fraunce' was loyal, but hardly realistic, as only Boulogne and Calais then remained under his dominion.

Apparently the testator had no son—certainly none is mentioned. His wife, Alys, was given '5 score shepe & a score lambys, 4 kyen, 2 heyfers, 2 oxen, 2 horsses . . . the best fether bed & all thyngs therto perteynyng, a cubbard, a broche, an andyern, 2 brasse panys & a brasse pott, 10 pesys of pewter, 10 quarters barly, 5 quarters whete, halfe of old halfe new, & a sow, in mony £20 sterlynge, and 2 stalles of beys & one tode of wulle'.

The next beneficiary, Rychard Mawndfyld, received a substantial legacy of £20 plus five quarters of wheat and 10 of barley, after which follow gifts of sheep ('yewys, wethers and lambys') and of bullocks and cash to Robert and John Leffe, Nycholas and Mary Langrysh, Thomas Smythe, Thomas Horton, god children and cousins. Servant John Wade was remembered, with three sheep and three lambs, as was the Church: 'To be put in the chest in the Church 3s. 4d.' and 'To Sir Rychard curat of Estmene 3s. 4d.'. Residue went to son-in-law William Bren and Johanne his wife, also named as executors. Lomer's inventory and its transcription are reproduced below, showing his sheep to be worth 2s. 0d. each, steers 13. 4d., cows 10s. 0d., calves 5s. 0d., horses £1 0s. 0d., ducks 1½d., geese 3d., and a hive of bees 5s. 0d.

PROBATE COPY WILL OF WILLIAM EDWARDS, VICAR OF EAST MEON,

6 June 1552

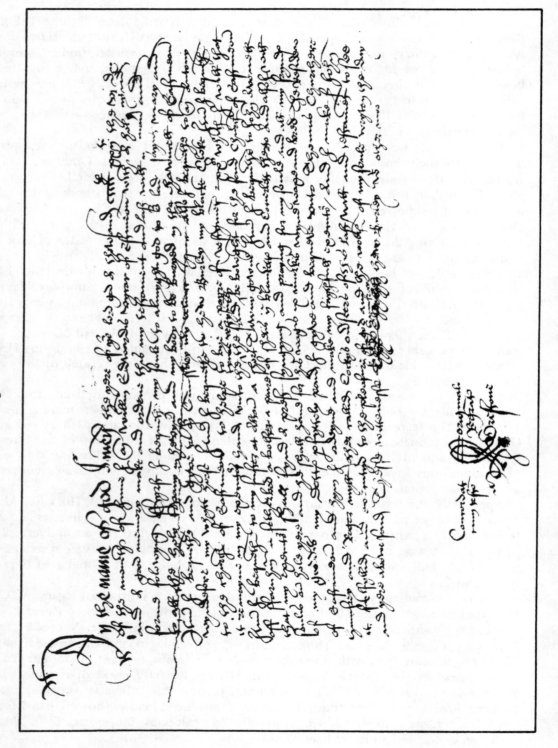

TRANSCRIPTION

In the name of God Amen the yere of your lord god a thousand cccccth xxii^{ti} the vi d[ay]
of the moneth of June   I Master William Edwardis vycar of Estmeon with a hol[e] mynd
and a good memory make and ordene this my testament and last will in maner and
forme folowyng ffyrst I bequethe my soule to almyghti God to our lad[y] saynt Mary and
to all the holy company in hevyn and my body to be buryed in the Chawncell of Eastmeon
Item I bequethe and gyve to Master Commissary my [   ] Also I bequethe to Master Antony
Wyndesore my whytt horse   Item I bequethe to Hew Burley my blacke Cloke   Item I bequethe
to the church of Eastmeon to helpe to bye a payre of vestymentes xx^s which I will that
it remayne in my executours hand unto the tyme the said vestymentes be bowght for the said Church of Eastmeon
Item I bequethe to my suster at Alton a short Tawny gowne   Item I bequethe to John Avenell
off ffarnham a fetherbed a bolstere a paire of shetis ii blankettes and Coverlett thereto and also I will
that my executour shall fynd a prest syngyng and prayng for my soule and all my fryndes
soulis on hole yere and he shall have for his wagis ix markis wyne waxe and bred The Residew
of my gooddis my dettes perfyctely paid I gyve and bequeve unto Thomas Churchere
of Eastmeon and hym I ordeyne and make my faythfull executour And I make Sir John
Humfrey and Roger myll other[wise] callid Cockys oversers of this last will and testament to see
it fulfyllid and executyd to the pleasure of god and the wolth of my soule wryton the day
and yere abovesaid   Thesse wittenesse John Humfrey Hew Burley with other moo

Concordat   originale

cum testo   Regrat

Orestone

Notes:

(1)   Use of capital letters and of roman numerals follows that of the manuscript.
(2)   Square brackets enclose words or parts of words indecipherable in the manuscript, and, in the case of 'otherwise', part of that
        word apparently omitted by the writer.
(3)   *See* glossary for meaning of 'commissary' and 'moo'.
(4)   Translated, the concluding note in Latin reads 'Corresponds with the original registered will'. This surrounds the monogram
        (or personal symbol) of the notary, whose surname is Orestone.

TRANSCRIPT OF THE PROBATE INVENTORY ON FACING PAGE

The Inventory of the goodes cornys & cattell
of Richard lomer of wes[t]bery in the paryshe of
Estmene in the County of Suthe[hampton] preysyd
indyfferently by Syr Rychard Alyn Curat[e]
John Boys   John Tyllborow

Item	*li*	*s.*	*d.*
In primis iiii cccc shepe	xi		
It. lxx tegges pc	iiii	xiii	iiii
It. iiii steres pc		iiii	markes
It. vii kyen & a bulle	iiii		
It. viii bullockes		vi	viii
It. v calfes pc		xv	viii
It. v horssys pc	v		
It. xx quarters malte	v		
It. xxiiii acres whete	vi		
It. xlix acres barly	xii	v	
It. hey		xxx	
It. the swyne of all sortes		xx	
It. one Carte one ploughe & harneys belongyge to them		xiii	iiii
It. xvi duckes		ii	
It. vi gese			xviii
It. x hennys & a cocke iiii capons		ii	iiii
It. iiii stalles beysse		v	
It. one byll ii axys			viii
It. iii peare of fethers with old yron			xii
It. ii flockbeddes ii Coverlettes i blanket		viii	
It. ii pare of shetes ii bolsters		iii	iiii
It. iii steynd clothis		ii	viii
It. one brasse potte one bell ii kettylles		iii	
It. ii platers ii candelstyckes one potynger i saucer		iiii	
It. one yowtynge vate a keve a kever a cowle			xx
It. iiii sackes a vyinshete		ii	
Sum total	lxxxv	xiiii	vi

Notes:

(1) Use of capital letters and of roman numerals follows that of the manuscript.
(2) Square brackets enclose parts of words omitted by the writer.
(3) '*li*', an abbreviation of the Latin 'libri', meaning 'pounds', preceded the '£' sign.
(4) 'pc', an abbreviation of the Latin 'precii', can be translated as 'worth' or 'valued at'.
(5) *See* glossary for meaning of kyen, stalles beysse, byll, flockbeddes, potynger, yowtynge vate, keve, kever and vyinshete.

PROBATE INVENTORY OF RICHARD LOMER, WHOSE WILL WAS DATED
18 April 1548

In 1550, Rychard Rynge of East Meon died, survived by a widow and two daughters, the introductory and closing wording of his will being so similar to Lomer's that both could have been prepared by the same draftsman—perhaps curate Sir Rychard Alyn, who received a 3s. 4d. legacy from Lomer, helped appraise Lomer's inventory, and witnessed Rynge's will. Rynge's inventory is notable because though farming stock was minimal—two acres of barley and two cows, indicating insufficient activity to constitute a family's livelihood—his household goods were more numerous and varied than the wealthy Lomer's. Among 150 items were a folding table, a form and four stools, six coffers, seven pairs of sheets, six brass pots, a posnet, six brass pans, four kettles, 15 platters, 12 potingers, five pewter pots, three salts, a carpet and a banker.

Why did a family of four, in times when household effects tended to be both sparse and spartan, need 15 platters and 12 porridge bowls? Possibly a clue lies in an inventory item, crossed out, but reading: 'The stuffe in the shoppe'. No value was shown, but apparently Rynge had been a shopkeeper, though one can but speculate why no stock-in-trade was listed. Perhaps the business had been closed due to his illness, or it may have been transferred to his family; and if preparation and sale of food had been involved the numerous culinary and eating utensils could have been needed.

In 1558, Elizabeth I's accession year, two wills deserve notice, those of Robert Wryte, a wealthy yeoman with widespread property, and of William Uppesdale, also a yeoman, but of lesser affluence. Wryte's will[5] commenced with customary religious bequests—6s. 8d. to East Meon church for his burial, 20s. towards church repairs, 4d. to Winchester Cathedral, and a cow to the Guild of Jesus. Gifts followed to his elder son, Edward, of a leasehold farm in East Meon (subject to payment of an annuity of £8 6s. 8d. to Margaret, his mother), together with 'the lord's stock of shepe', six horses, their harness, a cart, a plough, six quarters of wheat, 10 quarters of barley and 12 hogs. Next came provision for single daughters, Parnell and Johanne—£30 each, 'with honest apparell' for marriage, and his married daughter, Kateryne Jeffry, was to have 'fyve quarters of whete, 6 quarters of barley one irebounde carte of the mydell sorte & one cople of steres of 2 yeres age'. She must have been a farmer's wife.

Six male and female servants were then given barley, wheat, ewes, bullocks and cows (one also to enjoy a year's rent-free occupation of his cottage), and each godchild was to have 20d. at the testator's 'Monethes Mynd'. Younger son, Nycholas, possibly his father's favourite, was given 'all my lands . . . leases pastures woods . . . sett lying and beying in the paryshes of Clanfilde Catrington Warblington and Nutymber'—a scattered estate. Six overseers included 'John Horton Esquire', Nicholas Pynke and son Edward, of whom Horton received a black ox 'beying at fatting', and the others 5s. 0d. apiece. Finally, as a sort of codicil:

'Memorandum that my executors doo bestowe at my bureall and Monethes Mynde meate and drynke and money and to see the same honestly done'. Reference to 'the lord's stock of shepe' illustrates the practice of livestock as well as land being comprised in some leases, a practice that continued, to some extent, until comparatively recent years.

Wryte's lengthy inventory grouped household goods according to the rooms where kept—a hall, parlour, chambers over both, chamber 'where the wulle lyeth', inner chamber, buttery, kitchen, milkhouse and 'hynder' chamber—10 rooms in all. As would be expected of such a testator, some of his possessions reflected affluence—14 garments (doublets, jerkins, coats and jackets), seven silver spoons, four dozen other spoons, 28 pairs of sheets, 14 tablecloths, and five and a half ells of new cloth. He also had 'a payer of a[r]mour ryvetts a bowe and sheyff 8s. 0d.', and farm stock included 60 quarters of wheat, 100 of barley, 16 horses, numerous cattle and sheep, and the quaintly worded 'hey and vetchys for horsmeat', meaning, 'hay and vetches for horses' food'.

William Uppesdale's will[6] is typical of many, with frequent reference to sheep: 'I bequeathe to John Love my kynysman twoo ewe shepe I geve to Agnes Herring £10 0s. 0d. [worth] of woll I geve to George Herring one ewe shepe [I] geve to Margaret Grenell my servant one shepe I geve to evry one of my good children [godchildren] one ewe lambe'. Then follow provisions for the widow and five sons, the widow and eldest son benefiting most. The draftsman's treatment of the four youngest sons follows principles equally suitable to a 20th-century will: first, their cash legacies were to be paid in two instalments spread over a year, thereby reducing the risk of a sudden inheritance going to the heads of impetuous youngsters; and, secondly, the share of any son failing to attain 21 passed equally to his brothers.

Plague recurred periodically in England for well over three centuries after its 1348 devastation, and overwhelming circumstantial evidence points to its having struck East Meon in 1563. In that year London suffered what in proportion to its population may have been its most destructive visitation,[7] and deaths in Petersfield, from a population approximating to East Meon's, numbered 139[8]—nine times the previous 10 years' average. Either by chance or through practising isolation, East Meon deaths in 1563 were limited to 31,[9] 18 of whom died in August/September, as against a previous annual average of 12 and subsequent average of 15; so it seems that the number of plague victims was limited to about twenty. Nevertheless, a few families were particularly hard-hit, for between 17 July and 25 August Margaret, Thomas, Henrie, John and Nicholas Corps were buried, the last four within as many days; and between 27 August and 14 September Nicholas, John, Anthonie and Steven Steele succumbed.

When Nycholas Burwell signed his will[10] in 1566 he was rightly described as 'beynge syke of bodye, but hole and perfete of remembrance', because three days later he had died and his inventory had been prepared—by six appraisers, though the estate was not large. A small farmer whose wife, Dorothie, had died four years earlier leaving five children still under 20 years old, he directed that 'my brother Harry Grete shall have the government of my sayd chyldren and also to have the keeping of ther sayd goods . . . .'. Harry's different surname was probably due to his being a *brother-in-law,* but why so many appraisers? The answer may be provided by the testator's hoard of over £42 in cash, which, with only children surviving, could easily have 'disappeared'. The coins listed were 'souveraynes with 3 angeles £13 0d. 0d., Frenche crownes with one Ingeleshe crowne £10 3s. 0d.', shillings £13 0s. 0d., fourpenny pieces £3 0s. 0d., and sixpences also £3 0s. 0d. As angels were gold coins worth 6s. 8d., minted in 1464–65, and replacing the old version of the noble, they had been in circulation (or hoarded) over 100 years. Sovereigns, also gold and minted in 1489, were, by 1566, worth £1 10s. 0d.

The 1569 will of widow Jone Tyre[11] of Drayton reveals thoughts common to today's testatrices, who so often wish to pass on specific treasured possessions, such as rings or even garments, to named friends or relatives: 'I bequethe to my brother Nycholas Serell one silver ryng 12 owld silver grotes I bequeth to Jone Serell my sister-in-law one silver rynge I bequeth unto Elizabeth Tryvet my sister a lynan raile and a kercheve [and] my best hookes I bequeth to Elizabeth Lanman one kercheve and a raile'.

A few months afterwards John Strowder was so near death that he expired before his orally expressed testamentary wishes could be committed to writing, yet, as there were witnesses to those wishes, a nuncupative will[12] was admitted to probate. Being a small farmer of modest means, his legacies were limited to 6d. for Winchester Cathedral, 4d. to the 'poore mens box of the parish', an annuity of £1 10s. 0d. for his wife, £6 0s. 0d. for nephew John Strowder (payable by three annual instalments) and £1 0s. 0d., a bullock and a sheep to nephew Richard Strowder 'to be payde & delyvered at the terme [of] 7 years . . .', presumably because Richard was under age. Thoughtfulness was shown towards tenants John Raynolds and his wife, and Harry Mellys and his wife, permitted to continue dwelling in the testator's houses in each case 'so long as they both live payeng their rent & doyng their dutie'. It only remained for the two overseers to be named and rewarded with 2s. 0d. apiece, and for the residue to be given to son-in-law John Trybe.

Nicholas Pynke, yeoman of Oxenbourne, who had been one of Wryte's overseers, died in September 1570.[13] Yet another farmer, a substantial one, he owned eight horses, an unspecified number of 'rother bestes' (black oxen used for ploughing and other farm work) valued at £12 6s. 8d., 240 sheep, 38 tegs and 27 'hoggs and pyggs'. Corn comprised 40 quarters of wheat, 50 of barley, and 12 of oats. Other inventory items were 'Armar and wepon 13s. 4d.' and 'The lease of the farme—one hundryth marks'. The will gave a quarter of wheat 'to be dystrubythe amonge the pore people of the parrishe'; 20 sheep, 2 cows and a quarter of wheat and of barley to son Nycholas; similar live and dead stock to son Anthony, plus a 'masar' and three silver spoons; and 20 sheep to married daughter Magrett. The residue went to son John, whom we shall meet again.

Mathew Addarley of Coombe, who died a year later,[14] was a fairly small farmer, though with comfortable living standards as shown by household goods that included '3 lynnen testers, 8 payer of shetes, 3 tabylcothes, 4 napkyns, 2 tewells of dyaper and one other tewell; in bras 1 pan, 4 kyttylls, 4 potts, 3 belles, 1 chafyng dyshe, 6 candyllstyks and one owlde cawdron'. An interesting group of items in the inventory was 'a bow and halfe a shefe, a sword and dagger and a byll and hys parte in a gunne of the tythyng 6s. 0d.'.

As armour and weapons have appeared in several inventories, some explanation may be helpful. Starting with the Anglo-Saxon *fryd-service,* there was ever after an acknowledged obligation for able-bodied men to defend their country, or at least county, and subsequent legislation in 1181, 1285 and 1558 decreed the weapons men must keep according to their wealth.[15] The last of these acts obliged those with incomes of £5–£10 to keep a corslet, a bill, a halberd, a long-bow and a steel helmet, with proportionate demands on men with goods valued at £10 or more.

Between 1558–88 general musters were held at least every three years, when those liable for military service were bound to attend with arms and armour for public inspection of each county force. In addition, far more frequent *special musters,* of a more local nature, were held, their main purpose being *training* in the use of new weapons, for guns and pikes were replacing bows and halberds, and new strategies had to be adopted. Then, from 1573 'trained bands' came into existence, after which militiamen were divided into trained and untrained categories, only the former being regularly summoned.[16] Chapter Four refers further to this subject, but points needing to be made are: first, there existed certain publicly-owned arms and armour, often kept in the local church, an example being the 'gunne of the tythyng' in which Addarley held a share; and, secondly, an individual's duty to provide arms and armour arose from his financial or land-owning status, irrespective of his fitness for service, so the appearance of such items in an inventory does not necessarily mean the deceased was a potential fighting man.

So Wryte, Pynke and Addarley may or may not have been Elizabethan militiamen; Wryte had belonged to a generation of bowmen, though weapons were changing so rapidly that at Pynke's death in 1570 muskets were gaining ascendancy over bows, and his 'wepon' was most likely a musket. As for Addarley's 1571 inventory, he may have had a foot in both worlds—possessing his own bow, and sharing ownership of a communal gun, probably a musket, belong to his tithing.

It is time temporarily to leave wills, inventories and weapons, and return to the pipe rolls, though purists contend that after 1454 they were no longer *rolls*, but consisted of folios bound into annual volumes. In 1501,[17] when Thomas Style was 'reeve of the rents' and Thomas Corpus 'collector of the farm', Southmylle was 'farmed', as had been the case way back in 1207-08. Now, on payment of 15s. per annum, John Weston was the miller, successor to Thomas Holden. A lengthy list of rent defaults could be a further sign of slackening manorial discipline, though one defaulter, the Abbot of Burford, may have deliberately forfeited his copyhold due to its geographical remoteness from the Cotswolds. Another default concerned rent of 'one shope' near the cemetery, formerly held by Maurice Vale 'because it is in total decay'—a reminder that many houses (and the shop was doubtless a house as well) were not built to last, but till they fell down.

On a different plane, and headed 'Custom of the Park', is a declaration that Launcellet Baynbrygge was life holder of the offices of Keeper of the Park and Measurer of Tithe Corn, by virtue of letters patent granted by Bishop Langton and confirmed by the Prior and Chapter of Winchester Cathedral, his salary for the first office being 60s. 10d. per annum. Drayton Mill, like South Mill, was farmed—to Thomas Tyler at 26s. 8d. rent. Even the tithe corn of Oxenbourne and Ramsdean was 'farmed' to Thomas Holden (the former miller), whilst that of Langrish, Riplington, Drayton, Tigwell and Itedene (Jutish echo!) was 'farmed' to Richard Stempe. Clearly, entrepreneurs existed.

By the early 16th century, collection of tithes in kind by the lord was being largely superseded by farming out this cumbersome system of gathering Church revenue for cash payments representing substantial discounts, since the lord was relieved of the expense of employing staff and vehicles and maintaining barns to collect and store produce, quite apart from coping with attempted evasion. By 1520,[18] Nicholas Langrysshe was the tithe farmer of Langrish, specifically for corn, orchards, wool and lambs, paying 48s. 4d. per annum for the privilege.

A last glance at the pipe rolls, for 1550,[19] notes two curious references to nominal or peppercorn rents. Tenant John Dameane, whose theoretical obligation was 'the price of a pair of gloves', had, in fact, to pay 'nothing, by reason of his office because he is the lord's auditor'; and the rent (again theoretical only) of the Warden and Fellows of Magdalen College, Oxford, was '4d. for 1lb. of pepper'.

Manorial courts continued to function, and in 1556-57,[20] at the Turn of St Martin (1 October) John Style of Oxenbourne was presented because he allegedly 'made assault and attack upon Robert Sugget and extracted blood against the peace'. And at Riplington 'George French subverted his ploughland upon one boundary . . . between his land and land of Joan Heather and encroached himself on the land of the said Joan [by] an eighth part of an acre . . .'. The court tersely ruled 'He to amend'. Unsurprisingly, cultivation of long, narrow strips in the great open fields, without dividing hedges or fences, constantly involved disagreements.

The following spring, at the Turn of Hock[21] (the second Tuesday after Easter) a more widespread civil dispute came up, arguments having arisen between the copyhold tenants of Rydgland as to the extent of their rights to common pasture. With the concurrence of the parties, four 'arbitrators' were appointed (Walter Wryt, Jesper Daker, Anthony Style and Robert Hoker), who ruled, doubtless according to precedent, that the common pasture should be shared in the same ratio that the claimants' respective copyhold areas bore to one another; the outcome being that on one half of the common Margaret Westbrooke, John Corps, John Somer and John Bone could each pasture 16 sheep and Thomas Corps 20; and on the other half 'the tenant of Staveley' had the sole right to pasture 44 sheep. The roll concludes: 'And thus this controversy was determined and it was ordered by the Court that this ordinance should be strictly observed by the said tenants'.

Reference has already been made to arms and armour, to musters, to trained bands, and (in Chapter Two) to the 1327 Lay Subsidy. Now, as 1588 drew near, military and financial preparations to resist the threat posed by the Spanish Armada crystallised. Regarding taxation, it should be emphasised that innumerable, though not annual, subsidies were levied during the centuries after the 1327 Subsidy. Occasionally, in times of great need, a double rural rate of *two* fifteenths was imposed. But by the 16th century, with assessments completely out-of-date and expenditure rising, a 'full and entire' subsidy was periodically granted, based on ownership of land worth at least £1, or goods worth at least £3, producing £80,000 nationwide. With invasion looming, and consequently the need for armaments becoming increasingly pressing in the 1580s, parliament authorised such grants in 1585 and 1587 respectively. The earlier one was collected in two instalments, and the 1586 assessment roll[22] for East Meon's second instalment has survived.

Its artificiality and inadequacy is illustrated by only four *landowners* in East Meon Tithing and three in Coombe being listed, and *in every case* the value of their land was exactly one pound! No one was assessable in respect of land *and* goods, but the valuation of goods tended to be vastly higher than land. Thus, again quoting from East Meon Tithing, examples of goods' assessments are:

'Robert Wright, gent, £16; John Wright, gent, £10; Peter Tirrell £9; Margaret Langrishe £4; Anthony Cowse £8; Anthony Kerbye, alien, £10; Nicholas Langrishe £5'. Other members of the Langrishe family were well-off, with Edward's Bordean land assessed at £12, William's goods at Langrish worth £8, and Roger's goods at Ramsdean worth £3, the social status of each being marked by the appellation 'gent.'. In addition to finance provided from taxation, a voluntary fund was raised by the queen in 1588, and Nicholas Wright of East Meon, doubtless the youngest son of wealthy Robert Wryte, who died 30 years earlier, was one of the 80-odd Hampshire contributors.

Military preparations particularly affected Hampshire, a maritime county embracing Portsmouth and the Isle of Wight, both considered highly likely targets for invasion. From the viewpoint of army organisation, Hampshire had seven militia companies, matching its seven administrative divisions, and companies picked for service in 1588 were armed with the latest weaponry, 80 calivers and 70 pikes for each band of 150 men.[23] East Meon Hundred was one of the five hundreds making up the Alton Division, and, judged by surviving statistics of a few years earlier, may have had as many as 130 militiamen available for call-up.

Being adjacent to lofty Butser Hill, East Meon was also vitally concerned with the warning system provided by chains of beacons, both timber and fuel for Butser's beacon, being customarily supplied from Hyden Wood. When coastal look-out men, or crews of patrolling pinnaces spotted the approach of hostile ships, the plan involved beacons being successively fired in the Isle of Wight, on Portsdown Hill, on Butser, and then via Burnet and Crondall, over the county boundary into Surrey. In 1588, and again when further Spanish invasion attempts followed in 1596-97 and 1599, the beacons signalled neighbouring counties to despatch their forces to threatened areas; and the arrangement proved remarkably efficient, provided visibility was adequate.

In 1598 the Court Baron was still dealing with transfers of copyhold land—surrenders by outgoing tenants and admissions of their successors, though sometimes in harrowing circumstances and not actually within the court building. Yeoman Anthony Cowse, desperately ill on 30 May, took steps to put his worldly affairs in order. First came his nuncupative will,[24] giving 'all his landes and goods' to his wife Agnes for life, 'provided she sholde give and allowe unto his boye Robyn meate drinke lodginge and apparell sufficient and fower pounds a yeare towards his mayntenance', all such property to pass to Robyn on her death. Secondly, on the same day, for life was fast ebbing, he verbally surrendered[25] (from his sick-bed) to John Goddwyn the tithingman, representing the lord, 'his howse and all his lands in Eastmeane to the use of Robt. his boy which Robt. was then present in the sight of . . . Anthony his grandfather, kneelinge on his knees'. Apparently the will and surrender were inconsistent, perhaps understandably so in the circumstances, though the surrender, by reason of its immediate effect, would have taken precedence over the will, inoperative until death. Hopefully, the widow still received sufficient benefits for life to enable her to provide for the boy; but one can be sure the drama of that unhappy day, with the dying man surrounded by his wife, his old father, the tithingman, probably a priest and certainly neighbours, remained engraved on the memory of the youthful Robert (or Robyn).

As the 17th century got under way, the Court Barons of 1600-1601[26] faced a wide variety of business. The pitiful goods of felon Stephen Gunter in his wife's possession included two kettles, five pieces of pewter, an iron spit, two table-cloths, a cotton waistcoat and a gun. The whole, listed and priced at 19s. 6d., were declared forfeited to the lord, leaving poor Mrs. Gunter without even the means of cooking.

A year later the Langrish (or Langrishe or Langrysshe) family figured in two presentments.[27] First, William's partridges had been poached: it was recorded that 'Wee presente that George Compton did take partridges since the last Lawdaie in the ground of Mr. Willm. Langrishe by what authoritie or warrant wee knowe not'. Whether this was followed by a conviction and fine is unknown. And secondly: 'Wee presente that on Sundaie the 21th of Februerie laste about the hours of 7 and 8 at nighte came Thomas Potnell to the howse of Anthonie Langrishe at Ramsdeane, and there by throwing of stones againste the doore and howse caused the said Anthonie and his houshould to come foorthe and theie so coming the said Potnell offred to strike the said Anthonie with a cudgell hee had in his hand. Whereupon the said Anthonie sent for the tythingman whome also the said Potnell did resist, strike and otherwise greatlie abuse.

Potnell had previously defied authority by repeatedly poaching in the park and refusing to leave 'the Park pale' after he had 'kilde a counny with his pece'.[28] Whether drunk or sober, he must have been a tiresome character who was asking for trouble.

Alleged civil wrongs before the same court included failure to maintain hedges and stiles, and wrongful tree felling, whilst William Sutton had taken an undertenant 'without the consent of good liking of the parishe, whereuppon theie crave a paine for removing of him'. There was also a slightly vague presentment 'that the cattell called Rother beastes of Froxfild, Borden, Langrishe and Oxenbourne goeing about the lanes doe much harm and therefore wee crave a paine'. Recital of such seemingly trivial parochial events helps to explain the evolution of society, and for that reason is justified. On a far broader view, the reign of Good Queen Bess, attended by domestic prosperity and national formidability, was nearing its end. Great trouble lay ahead.

DEATH-BED SURRENDER OF ANTHONYE COWSE
30 May 1598

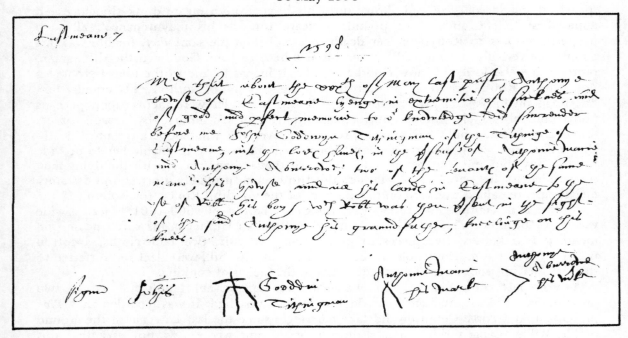

TRANSCRIPTION

Eastmeane   1598

Mem   That about The xxxth of May last past,   Anthonye
Cowse of Eastmeane (byenge in extremitie of sicknes   and
of good and perfect memorie to our knowledge did surrender
before me John Goddwyn Tithingman of the Tithinge of
Eastmeane, into the Lordes handes, in the presence of Anthonie Macie
and Anthonye Aburrowe;   two of the tenantes of the same
manor, his howse and all his landes in Eastmeane, to the
use of Robt his boy which Robt was then present in the sight
of the said Anthonye his grandfather, kneelinge on his knees.

Signed   John ✝ Gooddin   Anthonie Macie   Anthonye
                    Tithingman   ✗ his marke   ﹥ Aburrowe
                                                          his marke

Chapter Four

THE STUARTS AND THE COMMONWEALTH, 1603-1714

IN 1605 THE TUDOR monarchs had been succeeded by the Stuarts. For the Pinks (or Pynkes or Pincks) of Oxenbourne, the wheel of life was turning full circle. As we know, old Nycholas, who made his will and died in 1570, left the residue of his estate to his son John. Now, 35 years later, John was 'sick of bodie but of good and perfit memorie', and made his own will,[1] though he subsequently survived for 18 months. The Cathedral Church of 'Winton' was to receive 12d., 'the Church of Eastmean on wether sheepe', and 'I give unto the poore peopele of Eastemean on quarter of wheate to be made in bred and delivered at my funerall by the discretion of my overseers'.

The son had followed his father's example, giving a small sum to Winchester Cathedral (12d. as against 4d.) and had left the poor of the parish an identical gift, though adding the rather pleasant proviso for its distribution after his funeral in the form of bread. Having no sons, the bulk of his estate went to his nephews, sons of a late brother. No chattels in the inventory, dated July 1607, can be identified as inherited from Nycholas, though 'the Armyrie within the howse 16s.' could conceivably have comprised his father's 'armar and wepon'. If so, these had appreciated in value during 36 years from 13s. 4d. to 16s.! '2 duzen of wattles' may refer to hurdles for penning livestock—almost certainly sheep, though 24 hurdles would not have gone far in containing his total of 131 sheep. Another entry is of significance: it reads 'One lease of 9 yeres to come for certen shepe comon in the comon feildes 11s.'. So enclosure was still incomplete at this time.

When James I ascended the throne in 1603, thereby uniting the crowns of England and Scotland, the Church, at national and village level, remained powerful, notwithstanding previous upheavals. Vestries still annually elected Overseers of the Poor, whose duties included relief of native poverty and prevention of intrusion by aliens who might become a financial liability to the parish. Thus, when in 1623 a villager, one of the Pincke family, left East Meon (we know not whether temporarily or permanently) he had to obtain an official certificate—a sort of inland passport—to prevent his being hounded and returned to 'where he belonged'. It read as follows:

> These are to certify you to whom it may appertayne that Robt. Pincke is departed out of the parish of Eastmeon the 29th. day of May 1623 and hath in his custodye with him as by a certificate appeareth undere the hands of John Butler minister Richard Vinne Constable Raph Blanchard Tithingman Rob^{t}t Foule Nicholas Longe Agnes Pincke widowe and coppieholders.
> Dated the 28th. day of May 1623.[2]

In 1625, plague again descended on the village. This was also the year of the penultimate great outbreak in London. Annual deaths, having previously averaged 16, leapt to 57, the epidemic typically peaking in late summer and early autumn, as vividly demonstrated by burial figures:[3]

April	5 burials	October	8 burials
May	3 „	November	2 „
June	3 „	December	1 „
July	1 „	January	3 „
August	12 „	February	— „
September	16 „	March	2 „

Also typical was the way certain families suffered multiple losses or even annihilation; five Cagers and six Hencockes were buried during August/September, four Aburrows in September alone, and five Surketts in October/November. It must have been a time of great fear and grief.

The spate of house-building and re-building that began 50 or so years earlier proceeded apace, with bricks and tiles largely replacing traditional materials, partly due to increasing scarcity of suitable timber, formerly used in prodigal quantities. The *fine* book of Meon Church Manor for 1625-26[4] records the payment of 18d. by John Aylwyn for a licence 'to dig lutum and sand called in English cłay and sand upon the lord's waste called Le Stroude to make les tyles and backes' for the ensuing seven years. This may represent the birth of the first local brick and tile yard within the old parish boundary, a yard that was to remain in production for over three hundred years.

Another glance at the Court Rolls shows continuation of unneighbourly physical violence, when on 30 August 1626[5] a presentment alleged that 'John Ratleife, an inhabitant within the Hundred [since] the last Corte made a bludshed uppon Joan Jaye the wife of Anthonie Jaye gent. with his fist. Also . . . that the said John Ratleife did commit another bludshed since the last Corte uppon Anthonie Jaye the sonne of the sayd Anthonie Jaye with a buckett value of 2d.'.

Though the Overseers were primarily responsible for relieving poverty, whether due to illness, accident, old age or unemployment, individual benevolence also sometimes played a significant part. Charitable bequests to 'the poor', already an increasingly regular feature of wills, attained a new dimension when John Terrill, an East Meon butcher, and apparently either a bachelor or childless widower, died in 1627, having made his will[6] the previous year:

> I give and bequeathe fortie pounds to imploy and sett to worke the poor of the parish of Eastmeane aforesaid the said fortie pounds to be imployed according to the discrecion of Sir Francis Neale Knight whom I most earnestly and humbly intreat together with the chiefe inhabitants of the parish of Eastmeane as cheife and principall overseer for the imployment of the foresaid fortie pounds to the best benefitt that maie arise and accreu not by waie of uses but to keepe and imploy them the said poore and aged persons by waie of trading and at noe otherwise according to his and their discrecion.

Generously, Terrill also gave 'to a hundred poor people of Eastmeane twentie pence apeece to be paid and distributed amongst them at my buriall'.

Though King James initially favoured religious toleration, soon, troubled by the number of Roman Catholics, his attitude hardened, fines were reintroduced, and priests banished; then the Gunpowder Plot of 1605 exacerbated the situation, and Roman Catholics became outcasts. Broadly speaking, 'Church and King stood together. On the other side a party of Parliament and Puritanism was gradually being formed'.[7] Charles I succeeded James in 1625, and has been described as 'a sincere, Catholic-minded, anti-Puritan, artistic, not very intelligent, solemn, rather illiberal Anglican'.[8] The days of reasonable prosperity for most people continued. There was no standing army, and the decline of feudalism plus the use of gunpowder had outdated the days when yeomen were skilled archers and the gentry trained soldiers; and it has been said that 'the Musters were perfunctory, with many complaints of poor arms and non-attendance'.[9]

The earliest surviving East Meon muster roll, dated 19 May 1624,[10] names Wm. Bolde as captain, Wm. Harling as lieutenant, Anthony Langrishe and Thomas Fry as sergeants, plus two drummers and two 'fifes', There follow two lists, one specifying men due to wear corselets, together with names of those liable to provide of 'furnish' such armour; the other specifying each musketeer, and the name of his 'furnisher'. Occasionally arms or armour were to be furnished by the bearer himself, but usually by his father, by a stranger (male or female), or even a group. Typical entries include:

Edward Redding and Oliver Prouting	} furnished by John Witcombe
Anthony Terrill	furnished by his father
William Reeves	furnished by Sir Francis Neale
Anthony Corps and John Knight	} furnished by the tenants of Tygall

At the muster on Old Down in July 1626,[11] when Sergeant Fry had become 'churgion to the Company', there were 52 corselet wearers (though eight corselets were 'wanting'), and 77 musketeers. This substantial force was supplemented by 12 pioneers, 20 victuallers, 20 carters and 81 'spare men', pointing to the huge numbers involved nationally. One of the victuallers was Richard Smyther, whose subsequent death in 1633 is commemorated by a church tablet inscribed 'Heare lyeth the body of Richard Smyther, Who departed this life in hope of a better March ye 16, 1633'.

Following the 1626 muster, the captain penned a note:

Mr. Joy hath promised to provide his furniture with all convenient speed and I am contented to accept his promise and therefore return him not.
To the Constables of the Hundred of Eastmeane.
Willm. Bolde.

Perhaps the captain was particularly conscientious; the muster rolls certainly give no indication of undue slackness within his command. Meanwhile the struggle between King and Parliament intensified, Parliament's 'trump card' being its ability to raise revenue by legislation. Having dissolved Parliament in 1629, the King obtained money as best he could, but shortage of funds forced him to call a new Parliament in 1640. The point of no return was approaching.

In August 1642, civil war broke out. Over the next four years the fighting, confused and widespread, included sieges and battles in most parts of the kingdom, but, as a generalisation, a line from the Wash to the Solent divided the King's forces in the north and west from Parliament's in London and the south-east. East Meon, geographically more or less in 'no man's land', though not the exact scene of a battle, was very much in touch with events. No one can say with certainty where the allegiance of most villagers lay, though I suspect the majority, whilst maintaining outward neutrality, secretly sympathised with the King, as did most of the English countryside, market towns and cathedral cities.

Parliamentary forces under Sir William Waller captured Portsmouth, Farnham, Winchester, Arundel and Chichester in the late summer and autumn of 1642. A year later, with the King's headquarters at Oxford and Parliament's in London, and Winchester and most of the west in Royalist hands, the outcome remained wide open. That autumn, the Royalist Lord Hopton divided his army into three brigades, quartering them at Alresford, Petersfield and Alton.[12] Some of these forces, proceeded via Harting and Midhurst, captured Arundel in early December, thereby obtaining a springboard for a further eastward advance in the spring. En route, a skirmish occurred at Harting, five miles from Petersfield, when 120 of Hopton's cavalry were literally caught napping in that village by 400 dragoons under Parliament's Colonel Richard Norton.[13] At least three men were killed, Harting's oldest register recording 'There were 3 soldiers buried Nov. 24, 1643'. The threat to Parliament called for counter-attack; whereupon Waller, after a surprise night march from Farnham, captured Alton on 13 December, killing 40 Royalists and taking 875 prisoners; and then, four days later, he set off for Arundel, which was recaptured on 20 December.

By March 1644 a major clash was building up. Waller led his Arundel forces towards Petersfield, thence to a muster of his horse at East Meon on 26 March. Next day there was a rendezvous on 'the heath by East Meon' (probably the reverse slope of present Westbury Forest) of Waller's men, plus Sir William Balfour's from Petersfield, and Major-General Richard Browne's Londoners from Midhurst. Something like 10,000 men and a great number of horses were there, numbers that could not be kept secret from the enemy. Indeed, the Royalist generals at Winchester, assuming that city to be threatened, hurriedly marshalled their forces under Lord Hopton and advanced towards the Meon valley. The two armies, numerically well matched, were but a few miles apart, watching for an opening as minor skirmishes developed. Then Waller, hoping to sever the Royalists from their Winchester base, set off for Alresford, probably marching along Vinnall's Lane, West Meon, and thence to Bramdean. Hopton, reading Waller's mind, immediately headed in the same direction, the armies marching flat out in parallel columns, a mere mile or so apart, often within sight of each other. Hopton narrowly won the race, and the two armies camped for the night of the 27th near Cheriton.

After a day of skirmishing, the stage was set for battle on the 29th, Waller's forces drawn up between Bramdean and Hinton Ampner and facing north, where Hopton's army, on and near East Down, barred the way to Alresford. From 8 a.m. until well into the afternoon fortunes fluctuated, but by 5 p.m. the Royalists were in orderly retreat, passing through Alresford and heading for Basing. Though the numbers killed (approximately 300 Royalists and 60 Roundheads) were small compared with the total forces deployed, the outcome of the battle of Cheriton proved a turning point in the war. The following day Waller held the keys of Winchester. The Royalist threat to London was averted, the King had lost the initiative, and, in June was forced out of Oxford. In mid–1646 the King surrendered himself to the Scots, and the war was over— for two years.

The year 1648 saw a fresh attempt to restore Royalist fortunes, leading to the Scottish army being destroyed at Preston, following which the King was handed over, and, on 30 January 1649, executed. Sadly, that horrifying act failed to bring lasting peace, for the Prince of Wales, returning to Scotland from exile, was acknowledged there as Charles II. To forestall another Scottish invasion, Cromwell's 'Ironsides' headed north and met and defeated the Scots at Dunbar in September 1650. Even then, a final scene of the national tragedy remained to be enacted a year later, when the Scottish army, with the young king, penetrated England as far as Worcester, before again encountering defeat at Cromwell's hands on 3 September 1651. Charles escaped, travelling in disguise to Southwick near Brighton, whence he sailed to safety on the Continent aboard the barque *Surprise,* after spending a night on the way at a Hambledon cottage still known as 'King's Rest',[14] and meeting some of his followers on Old Winchester Hill.

Now it is time to pick up the threads of village life, and to seek clues regarding the impact of national events. As usual, wills and inventories deserve attention, first, because they afford a reminder that the ordinary working and domestic lives of ordinary people continued to follow predictable paths, on the surface at least; and, secondly, because there is always a chance of apparently routine testamentary items providing tantalisingly incomplete glimpses of current affairs that were far from ordinary. An East Meon man, Henry Goldfinch, made his will[15] on 11 July 1643, when he was 'weake in body', died within a few days, and was buried on 1 August. Though described in the will as a yeoman, he was an affluent farmer, employing at least six 'servants', and leaving an estate valued at £422 17s. 4d. The inventory, dated 'the laste day of Juli', shows the farmhouse accommodation comprised a hall, chamber above, pantry, parlour, servants' chamber, wool loft, milkhouse, kitchen and millhouse. Live and dead stock were valuable, including wool (£27), horses and harness (£42), cows (£35), growing corn (£160) and sheep (£110). Then comes a reminder that war was raging: 'One musket sowrde and bandlere and one foulling peese £1 05.00). Whether Henry Goldfinch had participated in earlier fighting, or merely furnished arms for others is unknown, nor can we say with certainty whether he was a Royalist or Parliamentarian.

Yet another affluent yeoman farmer, 'signed sealed and published' his will[16] four months later in November 1643. He was John Trybe 'of the Strowd in the parishe of Eastmeane', and his inventory, prepared in the same month, included 'One muskett, one coslett, one sword and one pike bandaleers and rest 30s.'. Again we are left wondering whether he participated in the war, as a foot soldier.

The will's contents tell us he was survived by a son (also John), by four of his five daughters (all five of whom had married yeomen—three Sussex men, and two Hampshire men) and by 19 grandchildren. Scrupulous fairness on the testator's part shines through the skilfully drafted document, and the rather charming wording of the appointment of overseers is noteworthy: 'And I doe intreate my loving freinds John Goodyer of Weston in the parishe of Buriton . . . gent and William Legge of Petersfield gent to bee overseers . . .'. Those 'loving freinds' also attested the will, John Goodyer being the eminent botanist who a few years later was described as 'the ablest herbarist [*sic*] now living in England'. Two further comments occur: first, though Trybe died in November 1643, probate was not granted till November 1645, probably reflecting the virtual closing down of many church courts during the war. Secondly, the hamlet of Stroud, where Trybe lived (previously called 'Le Stroude' in the manorial fine book), was referred to in the will as 'the Strowd'. Today, nearly three and a half centuries later, that same expression is widely used, probably due to its derivation from the Old English *strōd,* meaning marshy land overgrown with brushwood.

Goldfinch and Trybe apparently died of natural causes, though one or both could have sustained wounds before coming home to die. Which leads to the 'Amens Plenty' legend, the supposed story of four soldiers killed in the war having been buried beneath the floor of East Meon Church. The *facts* from which this legend arose were noted in a parish register by the then vicar, the Rev. W. Brodie, in 1870: 'During the repairs of this Church some very curious discoveries were made, which ought not to be forgotten. Under the stone in the South Transept enscribed "Amens Plenty" were found the skulls of 4 men—placed back to back, who, as the remains evidently showed, had been buried upright. The stone was then further south, underneath the present pews on the east. The stone being removed to erect a scaffold pole, the fact above noticed was ascertained. At present no sufficient explanation of the meaning of the stone—or of the burials— has been given'.

Predictably, a tradition soon grew to explain the discovery: one version published in 1877[17] being that during the Civil War four soldiers were killed during Hopton's march from Winchester to Arundel, and continuing: 'let the imaginative believe that four Psalm-singing knaves were killed on their way through East Meon into Sussex, and buried in grim jest as a quartet to sing Amens Plenty without interruption'. This writer adds: 'The lettering is very plain and precise, and might pass for a very modern [1877] effort; but it is almost identical with that cut on the grave of Shakespeare's wife Anne at Stratford-on-Avon 1623'. Nevertheless, the *V.C.H.* describes the lettering as 18th-century. A slightly different version of the tradition ascribes the 'curious discoveries' to a hurried burial service over the bodies of some of Waller's soldiers killed in a skirmish before the battle of Cheriton.[18] Nevertheless, whilst local traditions endure for long periods, and frequently have a factual basis, it is hard to accept this one at face value; first, because it is unlikely that unknown soldiers would have been buried in a place of honour within the church, as distinct from the graveyard; and secondly, why no mention of such a burial in the church register? Though the times were exceptionally disturbed, East Meon's burial register was maintained, but contains only one mention of 'military' burial: '1644 Apr. 2nd. A soldier buryed who dyed at Thomas Jarman's house'. The date, four days after the Battle of Cheriton, pre-supposes the likelihood of the unknown man having been wounded there, and, struggling back along the route he had followed a few days earlier, possibly with the help of comrades, found he could go no further. The burial was openly recorded, as was that of the three soldiers at Harting a few months previously, so the legend, obviously unheard of by East Meon's vicar in 1870, seems without foundation.

Apart from direct or indirect involvement in battles or skirmishes, East Meon people ran a real risk of their property being plundered by part-time, semi-disciplined soldiers, usually far from home, often hungry and unpaid. Light is shed on the problem by a Council of War proclamation dated 7 December 1644 and issued from Waller's Petersfield headquarters:

> Whereas many abuses and violencyes are dayly offerred and practiced upon countrymen both in theire dewllinge, and travelling on the road by soldiers in plundering theire horses cattle sheepe and other provisions from them some of wch intended for the markette: It is this day ordered by the Councell of Warr that no soldiers upon any pretence whatsoever shall from henceforth plunder, seise or take away any of the goods, sheepe, cattle, horse or horses whether by exchaning or otherwise from any countryman or other traveller upon the road, nor molest in theire person or goods any man or woman comeing to or from the markett without expresse order from the Generall or other superior officer haveing power thereunto, upon paine of death without mercy. This order to be published at the head of every Regiment.[19]

This amounts to pretty plain speaking, which doubtless had a salutary effect. However, though we are unaware of the extent of local plundering, much is known of

1.   Ramparts of the Iron Age hill-fort, Old Winchester Hill, probably dated to *c.* 250 B.C. The single bank and ditch still measures 18 to 23 feet vertically from crest to ditch.

2.   Bronze Age burial barrows within Old Winchester Hill's 14-acre enclosure. Grazing sheep help to preserve the natural downland turf.

HEAD OF A WOMAN,
from a statue in limestone,
the hair rendered in linear tooling
and dark paint (of which traces remain).
FOUND at REDWOOD, EAST MEON, HANTS.

Given by Messrs. E.S. & G.S. Jennings, 1937 (7-9.1)

3. (*left*) The head (rear view) is part of a limestone statue, dated to the second century A.D. It was accidentally discovered in the parish, and is evidence of Roman occupation.

4. (*below*) The face, less than lifesize, is largely destroyed.

5. (*opposite page, above*) A somewhat sombre Methodist Chapel group *c.*1893.

6. (*opposite page, below*) Fife and drum band at nearby Langrish Vicarage, 1896. Standing, are Robert Fisher (*second from left*) and his father, George Fisher (*on right*).

7.   Schoolboys *c.*1900, with headmaster William S. Tregear and assistant teachers Ada Hovell and Frida Kille.

8.   Schoolgirls *c.*1900. Back row (*left to right*): Isabel Budd, Miriam Nash, Mabel Pollard, May Kille, Dorothy Kille, Winnie Moody, assistant teacher Frida Kille. Middle row: Unknown, Lily Wilks, Kate Blackman, Nancy Micklam, Winnie Smith, Miriam Sawyer, Ellen Chivers. Front row: Beatrice Parfit, Emily Nicholson, Nellie Hockley, Rose Nicholson, Annie Moon, Nellie Moon.

9. Westbury House before its destruction by fire in November 1904.

10. Westbury House after the fire during which its owner, Col. H. Le Roy Lewis, performed heroic feats.

11. Westbury House staff in 1895. Judged by appearance, the smartly-dressed man (*seated right*) must have been the butler.

12. Westbury cricket team, 1909. Reference to 'West Meon' in the caption is probably explained by the club's ground and pavilion being just within West Meon parish, though Westbury House was (and is) in East Meon.

.Davis, G.Hale, G.Paice, R.Tulley, R.W.Read, R.J.Treble, F.Sedgwick, G.Longhurs
.Gregory, A.Beckingham, W.H.Treble, Mr.S.H.Le Roy Lewis, Col. Le Roy Lewis, Mijs Le Roy Lewis, W.Tulley, H.Forc
Westbury. Cricket Club. WEST MEON. 1909

13. Mr. T. A. Adams's premises look smart and efficient. Note the 'miniature' horses and human figures, so depicted to avoid obstructing the shop windows.

14. The same premises about 1919, then owned by Stephen J. Parsons, with the village's first motor delivery van outside.

15. (*left*) George Attwood, the almost immortal boot and shoe maker and sexton. His daughters ran a dame-school at 1 Westbrook Cottages.

16. (*below*) Nurse Kate Micklam and her family about to set off for a cycle ride *c.*1903.

17. (*opposite page, above*) All Saints' Church— a 1793 water-colour. Note the jettied Tudor cottages (*right*) in what later became part of the churchyard.

18. (*opposite page, below*) All Saints' Church *c.*1872, as seen from Park Hill. The original five Forbes Almshouses and *The George*, immediately beyond, are in the middle distance (just left of the Church tower).

19. The Court Hall—south elevation, showing the massive brick chimney.

20. The Court Hall—east elevation. The 16th- or 17th-century east wing is on the right.

21. Bryden etching of Church Street, 1905.

22. The same today. All the buildings are virtually unchanged.

23. Bryden etching of The Cross, 1905. The cow grazes in the present Vicarage garden.

24. The same today.

25.   Bryden etching of Chapel Street, 1905.

26.   The same today. Bert Warren's house (*extreme right*) was destroyed by fire. Heycroft House (*next-door*) luckily survived, and has been restored to reveal its timber-framed construction with herring-bone brick infilling to the east elevation.

27. (*opposite page, above*) Bryden etching of the Court House and Hall, with farmyard and farm buildings, 1905.

28. (*opposite page, below*) The same today.

29. (*right*) The thatched High Street cottages destroyed by the great fire of 1910, as viewed from The Square.

30. (*below*) The fire raging, furniture piled in the street, and a 'human chain' passing buckets of water from the river to protect the thatched roof of Potter's General Warehouse.

31. Smouldering ruins, with little more than chimney stacks standing.

32. Next day. Petersfield fire brigade, with the village policeman and boy scouts towards the left.

33. Potter's General Warehouse as it was when thatched.

34. Corner Cottage, with tiled roof as it now is, Heycroft House in the distance and Middle Barnards and Barnards Corner in left foreground.

35. High Street, looking north-west, *c.*1910. Centre, Forge Sound, a medieval house, possibly dating from the 14th century; on extreme right the canopy which projected in front of the old butcher's shop; and in middle distance on left the Tudor cottages that stood on Washers Triangle, demolished *c.*1920.

36. Today, Forge Sound (*left*). The butcher's shop (*right*) having ceased to be used as such since 1957, is now part of Riverside.

37.   Bread delivery by Savage and Parsons at Frogmore. Charlie Merritt leans nonchalantly against the bridge, with Mill Cottage in the background.

38.   Frogmore in the 1930s. Mill Cottage, formerly thatched, has acquired a tiled roof and dormer windows. The other cottage has been demolished.

39. The Forge *c.*1909. Master blacksmith Jim Hobbs (*fourth from left*) is flanked by his sons Donald and Harold. Employee Walter Lambert holds the pony (*extreme left*) and the little old man, Jimmie Lock, retired and blind, carries a travelling blacksmith's tool-box. The carter is unknown.

40. (*left*) Henry Curtis Gallup, owner of Bereleigh, mounted on his hunter. He enlisted in the Royal Artillery at the beginning of World War I.

41. (*opposite page, above*) Maypole dancing at the Vineyard Hole, *c.*1923, was followed by an outdoor tea.

42. (*opposite page, below*) The procession back to the village. One of the passengers in the leading wagon is Kate Masters (the Vicar's wife) wearing Red Cross uniform.

43. Nellie Aburrow outside Drayton Mill.

44. Aburrow's timber-yard at Drayton Mill.

45.   Leydene House, built by Eleanor Countess Peel, and now the ward-room of H.M.S. *Mercury*.

46.   A meet of the Hambledon Hounds at Bereleigh in the mid 1920s. The owner, Major Reginald Nicholson, stands to the left of the doorway (in hunting attire).

47.   The Home Guard, 1940 or 1941. Most of those armed with rifles are apparently World War I veterans, wearing medal ribbons, many with N.C.O.'s stripes.

48.   The Auxiliary Fire Service unit fought fires caused by bombing in Portsmouth and Southampton. The Stolk motor trailer pump delivered 180 gallons per minute.

49. Flooded High Street, *c.*1954.

50. More floods, *c.*1954—Church Street.

51. (*above*) The old East Meon Hall, originally East Meon Reading Room, Library and Coffee House dating to the 1880s, and later known as the Church Institute.

52. (*below*) The modern Village Hall opened in 1974.

53. (*opposite page, above*) The old school (*middle distance*) with Vineyard Hole beyond.

54. (*opposite page, below*) High Street, looking west.

55. Today's panorama of the village from Park Hill. In the middle distance are the new school (*centre*) and Village Hall (*right*).

56. Butser Ancient Farm, sited on a spur projecting northwards from Butser Hill.

57. Looking north from Hyden Hill, with South Farm in the foreground and All Saints' Church far beyond.

58. Large barn at Lower Farm being re-thatched with Norfolk reeds.

59. Sheep on Wether Down (part of Lower Farm).

60. More sheep on Wether Down, with shepherd Malcolm Painter silhouetted beyond.

64.   Clara Fisher, born 1902.

61.   Bert Smith, retired thatcher, born 1899.

63.   George Macdonald, born 1894.

65. (*above left*) George Kille, whose family 'have been around for 400 years'.

66. (*above*) The late Jack Cook was a shepherd.

67. (*below left*) The late Ethel Lambert, born 1892, sang to Queen Victoria.

68. (*below*) Jesse Tubb, retired farm worker, born 1904.

the impact of Puritanism on both religious and secular daily life. Even before the war, in January 1641, parliament ordered commissioners to remove 'images, superstitious pictures and relics of idolatry' from churches throughout the country. Some months later came the abolition of Deans and Chapters, followed in May 1643 by a requirement that 'the basons and candlesticks of late years made to be used upon the altar be lent upon the publique faith [and] the rayles about the table and crosses about the church be pulled down and the table removed from standing altarwise and the ground levelled'. Innumerable churches and many cathedrals, including those at Chichester and Winchester, were desecrated, and at Winchester troops carried 'great store of popish books, pictures and crucifixes . . . up and downe the streets and Market-place in triumph'.

In 1646 the humiliation of the Church of England was carried a stage further by the abolition of the episcopacy, many bishops were charged with treason, and those who escaped that ordeal were ejected from their houses and deprived of their possessions. From 1647 marriages had to be civil, burial of the dead 'without any ceremony', and even observance of Christmas, Easter and Whitsunday was forbidden. Puritanical grimness put an end to bear-baiting, cockfighting, athletic sports, horse racing, betting, gambling, wrestling and even taking a Sunday walk! Swearing became punishable by a fine, and adultery by death.

The year 1647 saw the Parliamentary Survey of the Manor of East Meon.[20] Belonging to the bishop, and therefore to be sold, a preliminary survey to establish its extent and value was necessary. Painstakingly and skilfully prepared by sworn jurors, this lengthy document contains a vast amount of reliable information about places, people and customs. An example of its detail is its description of:

> The Mannor house called the Court house beeinge strongly built with stone, havinge a large hall, a large parlor, a dining roome, a kitchen, a buttery, a larder, a dayhouse, a kill, three lodginge chambers, a corne chamber, a cheese chamber with some other little roomes. Before the entrance of the house is a gatehouse with three roomes thereunto belonginge. The scite consistinge of two little gardens and one hopyard, and two little courts west beefore the house, lyinge altogether between the streete of Eastmeon on the west, and a feild called the Berry Garden on the east, neare unto the same on the northwest is the Church, on the north is a highway called Hide Lane, and on the south is a peece of ground called Dove garden containinge together one acre. Belonginge to the said house is a large barn and yard which lyeth on the west of Eastmeon Streete, and over against the same on the east side the foursaid street is a stable and yard beefore the same.

Particulars follow of the 635-acre Court Farm, some of whose field- and place-names still survive—e.g. 'one inclosed pasture called Small Down containing 120 acres, one sheepewalke not inclosed which will sumer 400 sheepe containing . . . 150 acres and known as Wether Down, Lay Down and Shrubs', and Duncombe Wood.

The landlord and tenant relationship can be summarised as follows: the Manor House (or Court House) and Court Farm, and livestock consisting of 300 'multons' and 300 ewes (valued respectively at 16d. and 14d. a piece), had been leased in 1614 by the then bishop to Sir John Pessall, for the lives of Sir John's sons, William, John and Robert, or the longest liver of them. Annual rent was £10 10s. 0d. for the house and land, and £11 13s. 4d. for the stock, subject to the tenant's liability to replace dead sheep. The tenant was obliged to repair buildings (being supplied with 'great timber . . . by appoyntment of the wood[w]ard' and also entitled 'by like appoyntment [to] fireboote, cartboote and rodds to make hurdles . . .'), and also to 'find for the Steward and other the officers at the keepinge of the Courts lodgings, hey, litter and fower bushells of oates'.

Sir John had died before 1647. The lease consequently vested in his son, Sir William Pessal, for two lives, namely his own and that of his brother John, as Robert had also died. However, to complicate matters, Sir William granted a sub-lease to Marmaduke and John James, as trustees for Nathaniell Hallowes of Derby. The date of this sub-lease, '29 of May 23 Car.'—i.e. 29 May 1647, was only two months before the survey commenced. As Hallowes bought the freehold in 1648, after four and a half centuries of continuous ownership by successive bishops, there was an obvious connection between that acquisition and the recent sub-lease in his favour. Perhaps Sir William Pessall sold his leasehold estate because he could not bear his ecclesiastical landlord being replaced by an unknown layman; or possibly he had become unpopular with Cromwell during the war, and, in consequence, was put under pressure to act as he did; there could be other explanations as well.

The Survey, having dealt in detail with the Court House and farm, next describes the 163-acre Church Farm, which included 13 acres in 'the comon feild called Westfield', and was leased (also for lives) to Richard Hildersham at £4 13s. 4d. per annum. Then, 'there is allso belonginge to this Mannor a Parke scituate and lyinge near the town of Eastmeon and known by the name of Eastmeon Parke lyinge' north-east of the church and south of 'the Mannor of Berley'. Having defined the boundaries of the 500-acre bishop's deer park (still commemorated by the name of Park Hill and Park Farm), the Survey records that it was 'paled about' [fenced]; 'stored with conies'—i.e. stocked with rabbits, as distinct from deer—and, finally, that Sir William Lewis was in physical possession, and claimed to hold the two posts previously mentioned, namely keeper of the park and measurer of 'tithe corn and wheat' of the rectory of East Meon, with all profits belonging to those posts. The Survey then recites the various legal documents evidencing Sir William's title, which included a lease granted by Bishop Watson to Queen Elizabeth I in 1581 (and assigned by her three months later), and mentions three other interesting points: first, that the annual 'rent' due to the bishop was '200 conies at such time and place the bishop shall require at any of his three houses of Waltham, Wolvesey, or Farnham' (non-indigenous rabbits having almost certainly been originally introduced by the Normans in the late 11th century); secondly, that the fee payable to Sir William for his 'offices' was £6 1s. 8d. per annum; and thirdly, that the lessee of the park was entitled to 'sufficient and competent fire boote, house boote, post boote, pale boote and raile boote'. Returning again to the Survey:

> There is belonging to the lord of this Mannor two corne mills under one roofe commonly called and knowne by the name of Shutt Mill which mills lye west from Eastmeon, and are worth upon an improvement £20 p.anno. Those mills are in the possession of James Hunt of Popham in the County of Southampton Esq. And there are severall coppices called Hiden Woods adjoining south-west on Wether Downe, Laye Downe and Shrubbs before mentioned in the particulars belonging to the Mannor house contayning by estimaton 120 acres and are worth p. ann. £25. The beacon on Butser hill hath beene usually suplyed out of these coppices both with timber and fewell.

Shutt Mill, let at 10s. 4d. per annum, was the mill listed in the Domesday Survey as belonging to the Bishop of Winchester 561 years earlier, then worth 30 pence a year; and was destined still to be a working water-mill, known as Drayton Mill, in the 20th century. Next:

> Belonging to this Mannor in the towne of East Meon is a Church and Viccaridge house . . . and 2 Churches or Chappells or ease the one in Froxfielde the other in Steepe which have been usually served by the Viccar of Eastmeon; all worth with all tithes belonging to the same p. ann. £120. The present incumbent is one Mr. Downes; the guift of the same hath beene in the Bishop of Winton but whether as Bishop or lord of the Mannor it doth not apeare.

Next follow separate descriptions of 21 freehold and over 330 copyhold properties in the manor, with the names of owners—still called 'tenants', since each owed some obligation to the lord. Those obligations, which, as we have seen, usually originated in a duty to render so many days free labour, had long since been commuted to an annual monetary or other payment, but in the succeeding centuries the value of money had so changed that there was nothing unusual in a rent of 3d. for a cottage, or, in one case, 2d. for three acres of land. However, the annual obligation was not always rendered in cash, a delightful example to the contrary being Sir William Lewis's land called Rosecroft, held by the yearly rent of one rose! Quite a few other copyholders had to render a hen, or a specified number of hens, to the lord, either in lieu of or in addition to money, and one or two paid in wheat.

Not content with these almost endless individual descriptions of hundreds of properties, the surveyors then summarised the overall manorial income, converting payments in kind into their equivalent cash value, and specified the annual payments, or outgoings (called 'reprisals') due *from* the lord. Thus:

There is a rent paid by the sevrall tennants of cocks and henns called churchets besides the rebates to widdowers and widdows	£6 11s. 0d.
There is allso paid a rent wheate of three quarters paid by the said tennants vallued to be worth p. anno.	£3 16s. 0d.
There is belonging to this Mannor one fayer every yeare which is kept at South Farme, in a feild called Fayer Feilde or Chappell Close in the parrish of East Meon. This fayer is kept on the Ladyday in Harvest. The profits thereof belonginge to the lord are	£1 10s. 0d.

Then, under the heading of 'reprisals':

Nicholas Pinke claimeth the office of baylife of the bayliwick of East Meon for his own life and the life of Will. Heycroft, granted to them by patten from Lancelot Andrewes late Bishop of Winton. The fee for the same is chargeable out of the Mannor of the said bayliwick and is p. anno	£10 0s. 0d.
The reeves and beedells have been equally payd out of the rents p. anno	£2 0s. 0d.
There have beene equally payd to the Vicker of East Meon for five quarters of wheate p. anno	£1 0s. 0d.

The time taken by the surveyors in compiling the Survey must have run into weeks, or even months; but its object was soon achieved, since, as stated above, the Court House and farm were sold to Nathaniel Hallowes in 1648, the year in which South Farm was bought by Richard Dannald; and in 1649 East Meon Manor, the Park, Church Farm, the Shutt Mills and other premises were purchased by Francis Allein. The ordinary people of East Meon were living in times of great change, for now, in addition to the impact of Puritanism on their religion, the manor courts that had functioned since time immemorial under the aegis of successive bishops were held and administered by the layman who had bought the manor, or by his steward. Indeed, we know that a court was held on 24 September 1649, when a William Musgrave was fined 6d. for emptying his lime-pits and throwing skins into the water.[21]

In 1653 the government decreed that henceforth marriages should be solemnised before a justice of the peace, after the publication of banns. A 'Register' [registrar] was to be appointed, with the duty of attending such marriages, and having the custody of a book in which 'births, marriages and burials should be entered'. East Meon's church register, whose parchment pages had been in continuous use for nearly 100 years, even throughout the Civil War, speaks for itself:

> Memo. that John Earwaker was elected and chosen Register for the Parish of Eastmeane. And was sworne into that office before us this 9th day of December 1653.
>
> Tho. Coke
> Edw. Hughes.

Nevertheless, the same ancient register was maintained much as before in respect of baptisms and burials. Marriage entries temporarily followed a different pattern, recording the publication of banns, and, usually but not invariably, concluding with a statement of the date when each marriage was performed by a named J.P. Banns were still published in the church, except for two cases when Petersfield Market was preferred:

> The purpose of marriage betwixt Anthony Barlowe and Elizabeth Haycroft booth of the parish of Eastmeon of the Countie of South was published three severall marcat dayes in the marcat of Peetersfeeld. And ther was noe exception or obiection made but they weare lawfully married by Justis Michell the one and thirtieth of July 1654.

Between 1653–57 the register records 31 such 'non-religious' marriages, 'Justis Collens' officiating in 10 such cases. The same register confirms that the troubles of other folk as far-off as Marlborough could still be charitably remembered:

> The 15 day of March 1653. Collected in the Parish of Eastmeon the sume of three pounds and one penny towards the loss by fier at Marlburrow.

On 3 September 1658, the anniversary of the battles of Dunbar and Worcester, Oliver Cromwell died without having named a successor, leaving a vacuum that no other parliamentary leader was capable of filling. The Long Parliament dissolved itself after nearly 20 years, a new parliament assembled in April 1660, agreed terms for Charles's return, and proclaimed him king. On 26 May he landed at Dover, and entered London three days later, his 30th birthday. Constitutional monarchy had begun.

To a great extent, there followed a putting back of the clock by nearly 20 years; Puritanism collapsed, some of the regicides were hanged, and confiscated Crown and Church lands were restored. East Meon's manors reverted to the Bishop of Winchester, who spent the enormous sum of £8,000 repairing Farnham Castle, and in addition built Wolvesey Palace at Winchester, which remains the home of 20th-century bishops. Locally, enclosure proceeded, an agreement being entered into on 23 February 1661[22] between the occupiers of the Oxenbourne common fields to pay rateably for the lord's licence 'to enclose, exchange and take into severalls the said comon feild lands'. The nine subscribers included members of the Pyncke, Longe, Aylward, Hobbe and Downes families, as well as Charles Cranley, a member of the gentry who was to be murdered six years later. The next year East Meon's parish constable faced a formidable task, preparation of a list of all dwellings, specifying how many hearths [fireplaces] there were in each. This arose from parliament's decision to raise revenue through a new form of taxation, called hearth-tax, which, subject to certain exemptions, obliged all house-holders to pay 2s. per annum for each hearth. Exempt from this imposition, which was to continue till 1688, were parishioners in receipt of poor relief, or residing in houses worth less than 20s. per annum and not paying parish rates. Payments were made by half-yearly instalments at Ladyday and Michaelmas, and the recorded returns prepared by parish constables are of special interest, telling us the number and size of dwellings, and the names of occupiers.

In East Meon village (the tithing) there were 59 homes, of which 32 were chargeable, the largest houses (or at least those with most hearths—eight in each case) being occupied by William Randoll and William Parvin. Anthony Terryl came next, with seven hearths, then Robert Randoll (six) and the vicar, 'Mr.' Richard Downes, had five, whilst even occupiers of modest dwellings with but one hearth were chargeable in nine cases. The total of chargeable hearths was 102, yielding an annual revenue of £10 4s. 0d., that for the whole Hundred being far higher.[23]

Fortunately for lawyers, litigation between some neighbouring landowners or occupiers seems inevitable; an example occurring in 1664 when Nathaniel Long, lord of the manor (or sub-manor) of Langrish, had a dispute with Edmund Bruning, lord of the nearby manor of Rothercombe, about a right-of-way through certain land at Rothercombe, to woods called Beechenleith Woods, also concerning his right to timber in the woods. The Chancery Court's judgment in favour of Nathaniel awarded him £500 damages, to be paid at East Meon 'at the sign of *The George*'. One can imagine the scene as villagers crowded into the inn to witness the counting and payment of this huge sum of cash (more than most onlookers could earn in a lifetime), doubtless hopeful of 'drinks all round' at the successful party's expense.

The years 1665 and 1666 were disastrous for Londoners, with first the plague which killed an estimated 100,000 or more, only to be followed by the Great Fire. Predictably, plague was transmitted to Petersfield, curiously not till 1666, though in that year 235 victims died there between April and December. Many of East Meon's inhabitants, recalling the events of 1625, dreaded a repetition, but either by luck or judgment, the village escaped. One cannot of course dogmatise that no single case of plague occurred, for, apart from exceptional circumstances such as murder, parish registers did not usually state the cause of death; but annual burials afford strong, sometimes overwhelming circumstantial evidence. The village burial register shows that burials for the four years before 1666 averaged under 16, and for the four years after 1666 under 19; but for 1666 itself, burials were only 13, well *below* the previous and subsequent figures. Perhaps, throughout Petersfield's visitation, physical contact between the inhabitants of East Meon and Petersfield was virtually suspended. If villagers supplied vegetable or dairy produce to the town, it may be that goods were left at an agreed spot for collection, and, in exchange, coinage payment deposited in a bowl of vinegar, as was done at Winchester in the same year. Such precautions against transmission were likely to prove effective, even though another 200 years were to pass before it was realised that fleas spread the disease.

Apropos coinage, no authorised copper coins were issued during the Commonwealth, whereupon towns and traders took it upon themselves to issue small change. These trade tokens, mostly farthings and halfpennies, and probably manufactured in London, were issued on a large scale. One such East Meon 'farthing' is known,[25] having on its obverse '1OHN WITCOMBE AT YE . . .' (this blank being filled with a pictorial representation of an angel), and on the reverse 'IN EAST MEANE .66 1 MW'. At the time John Witcombe was probably mine host at *The Angel* inn (now 1-3 Cross Cottages), .66 refers to the year 1666, and the initials '1 MW' stand for husband and wife 'John and M. Witcombe'. Their descendant, Arthur Witcombe, will be encountered in Chapter Five. Another East Meon tradesman carrying on business during Charles II's reign was John Aburrow, a tailor. He must have had a good business and reputation, for in May 1678 the trustees of a Petersfield charity (created by John Goodyer), paid him a premium of £6 10s. 0d. to have a boy, William Pinke of the tithing of Weston, apprenticed for eight years.[26] More will be heard later of the saga of the Aburrows.

Charles II died in 1685, and was succeeded by the Roman Catholic James II, who three years later lost the throne and fled to France. By that time Dutch William of Orange, the king's son-in-law, had landed in England with an army of 12,000 men. Parliament declared that James had, by implication, abdicated, and conferred the crown jointly upon William and his wife Mary. The revolution, for it was that, 'came suddenly and unexpectedly upon a nation which was enjoying unprecedented prosperity and social tranquillity'.[27] The queen's death from smallpox in 1694 is a reminder that the fatality rate of this disease, though less than half that of bubonic plague, was nevertheless high at 30 per cent. A few years later, in 1703, East Meon's purpose-built pest house was erected just within what was then the extreme north-eastern parish boundary, at Stroud. Such institutions (if that be the right word for a dwelling-house used as a primitive isolation hospital) had become a feature of many towns and villages from about 1600 onwards, when plague was the most frightening and devastating of infectious diseases. Then, when plague left Britain around 1671, smallpox became the greatest scourge. It is not known whether East Meon had a pest house before 1703, but the house of that date continued in use, either for its primary purpose, or, in the absence of current epidemics, as a parish poorhouse, for well over 100 years; almost certainly until made redundant by the Petersfield Union Workhouse with its isolation ward, built at or soon after 1834. The remote site chosen for the pest house, over two miles in a direct line from the village centre, represented a deliberate attempt at maximum isolation, and the north-eastern boundary may have been selected in the belief that, being downwind of the prevailing south-westerlies, germs would normally be blown *away* from the village. Today, the house formerly imbued with so much suffering is a happy family home, ironically re-christened 'Mount Pleasant Farm'.

Chapter Five

GEORGIAN ENGLAND, 1714–1837

THE GEORGIAN ERA was one of great change and stark contrasts. Elegance of design, whether of buildings, furniture, silver or glass, reached new standards of aesthetic perfection; yet, at the same time, poverty, squalor and disease plumbed the depths. Between 1700 and 1800 the population of England and Wales doubled from five million to 10 million. Many country families were housed in dwellings with walls of mud and straw, floors of beaten earth, virtually no washing facilities, sparse furniture, and but little privacy. Fuel became scarce, food largely consisted of bread and cheese, and water was often polluted. In 1762 54 per cent. of children died before they were two, and in the early 1800s almost 50 per cent. failed to survive beyond the age of twelve.[1] Inoculation against smallpox, first tried in 1721,[2] gradually gained popularity, but the great breakthrough came in 1798 with Edward Jenner's discovery of vaccination, substituting the cow-pox virus for that of smallpox. For some years after, many parishes practised both methods, occasionally pressurising the poor into opting for one or the other.[3]

After 1714 the pace of enclosure of open fields, previously almost entirely dependent upon voluntary agreement, gathered pace dramatically. Over four million acres of common fields were enclosed by 2,500 Parliamentary Acts between 1761–1844, and a further three quarters of a million acres of so-called waste between 1760–1801.[4] These changes contributed towards the continuing degradation of many copyholders who had tilled a few acres, kept a cow, a few sheep and the odd pig or two. Agricultural mechanisation, begun in the early 18th century with Jethro Tull's invention of a seed drill, was followed, first by winnowing machines, then threshing machines, and, by the end of the century, embryo mechanical reapers appeared. Realisation of the threat to manual employment sank in during the 1820s and the early 1830s.

Thus, while agricultural efficiency was being improved by enclosures and mechanisation, the cost in human casualties amongst an expanding population was severe. To make matters worse, war with France raised the price of many basic commodities to famine heights; while wages remained static. This led to the infamous Speenhamland Resolution of 1795, declaring that the deserving poor should receive parish relief related to the current price of a gallon loaf. The system, though well-meant, resulted in farmers refusing to increase wages in line with the high prices realised by their products, while the demoralised labourers lost their self-respect and former sturdy independence.

By 1727 East Meon had its own workhouse. An Act of 1722 had authorised overseers and churchwardens to buy or rent buildings for the lodging, maintenance and employment of the poor; and those who refused to enter such houses were to become disentitled to relief. East Meon's workhouse, situated in Workhouse Lane, where the Police Cottage and 'Meonside' now stand, was adapted from a terrace of ancient thatched cottages, probably similar to the 17th-century Kews Cottages still standing nearby; and was in existence, though by then disused, till accidentally burnt down when a spark from a passing steam wagon set it alight on August Bank Holiday 1910.

Fortunately, the overseers' Workhouse Account Book for 1727–33[5] is still available, specifying literally every farthing received and expended during six years, throwing much light upon social and economic conditions, diet, clothing and the state of medical knowledge, as well as naming many inmates, local traders, and all who paid the Poor Rate. Whilst it is impossible to judge the *quantity* of food and drink *per person* supplied to the inmates, its wide variety included, mutton, beef, veal, bacon, bread, milk, butter, cheese, turnips, cabbage, carrots, parsnips, peas, french beans, apples, rice, oatmeal, wheat, prunes, treacle, sugar, salt, pepper, caraway seed, allspice, nutmeg, mace, cloves, vinegar, saffron, ginger, currants, raisins, honey, cakes, biscuits, malt, yeast, hops, spearmint water, elder syrup, sack, beer, tent wine, rum and brandy. Some food was bought in considerable bulk, e.g. 10 cwt. of cheese at one time, three sides of bacon (purchased at Winchester Fair), 11 hogsheads of smallbeer, innumerable 'buttocks & flanks of beef' weighing up to 106 lbs., and 26 quarts of milk weekly.

Other food was 'home produced', evidenced by purchases of cabbage plants, and seeds for dwarf beans, carrots and parsnips; and pigs were kept (indeed, on 9 July 1732 five surplus ones were sold for 5s. each). Bread was baked on the premises, beer brewed, and even ointment and elder syrup prepared. Most inmates' clothing was made at 'the house', though hats were bought, usually in hot weather, presumably to protect heads from sunstoke. Clothing to fit-out girls entering service, and stockings were sometimes purchased, and, very occasionally, items such as breeches and gloves.

Limited medication was certainly provided. For example, in October 1727, 'peper and honey' were acquired for an inmate's sore throat, and, 10 days later, honey and treacle. Time and again, over a period of five years, ointment was bought 'for Peter Stigants leg'. On 13 January 1730 10½d. was spent on 'things to make Goodman Noice a drink for his cold', and three weeks later on 'one woolen cap for Goodman Noice 6d.'. Clove syrup was obtained for Goody Gennens, ruewater for 'Good Harises child', 'a purge for Mary Vallar', 'one blister plaister for Bety Guy', and 'alum for Peter Stigants'. Sometimes descriptions were vague, such as eyewater, a cordial and 'one bottle of stuff for Goody Bones child'. Possibly, attendances by the local doctor were gratuitous, since his more affluent patients would have been the very people who largely financed the workhouse. At any rate, only once in six years was a payment made to a doctor: 'April 2 1730. Doctor Wheeler for leting Goody Ford blood 1s.'. The previous year Goody Richards had been supplied with spectacles (cost 6d.)., and in 1733 another pair was bought for her at Arthur Witcombe's village general store (cost 4d.). In 1728 2d. was spent at the same store 'for tape and a piece of cork to make a truss', the next entry showing a payment of 6d. to Goody Kent 'for making a truss for John Selbey'. One hopes it fitted.

In December 1727 a cash debit appears: 'What we have paid for the people with the small pox 10s. 10d.'. Similar entries follow, usually at weekly intervals, over the following two months, such payments steadily rising to a peak of £2 1s. 4¾d. at the beginning of February, and then dropping off sharply. An epidemic had struck the parish, and continued for over two months, the payments representing money laid out by the overseers on food, medicine and nursing for the victims, who would have been isolated (probably compulsorily), either in their homes or at the pest house. At the latter, an amateur 'nurse', who had acquired immunity by previously suffering and recovering from the disease, would have been employed to do her limited best. Nevertheless, some parishioners probably died from the epidemic, since annual deaths which had averaged 13 for the previous three years, almost doubled to 24 in 1727, with five burials in each of August, January and February.

As the word 'workhouse' implies, inmates capable of doing so had to work, either on the premises, in the village or on surrounding farms. Spinning was the most usual task for females, the product being sold (usually to William Pink) at a price varying, according to quality, between 10d. and 1s. 2d. a pound. Several women went to houses in the village 'a washing' at 6d. a day, and occasionally women worked in the fields. Thus, on 24 May 1730: 'Recd. of Mr. Bonham for Goody Hall and Mary Vallars weeding 10s. 5d.'. At the current wage of 6d. a day, the two women must have worked for Mr. Bonham at least 10 days. Making and mending garments occupied considerable 'women hours', sometimes small sums being realised by selling articles. In January 1728 John Pritchet paid 8d. 'for knitting', and in March 1729 Mary Alderslade was charged 4d. 'for making a blue shirt'.

Understandably, male inmates were the bigger earners, carrying out such diverse tasks as harvesting, digging, threshing, winnowing, faggotting, hedging, stone picking, mowing, haymaking, weeding, dung-spreading, burning couch-grass, 'waymending', and even 'turning the grindstone'. Children were employed 'keeping cowes' or 'keeping of sheep'. Earnings were divided between 'management' and labour, usually 10d. in the shilling for management, and 2d. for labour. Sometimes labour's share was even more meagre, as when Goody Hall and Mary Vallars jointly received only 10d. out of the 10s. 5d. they earned weeding.

Birth and death, and possibly even marriage, took place at the workhouse. On 8 April 1730: 'paid to the midwife for laying Goody Haris 5s.', and the same day: 'paid for beer when Harrises child was crisened 2s. 6d.'; and the next day Goodman Harris received 4d. of his previous earning of 4s. working for John Pratt. But death occurred far more frequently, often preceded by purchase of medicines, special food, or drink for the sick inmate. On 23 April 1728 'a cordial for Goodman Richards' was bought from the general store for 6d., followed three days later by a pennyworth of brandy, though neither potion saved his life, for on 27 April:

Paid for Goodman Richards Coffin	7s. 0d.
Paid for ringing the nell and diging the grave (to J. Richards)	1s. 6d.
Paid to Mr. Downs	6d.
One dozen of bear for them that carried him to church	1s. 0d.

So, including the fee of Mr. Downes the parson for conducting the burial service, the funeral expenses totalled ten shillings.

In 1729 there were two deaths within a few days:

Aug. 11th.	Paid for the coffin boards for Goody Ford [to] Jon. Collins	..	3s. 6d.
	Paid to Mr. Downs	..	6d.
14th.	Paid for coffin boards for John Restalls child	..	1s. 0d.
	Paid for the buring of[John Restalls child	..	2s. 2d.
18th.	Paid out of the making of two coffins [to] Peter Stigants ..	..	8d.

With the help of inmate Peter Stigants, a joiner, who made two coffins for 4d. each, and with Downes presumably waiving his fee in the case of the child, the two funerals together cost 7s. 10d. Whether or not the coffins were the first made by Peter Stigants, he certainly made all workhouse coffins, except when incapacitated, for the following five years. Indeed, he seems to have acquired a unique position amongst the inmates, being a skilled artisan who, apart from coffin-making, undertook other joinery work such as, 'making a wooden casement' for Goodman Lide. A shilling was paid to the Overseers for this job, and 2d. passed to Peter. I think he must also have acted as handyman carrying out repairs and maintenance at the workhouse.

After 1729, funeral expenses tended to follow a regular pattern—coffin boards 3s. 6d., making coffin 6d.—Peter's allowance had been increased by 50 per cent.!—laying out the body 4d., digging the grave 1s. 6d. to 2s. 6d., parson's fee 6d., and, sometimes, a shillings-worth of beer for the bearers. Peter was not a fit man, though, being trusted, he was allowed to travel personally to Petersfield to buy medication unavailable in the village, as on this occasion: 'Feb. 2nd. 1730 Let Peter Stigants have to buy phisick and metson [in] Petersfield—2s. 6d.'. On 13 April he was still unwell: 'Paid for purging stuff for Peter Stigants [in] Petersfield—6d.'. The next day: 'One bottle of stuff for Peter Stigants' was purchased for 6d., but on 4 May he was bouncing back: 'Let Peter Stigants have to buy tooles—£1 0. 0.'.

Nevertheless, on 12 February 1731, the village store ominously supplied: 'One bed-pan [i.e. a warming-pan] for Peter Stigants—6d.'. Purges and 'metson' continued to be bought for him, and when Goody Short died in the following June, an outside carpenter, Thomas Earwicker, made her coffin. Events were, however, to prove Peter's resilience, for, on 20 December 1731 'one large awgar for Peter Stigants' was obtained in Petersfield; and a couple of months later he was back in the business as the coffin maker.

Betty Guy was another character to make her mark amongst the inmates. Probably elderly, and less than robust, for no earnings are credited to her, she was in 'the house' for several years. We first meet her on 2 March 1728; 'For ointment for Bety Guys face 2d.'. In June 1730 she must have been poorly, as 'one white loaf and 2 biscakes' were purchased for her from Mr. Alderslade, an indulgence to be repeated a month later. However, in June 1732, there is a somewhat startling entry: 'one ounce of tobacco for Bety Guy 1d.'. And thereafter, time and time again, tobacco was provided for Bety Guy, averaging about an ounce a fortnight. It would be intriguing to know why this pipe-smoking lady was thus favoured.

'The house' was, of course, heated by log fires, this fuel being far from cheap at 16s. a cord. Illumination was by candles and 'watchlights', and the periodic buying of chamber pots describes the 'indoor sanitation'. Miscellaneous purchases included leather, buttons, needles, thread, beeswax, 'a pair of breetches for Thos. Stigants', a ladle, a skimmer, an axe, brooms, a scrubbing-brush, soap, ink, quills, 'fine tooth combs', hour glasses, a mousetrap, and lamp-black and glue (these last two for coffin-making). Once a year 9d. was due for 'the Lord's rent for the workhouse' (the premises being copyhold), and there were periodic payments to an unnamed individual, 'the tinker', who mended 'the keetell & skilet', a bowl and other articles.

As for income, apart from examples of the kind already mentioned, and sporadic sales of bran and ashes, occasional credits appear such as:

1729 June 8th. Recd. of Anthony Bulbeck ten pounds which is to excuse him from taking an apprentice untill it comes to his turn again.

1729 Dec. 28th. Recd. of Daniel Ford keeping the children 1 week 2s. 6d.

1730 March 20th. Recd. of Edward Lide for one month's pay for his father which was due March the first 3s. 4d.

Regarding the first of these entries, children over a certain age who were orphaned or otherwise destitute were apprenticed or put out to service by the Overseers, and farmers were obliged to accept them on a rota basis unless exemption was bought at £10 a time; which is just what Bulbeck did. The other entries show 'the house' could be used, upon payment, for the boarding out of young and old members of families, but only, no doubt, when a compelling reason precluded their remaining at home. As previously indicated, the more affluent parishioners made periodic payments, based on the Poor Rate assessments of their farms or other properties, for instance: '1730 March 8th. Recd of Robt. Steale £2 2. 0.'.

By an Act of 1743, illegitimate children were thenceforth deemed to have acquired their mother's settlement, an improvement upon the previous rule that made place of birth the governing factor, which sometimes led to an unmarried pregnant woman being hustled from parish to parish as her confinement approached. Nevertheless, a putative father, unable or unwilling to marry, was if possible made responsible by bond for the maintenance of mother and child. Later, by another Act of 1757, responsibility for raising quotas of militiamen was placed on the parish, men being chosen by lot to serve for three years, unless able to buy a substitute, again for ten pounds. If such a man had a wife and dependent children it was often more economical for Overseers to provide the cash for his release rather than support his family for three years; and sometimes this was achieved for less than the prescribed ten pounds.

Moving on to the 19th century, further information concerning the poor is provided by the East Meon Overseers' Relief Book 1819–1826,[6] by which time the population had grown, poverty was far more widespread, and the village workhouse could no longer cope. During these eight years, outdoor relief was afforded to 333 individuals, a great many of whom were heads of families. Accordingly, the total of direct and indirect recipients may have exceeded a thousand. Certainly, the scale of payments was modest enough, even at then current money values, typified by a labourer's weekly wage of about ten shillings. As examples of payments, widows were usually granted 6s. to 8s. a month, 'maternity allowance' was 5s., and the contribution towards fitting-out a girl for domestic service was normally 10s., occasionally one pound. Often, relief was in kind, particularly when consisting of fuel, such as '¼ hundred bunts' or so many faggots.

Random entries from the book's 420 pages of beautiful copperplate writing include:

DENNIS—Richard and Wife etc.
    1819 20th. January   Extra allowance to purchase a plough   ..   ..   ..   6s. 0d.

NEWLAND—William and Wife etc.
    1819 17th. April   A shirt for himself and being ill   .. ..   4s. 0d.
           15th May   For his lame girl an Iron leg .. ..   —

GOODALL—Robert and Wife etc.
    1819 31st. May   Extra allowance to buy a scythe .. ..   5s. 6d.
          12th. June   Casual relief to his wife during her husband's absence
                        grass mowing .. ..   16s. 10d.

BRAMBLE—Edward and Wife etc.
    1824 13th. March   One months allowance to his family during Bramble's
                      imprisonment.. .. ..   £1 4s. 0d.

Other aspects of the Overseers' functions are illustrated by receipted accounts (framed and displayed in the private bar of *The George*), including:

The Overseers of Eastmeon		£	s.	d.
1818	To P. Luff Dr.			
August 16th.	To 1 box and stool going to Pesthouse for Henry Browning		4	6
	To coffin for Dame Norgate		12	0
19th.	Serving summons on Eliz[th] Gregory and Thos. Crockford ..		2	0
22nd.	Going to Trooper to Justice Meeting		3	0
Sept. 25th.	To coffin for John Kingshott's son		10	0
	Paid for bread cheese & beer for the bearers		4	0
		£1	15	6

Peter Luff was the village constable. In October, helped by James Lock and a posse of 'assistants', he was pursuing gypsies, an incident referred to in his next account.

The Overseers of Eastmeon		£	s.	d.
1818	Dr. to Peter Luff			
October 14th.	Going to Justices Meeting at Rogate with Waller		6	6
	To 1 day myself 1 day Peter & 1 day James Lock after the gypsies		8	0
	To beer bread & cheese for assistants		7	6
		£1	2	0

The constable's duties included keeping alleged wrongdoers in custody pending trial: 'Expenses in keeping Windibank & Ayling 2s. 6d.'.

In 1830 grinding poverty and unemployment drove normally peaceable men in the southern counties to indulge in machine-breaking and rick-burning, a sort of peasants' revolt. 'To break all the threshing machines in the county', was their war cry: 'to have two shillings a day wages' the ideal of their hopes.[7] The so-called 'Swing Riots' led to the trial at Winchester Assizes in December 1830 of 270 prisoners, 14 of whom were found guilty of capital offences. Revolution had seemed imminent, but following a general election and reforms, wages gradually rose, and, with the repeal of import tax on foreign corn, the price of bread came down.

By now parochial units were too small to cope efficiently with poverty, and therefore the Poor Law Amendment Act of 1834 was passed, bringing about the greatest changes for centuries. Three Commissioners were appointed to organise the poor law countrywide, and, where appropriate, to provide for groups of adjacent parishes to combine in a 'union', to be controlled and administered by an elected Board of Guardians whose duties included provision of a workhouse. Nevertheless, each parish remained financially responsible for its own poor. Large and forbidding workhouses sprung up at Petersfield and other nearby towns, their accommodation, diet and rules deliberately aimed at making occupancy so unattractive as to deter all but the desperate needy. Indeed, for many a year 'ending up in the workhouse' was to become a social stigma, and a threat by anxious parents.

Having touched on the Overseers' role in village affairs, and particularly concerning the poor, it is time to consider the churchwardens, who were likewise appointed by the Vestry. Again, detailed records exist, the Church Rate Book covering over 60 years from 1753–1814. This shows the Vestry met each Easter to appoint two churchwardens for the ensuing year, and to fix the church rate for that period, usually a round sum varying from £20 to £70. Very many properties were assessable, the two largest assessments being those of Court Farm and South Farm, each liable for about one-tenth of the rate, whilst countless small properties paid a mere sixpence, and a few even less.

A lighter side to the Vestry's annual meeting was the social gathering (or perhaps, calling a spade a spade, drinking session) that followed. Most of the remainder of the church rate was spent, as would be expected, in repairing, maintaining, and improving the church. These accounts show that a plumber—namely a worker in lead, and apparently a master-man employing assistants—undertook substantial roof work in 1764, probably repairs or replacements to the roof. A notable event, involving even greater expenditure, occurred in 1771, following a resolution passed in September 1770:

> We whose hands are hereunto set being the majority of the Vestry this day holden do agree that the bells shall be now hang'd and to authorise Joseph Tirrell and John Clark Churchwardens to contract with any person for doing the same.

One can imagine Messrs. Tirrell and Clark (the latter then of South Farm) to whom the organisation of this important task was delegated, conferring anxiously as they sought out, interviewed and obtained an estimate from one Sam Turner, who must have been a specialist 'bellhanger'. Joseph Aburrow, the carpenter, was the other key 'contractor', though the churchwardens knew him well as a local and reliable craftsman regularly employed on church repairs.

Not all churchwardens' expenditure related to obvious church repairs, maintenance and improvements, but included regular unexplained annual payments, usually £2–£4, made from 1753–91 to John Collins. As it is known there was a church clock at this time, Collins, who professed to be a clockmaker, may have been employed to wind and maintain it. (The John Collins who supplied boards for workhouse coffins in the 1720s was probably his father or grandfather.) There was also the clerk's customary fee for washing and mending the linen and cleansing the church vessel. Each year, between a few shillings and £5 was paid for 'sparrow heads', and communion wine was bought periodically, usually 18 bottles at a time for three guineas. In 1763 sexton Thomas Habin received a guinea 'for ringing days', and two years later 'a tune book and reeds for the bassoon' cost one pound. (The organ was not acquired until 1794.) Only once, in 1769, was there a payment, of 11s., for 'the carriage of the dead', though in 1775 'Paid for beer for the carrying the dead to Church 4s.' appears. Finally, a flagon (probably of silver) cost four guineas in 1778, and, as from Easter 1810, an entry recurs, 'Paid the singers £1 1s. 0d.'.

Thomas Habin, sexton in the 1750s and 1760s, was also parish clerk. Appointment to this ancient office, normally by the incumbent, was based on the 91st canon of 1603:

> And the said clerk shall be of 20 years of age at the least, and known to the said parson
> . . . to be of honest conversation, and sufficient for his reading, writing and also for his competent skill in singing.

His duties were to assist the clergy in conducting Divine Service by singing and saying the responses, and by playing the same part at marriages and burials. Habin, almost certainly when getting on in years and becoming eccentric, decided to fill up a few parchment pages in the church register which had been left blank way back in 1665. So, in a large, bold hand, he made his mark for posterity:

> Frances wife of Tho. Habin died the 8th. day of November in the yeare of our Lord God 1717 aged 41 years,

and

> Zealous of good works were the good men of old,

and, lyrically,

> Thomas Habin is my name   Eastmean is my dewling [sic] place
> And England is my nation   And Christ is my Salvation.

Grave-digging had become too much for the poet by 1769, when Thomas Wells succeeded as sexton; but it was not till after Habin's death in July 1777, that another parish clerk was appointed—none other than his son, John, a cordwainer. Later in 1807, the two offices of sexton and parish clerk were reunited, in the person of Robert Smith, son of one of the village publicans. He was destined to remain parish clerk for what must have been a record term, and, with understandable pride, left a note for future historians:

> I, Robert Smith, was first Clerk of our Church in the year 1807 to the year 1870, which is 63 years of singer at Church.

Then added, wistfully:

> When I depart this life I should like to have a hymn sung at my funeral as I have sung so many years.

Having at the very start of this chapter mentioned the elegance of Georgian buildings, and then proceeded to write almost exclusively about *people,* I must try to restore the balance: though, in looking at homes, especially the parish's 'big houses', their history tends to be inextricably interwoven with that of their owners.

Westbury House and estate was bought in 1722 by its tenant, Admiral Philip Cavendish, for £7,400. His naval career has been described as 'long and unremarkable',[8] yet he became a full admiral in 1736, Commander-in-Chief at Portsmouth from 1739-42, with a seat on the Board of Admiralty, and Member of Parliament in 1721, 1722-27, and 1734-43.[9] Following his sudden death in 1743, his widow remained at Westbury for four years before commissioning a 'particular of the estate'—a surveyor's detailed description and schedule—preliminary to sale. The document[10] says the mansion was 'very pleasantly situate containing upon the first floor . . . a parlour, small study, hall, saloon, and large parlour. Up one pair of stairs 5 chambers and a dressing room, and upon the attick story six good bedchambers . . . Below stairs are the house keeper's and butler's rooms, wood rooms, cellar, valts etc., and about 40 yards distant from the house to which there is a communication by a collanade is a very good kitchen, brewhouse, wash house, dairy, laundry, pantry and servants' hall, and several lodging rooms for servants, and also a coach house and stabling for 12 horses'.

This impressive establishment was set in 11 acres of pleasure grounds 'wich were laid out by Mr. Bridgman', with a one and a half acre kitchen garden, five acre Chapel Meadow and 16 acre Coney Garden all adjoining and in hand. The rest of the estate comprised 143 acres of woodland and 391 acre Westbury Farm (later called Westbury Manor Farm), the latter having previously been let to John Stone for £160 per annum. Coney Garden was a fenced rabbit warren, such as became increasingly popular on large estates during the 18th and 19th centuries, the primary object being an all-the-year-round supply of fresh meat for the table. Charles Bridgman, the landscape gardener, was at the top of his profession, had worked with Vanburgh at Blenheim, invented the ha-ha, and was appointed Royal Gardener in 1728.[11]

In 1747 Lady Cavendish sold Westbury House, its furniture and the estate to another admiral, Sir Peter Warren, for £9,000. Though coming from a humble Irish background, and commencing his career 'on the lower deck', he attained admiral's rank, fought gallant and successful actions, and, as well as collecting a fortune from prize money, married a New York heiress, Susanna de Lancy. Retiring from active service in 1748, he received many civic honours, became M.P. for Westminster in 1750, and died in Dublin of a 'violent fever' two years later, 'scarcely 50 years of age and in the full tide of prosperity'.[12] During his brief ownership of Westbury he carried out improvements that included walling the kitchen garden, and, by means of land purchases that took in sizable Langrish Farm, more than doubled the estate's area to something like 1,233 acres.

Of his three co-heiress daughters, Anne married Lieutenant-General Charles Fitzroy, later the first Baron Southampton; Susanna married Lieutenant-General William Skinner; and Charlotte married Willoughby Bertie, fourth Earl of Abingdon. In 1772 Susanna and her husband (or, to be precise, the trustees of their marriage settlement) bought out the other sisters' shares, and made Westbury their home. Preceding that transaction a lengthy and informative independent valuation[13] was undertaken by Thomas Browne, pricing the whole estate, still including the furniture, at £15,300. The Skinners' daughter and heiress, Susanna Maria, married her cousin Major-General Henry, third Viscount Gage in 1789, and the estate subsequently passed to their son, Henry, fourth Viscount Gage, born in 1808. More will be heard of Westbury in succeeding chapters.

The 1772 valuation deserves more than passing mention, since it illustrates the extent to which a substantial farm could still include many small, scattered pieces of land, some surviving as common field strips probably created before Domesday. Langrish Farm is an especially apt example; its 245 acres comprised 50 separate parcels spread over four manors, all in East Meon parish, and included 11 parcels in 'West Comon Field' and five in 'Lindworth Comon Field'. One third of the farm was freehold, the rest copyhold, and almost the whole leased to Richard Eames at £92 per annum. The fragmentation made the farm awkward to work, and so affected its worth, the point being specifically referred to by the valuer:

> This [farm] of Langrish is a good farm and well tenanted but does not lie well together, it is held of 4 Manors viz: Meon Manor and Meon Church belonging to the Bishop, Langrish belonging to Sr. Thos. Ridge and Riplington in wch last the Copyholders themselves are Lds. of the Manor and divide the heriots among themselves . . . the whole was purchased by Sr. Peter Warren at £2,400 which was a fair and reasonable price, but as it is so mixed, held of so many Manors, quit rents £3 7s. 5d., subject to 4 heriots and to large stewards fees, I cannot deem it at more than the price given.

Valuer Browne was not quite up-to-date concerning the ownership of Langrish sub-manor, since Sir Thomas Ridge, a brewer, distiller and wine merchant of Portsmouth, had become bankrupt eight years earlier, following which the estate was sold by auction in 1771 to William Jolliffe of Petersfield for £4,400. However, it is abundantly clear that further enclosure in East Meon parish was overdue.

In the last chapter we left Bereleigh sub-manor jointly owned by Bartholomew Smith's daughters, Elizabeth, Frances and Anastasia, the first two of whom died later without issue. In 1728 Anastasia became the second wife of William Sheldon of Winchester, whose father, Ralph Sheldon, had been equerry to King James II and accompanied the king when he fled to France 40 years before.[14] Unsurprisingly, the Sheldon family were strictly Roman Catholic, and many entered the Society of Jesus. By 1775 the manor had passed to Edward Sheldon, grandson of William and Anastasia.[15]

However, by this time the Eyles family of East Meon, who were destined to become owners of Bereleigh, were acquiring local prominence and prosperity. Richard Eyles, appointed churchwarden in 1756, was already rated as occupier of Court Farm, and 10 years later became the parish's biggest land occupier when also rated in respect of

'Beerly Farm'.[16] In 1775 Eyles, again churchwarden, had still further increased his land occupancy; but by 1780, Richard Eyles II, then aged 26, began taking over his father's land, starting with Bereleigh and adjacent Tigwell, and continuing with Court Farm in 1784, four years before his father's death.

The date when ownership, as distinct from occupation of Bereleigh, was acquired by the Eyles family is unknown, though it must have been between 1775 and the beginning of the 19th century when the old manor house, which had probably fallen into decay, was rebuilt by Richard Eyles II in the Regency style and on quite a grand scale; the accommodation comprising, in addition to spacious reception rooms, no less than 20 bedrooms. Richard II was a prosperous and locally important man, elected mayor of Petersfield in 1800, and presumably owner or part-owner of Patrick Eyles and Co., the 'Petersfield and Hants. Bank'.

By 1809, though he continued as churchwarden and still occupied Court Farm and other property, he had either sold or leased Bereleigh to Jacob Fitt, who was then rated as occupier. When Eyles died in May 1814 he was survived by a son, Joseph, who for the hunting season 1814–15 held the mastership of the Hambledon Hunt; but neither Joseph's mastership nor his life were to last long, for he died in March 1815, the year of the Battle of Waterloo, at the young age of twenty-nine.

If the period 1570–1640 is rightly called 'a great age of rebuilding', then the Georgian period (strictly speaking, the reigns of the four Georges from 1714–1830), the preceding reigns of William and Mary, and Anne, and the succeding one of William IV, were even more significant. Hitherto, the vast majority of ordinary dwellings were timber-framed and thatched, but by the time Dutch William came upon the scene in 1688 oak had become increasingly scarce and· expensive and 'brick building started to go with a swing'.[17] Over the following one and a half centuries hundreds of thousands of brick or stone houses, ranging from 'stately homes' to small terrace cottages, were erected, and are still universally admired for the simple yet pleasing symmetry and balance of their design. Plain and 'square' elevations, usually with a number of identical, white-painted sash windows, were relieved by prominent cornices where walls and roof met, and ornamental front doors surmounted by small, triangular cornices called pediments.

Yet the builders prevented simplicity becoming dull by employing various methods of 'bonding' bricks which resulted in a design or pattern in the exterior brickwork, especially of front elevations. Bonding—the technique of laying successive courses of bricks to achieve walls of maximum strength and durability—had prior to 1688 commonly involved one course of bricks laid lengthwise (stretchers), and the next course endwise (headers), and so on alternatively, this style being known as 'English bond'. During William's reign, the Dutch style, or 'Flemish bond', was introduced, alternative *bricks,* as distinct from courses, being laid as stretchers and headers; and when stretchers were of a mellow reddish pink colour, and headers purplish grey, the chequered appearance of such walls was, and still is, particularly attractive.

As the fashion and popularity of classically designed dwellings spread, many a house owner 'cheated' by replacing or encasing the old timber-framed front elevation of his home with a new, 'modern' facade, sometimes even constructing an entirely new 'shell' for the house; which explains why so many houses in town and country alike appear at first sight to be Georgian, but, on closer inspection, reveal an earlier origin.

'Glenthorne', an excellent William and Mary example of a substantial village house, dominates East Meon's High Street. Its front elevation could hardly be more pleasing, with Flemish bond chequered brickwork, rusticated quoins, bold cornice at roof level, symmetric sash windows and a splendid doorway that includes brick pediment and moulded surround. To complete its typicality, the house's rear elevation is timber-framed and of an earlier period.

'Brooklyn House' next door (the home and surgery of village surgeon George Pink in the 1850s, and more recently of writer Adelaide Manning) has been much altered. Its Georgian facade, constructed of course after course of purple headers, relieved by a flat band of stretchers between storeys, gives no hint of the *two* cottages formerly within; though two chimney stacks, one at each end, do just that. Two ground-floor bay windows were added in Victorian times, and a Regency-style balcony at the rear; so this attractive, medium-sized house has successfully evolved over many years without looking a hotch-potch. Immediately beyond 'Brooklyn House', the front elevation of semi-detached 'Clare Cottage' and 11 High Street also consists of purple headers and a band of stretchers, perhaps indicative of the same bricklaying hand having worked on each of these elevations. Certainly, the sequence of four brick-built 'Georgian style' houses plays an important part in the agreeable streetscape.

On the opposite side of the High Street, the former 1–6 'Barnards Cottages', now 'Barnards', 'Middle Barnards' and 'Barnards Corner', are all 18th century, well maintained and charming; being colour- or white-washed, they avoid uniformity. As the High Street bends south-east, leaving the heart of the village, other Georgian dwellings include 'Fern Cottage' (modestly constructed of inexpensive flint, with brick dressings and a slated roof, the latter probably dating it to the 1830s); the far larger 'Wheelwright Cottage', having a considerably earlier timber-framed interior; pretty 'Farriers', with rendered facade of malmstone and brick quoins, and delightful 'Ivy House', whose chequered double-fronted elevation with cambered arches to sash windows and simple latticed porch hides a far older village farmhouse behind. Before leaving the High Street we should note a 'non-dwelling' building, namely 'Glenthorne's' former coach-house, now Goddard's Garage, well constructed of coursed knapped flints, with a galleting of flint flakes on the south elevation and of bottle glass on the east. The passer-by who gingerly fingers the embedded flint flakes will readily appreciate why their razor-like sharpness made such formidable weapons and versatile tools thousands of years earlier.

The manifold other village houses of this period forbid individual reference. Yet the lovely, quiet, narrow little road called The Cross is made by Georgian 'Cross Keys' and 'Vicarage Lodge', harmoniously contrasting with the three ancient 'Cross Cottages'; and Church Street equally owes its charm to the combined appeal of *The George,* Post Office, 'The White House' and 'Church Cottage' (all 18th-century, the latter Queen Anne), and to the original Victorian five Almshouse Cottages and the Edwardian bungalow pair opposite.

Frogmore, 200 yards upstream, and generally regarded as a separate hamlet, also exemplifies harmonious contrasts of building materials, style and colour. Roofs of thatch, tiles and slates, and walls of flint, brick, and timber-frame plus infill, all seem in place, as does white, pale yellow and pink colour-wash. Almost by accident, and with little help from planners, Frogmore's 18 houses, whose building has spanned at least four centuries, have achieved a happy blend.

What of the farmhouses? Though the origins of several go back to Tudor or even earlier times, practically every farmhouse in the parish is either entirely or partly of 18th-century date, reflecting the change from earlier times when farmers tended to live in the village (and even have farmyards there), to Stuart and Hanoverian days when, following enclosures, old village farmhouses were pulled down or sold, and new ones built where most convenient and necessary, namely on the land their owners farmed, often two miles or more from the village centre. Yet another change is currently under way as progressively larger farming units lead to many farmhouses becoming the homes of non-farmers.

Finally, and pursuing the theme of Georgian contrasts, I propose to come down to earth again by quoting a letter written anonymously in 1837 to Mr. and Mrs. John Bonham Carter. At that time M.P. for Portsmouth, John Carter IV, having obtained a royal licence to change his name from Carter to Bonham Carter, had inherited much property in the Petersfield and East Meon area from his cousin once removed, Thomas Bonham:

> We feel we have a duty to give you our thanks for gifts bestowed on us both for schooling our little ones, and the wood you paid for us, but W. Guy wont give none till we first pay 1d. each for carriage from his farm Farefield. When we can buy at other places and our masters will bring it for us who says they should at any time be glad to do it, but this time they had not the chance because Guy made up all his odd time for his horses this wet wether thereby and selling all his own inferior things he made a good job of it. Besides, if we hired a teem for 10s. a day we could bring 3 hund. in a day which is but little more than three shillings a hund. instead of 8s. 4d. saving us poor folk 15s. in one day. There is grate complaint both among us as well as our masters who tell us its not your fault. We think so too. Mr. Padwick of a liberal spirit brings numbers of loaves gratice every year and we thank you whether we had one or no. I leave it to your good sence to juge according to the justice case. We do not mention our names because of our livings and we know what his spite is.
>
> We are your humble servants by night or day.
>
> Eastmeon Poor

The benevolently-inclined M.P. and his lady had evidently made a gift of fuel, subject to its being collected from Fairfield Farm (otherwise South Farm) when it had been cut. The wood in question must have been in the form of bundles of sticks or brushwood, often called faggots elsewhere, but, in East Meon 'bunts', and used, especially, for heating bread ovens. The hard-hearted Fairfield Farm tenant, William Guy, apparently charged 1d. a bunt for wagon transport, making the cost of delivering 300 bunts £1 5s. 0d., as against only 10s. if a team were made available for hire to the poor. Possibly there were two sides to the story, but in the 1830s many well-to-do people certainly showed a terribly harsh attitude towards the poor, and it is understandable that resentment very occasionally boiled over into arson and rioting. However, the 'humble servants by night or day' must have been delighted when, some years later, the liberal-spirited Farmer Padwick succeeded Guy at Fairfield.

Chapter Six

SCHOOLING

ORGANISED EDUCATION (except that of aristocrats and apprentices) was provided by the Church for nearly 1,000 years from St Augustine's arrival till the Reformation, all teachers having to be licensed by a bishop. After the Reformation many grammar schools were re-endowed by lay benefactors, and by 1740 there were nearly 2,000 charity schools in England.[1] Nevertheless, during the 18th century university and grammar school education fell to a low standard, and prior to 1800, when only one out of every 30 children of school age received organised schooling, the state neither aided nor controlled education.[2] It was the Sunday School movement which pointed the way towards universal popular education. Sunday school aims were religious and social rather than intellectual, specifically teaching reading and spelling as a prelude to Bible reading,[3] though some Sunday schools provided secular instruction, and some opened on weekdays also. With the benefit of publicity given by the *Gentleman's Magazine* and other contemporary periodicals, the number of children attending Sunday schools rose to nearly 250,000 by 1795.

In the early 19th century the monitorial system, by which younger children were taught by older children, led to an increased number of pupils receiving education of a sort, but the state continued to stand aloof. Indeed, when a bill was introduced in the Commons in 1807 to establish rate-aided parochial schools, it was defeated following arguments that such a step would undermine the Church's educational monopoly, and might make the lower classes discontented.[4]

The date when schooling commenced in East Meon is unknown, but an article dated 7 February 1816, written by one Charles Walters, and published in the *Gentleman's Magazine* in 1819, describes East Meon Church in considerable detail, before continuing:

> The north transept is now used as a Sunday and day-school for the neighbourhood. I was much gratified to learn that on Sundays no less than 160 children are collected in this room for religious instruction,—a considerable number, when it is recollected that the neighbouring tithings or hamlets, from which many of the children come, are, some of them at least, three or four miles from church. It cannot but be a matter of regret, that when this room was first devoted to the purpose of instruction, it was not done with more taste and care. The present deal floor is raised six or seven feet from the ground, and a communication is made with the Church by means of a narrow staircase. The east window has made way for a door, and the place of the north door is now occupied by a chimney. Underneath the above mentioned deal floor is a dark room, in which fuel is kept for the use of the school.

This picture of the school within the church is tantalisingly incomplete, though the thought of 160 children crammed into such a limited space on Sundays is staggering, and compels admiration for teachers facing such conditions. The number of weekday attenders is uncertain, but there is little doubt as to the identity of the schoolmaster in

63

the 1790s, since the Church Rate Book refers to a meeting of the Vestry in August 1794, when 'William Vinn, schoolmaster', was appointed to be parish clerk; and the Burial Register records the burial of 'William Vinn, school teacher', in 1806.

Another Mr. Vinn—probably Randall Vinn, son of the schoolmaster, baptized in 1794 —was apparently an overseer in 1823, as is evident from the story which follows. An asylum, or school, for 'deaf and dumb' children, the first in England, had been opened in Bermondsey in 1792. Fifteen years later, in 1807, the foundation stone of a new school building was laid in the Old Kent Road, whither the establishment was moved in 1809. The pupils, male and female, were such children as were deaf and dumb, not being deficient in intellect; and the term of their stay was five years, during which time they were taught to read, write, draw, and cipher, to speak by signs, and in many instances to articulate so as to be clearly understood.[5] 'The teacher, Joseph Watson, LL.D., held the situation 'upwards of 37 years, and counted over 1,000 pupils; such pupils being elected without reference to locality, sect or persuasion'.[6] Which is all most interesting, but what is the connection between this splendid pioneering institution and East Meon?

To Mr. Vinn or   Asylum for Deaf & Dumb
The Officers of the Parish of East Meon,   Kent Road [sic]
Warnford, Hants.   Sept. 23rd 1823

Gentleman,

I am sorry to say that the state of Wm. Weller's health renders him unable to attend in School, and as the medical attendant recommends change of air his removal into the country is very desirable. His health being restored he may return to finish his education.

I am, Gent[m]
Your Hb. Serv.
J. Watson.

On the same sheet of paper was an account:

Expenses incurred by Dr. Watson for the clothing of Wm. Weller in the Asylum for Deaf and Dumb

1823				
Jany.	21	A pair of shoes		6 - -
		Two neckcloths		1 - 4
Mar.	17	A coat 19s. A waistcoat 5s. 6d.		1 - 4 - 6
Ap.	7	A hat		4 - 6
July	3	A pair of shoes		5 - 6
	25	Four shirts		16 - 0
Sepr.	18	Repg clothes, shoes		15 - 4
				£3 - 13 - 2

To have been plucked from obscure East Meon and given the chance to overcome his grave disability in distant London had seemed good fortune for William Weller, but there is poignancy about his own accompanying letter to his parents, written in a neat 'copy-book' hand, and reproduced on page 65.

Sadly, the change of air failed to bring about a recovery, and William's young and silent life ended in the following January, when he died aged 14 and was buried in East Meon churchyard. Society at parochial level, had shown compassion, and had apparently borne the expense involved.

LETTER WRITTEN BY WILLIAM WELLER, 1823

My Dear Parents

D' Watson desires me to write this to you. I am very sorry to inform you that I have been poorly and do not get any better and if you please I should like to go home for the benefit of my health. I hope you my brothers and sister are well at present. I think of you all every day. I love you. I can speak a little and read write and understand many words. Give my love to my brothers and sister and accept the duty of

Your affectionate Son

William Weller

Eventually in 1833, parliament allocated £20,000 for the erection of schoolhouses—a niggardly sum for the whole of England and Wales. East Meon's first purpose-built school was constructed in 1845 at a cost of £696[7] following the gift of a site from the Bishop of Winchester in 1844. The convenance transferred a strip of roadside waste of the manor plus an even narrower strip of Church Hill Field, to 'the Minister Church Wardens and Overseers of the Parish of East Meon' upon trust for 'a School for the education of Poor Children' and as a residence for the schoolmaster. The deed adds that the 'school shall always be conducted upon the principles of the Incorporated National Society for Promoting the Education of the Poor in Principles of the Established Church and shall be under the general management and control of the Committee for the time being of the Subscribers to the said School'. The combined school and master's house was constructed mainly of knapped flints with a slated roof, 'in the Elizabethan style', the site having been reasonably well chosen, with Park Hill towering to the north, a splendid and extensive view to the south, and the church and village centre a few hundred yards away. Private subscriptions provided some or all of the capital outlay, though possibly with a government contribution.

In the school's early days the pupils taught by schoolmaster John Jones[8] totalled about 60–70 boys and 50 girls, a tiny minority paying 3d. a week and the rest 1d. Income from 'children's pence' was augmented by annual payments from benevolent 'subscribers', who included the bishop (£2), Magdalen College (£2 2s. 0d.), Lord Gage (£2), Sir William Jolliffe (£2), John Bonham Carter (£4), G. T. Nicholson (£1), and the vicar (£5). In 1848 John Forder and his wife Sarah were appointed master and mistress in succession to Jones, at a 'stipend of £50 together with four tons of coals and the use of the house and gardens'. At the same time it was decided 'that a paid Monitor be had at the sum of sixpence a week'.[9] In 1851 total income was £62 2s. 2d., and expenditure of £59 13s. 3d. included:

Mr. and Mrs. Forder ..	£50 0s.	0d.
Woman Jacobs for cleaning schoolroom		8d.
Jane Bramley, monitor 4 weeks ..	2s.	0d.
Emma Pile, monitor 9 weeks	4s.	6d.
1 ton of coals ..	1 1s.	0d.
Mr. Greentree for cleaning the clock	1s.	6d.

By 1856 receipts had risen to £128 8s. 7d., including 'Capitation Grant' £12 15s. 0d., grant aid for new floor and fittings £35, and a quarterly record sum of £8 1s. 8d. from children's pence. The main additional expenditures were on desks bought from Norwich for £24; Mr. Kille's account (presumably for the new floor) £25 7s. 8d.; and 'Well and rope £3 1s. 0d.'.[10] The following year the school committee decided 'that a map of Europe be obtained also a water tub for the girls to wash with'.

School attendance was not yet compulsory. Indeed, in 1858 it was estimated that nearly 40 per cent. of the country's total school population attended for less than a year. The name of George Forbes of Bereleigh figures amongst the subscribers from 1852 onwards, and his name occurs a second time in the 1860 treasurer's accounts: 'March 16th. G. Forbes Esq. Making waistcoat 5s. 0d.' Presumably the garment was made by pupils, and was considered successful, for a few months later we find 'July 24th. Mrs. Forbes for waistcoat 5s. 0d.'.

At national level, pupil teachers originated in 1846, being apprenticed from the age of 13 to eighteen. They spent five and a half hours daily teaching or in some kindred activity, and themselves received seven and a half hours weekly instruction outside school hours. Sarah Green and Elizabeth Beagley, both apprenticed in 1863, were the village's first pupil teachers, each with an annual salary of £12 10s. 0d. to be followed by yearly increments of £2 10s. 0d. The East Meon master's log-book also commences in 1863, providing innumerable brief but vivid pictures of mid-Victorian life. Entries tell of simple pleasures, of work (child labour, as we now call it) taking predecence over education, and of mere part-time schooling for some:

March 10th.—The children had a whole holiday, being the Prince of Wales' Wedding day.
May 4th.—117 in attendance. The children went out at 11 o'clock to go to Bereleigh with May garlands.
May 13.—The children had holiday, being the village club festival.
June 29th.—Holiday. The celebration of the Queen's Coronation.
July 9th.—Attendance rather small, being the hay season.
Aug. 6th.—Attendance small on account of harvest.

Sept. 7th.—Opened school after the Harvest vacation, but owing to much wet the Harvest not completed, consequently scarcely any children present.

Sept. 28th.—Attendance not yet very good, some of the children not having finished gleaning.

Nov. 9th.—Winter cloaks given out.

Nov. 16.—Elizabeth and Thomas Mellersh left for winter.

Earlier in the year 'winter cloaks' had been presented by John Bonham Carter II for the use of the scholars of Eastmeon School as a memorial token of the interest taken by the late Mrs. Bonham Carter in the school'. H.M. Inspector (Mr. Wm. Warburton) visited the school in January 1864, when the children must have been well-behaved, since next day they had 'a game of play in the afternoon, as a reward for their good conduct at the Inspection'. Mr. Warburton seems to have been ahead of the times in his views, for he daringly suggested the mixing of boys and girls occasionally, which led to the master noting some months later, 'Find the mixing of boys and girls daily tends to soften the manner of the boys'.

The following year's entries record an occasion when the pupil teachers were admonished 'for playing with the children during school hours', though they were, of course, but children themselves. In October, evening classes for men and boys, funded by £5 15s. 0d. in 'pence', commenced, the main expenditure items being Mr. Forder's £3 per annum stipend, copy books 10s. 8d., and candles 18s. 9d. The next month two members of one family 'left—parents cannot afford to pay the school fees'. So, only 120 years ago, two children were deprived of schooling for the sake of two old pence a week. Christmas holidays lasted a week:

1865 Jan. 3rd.—Many late, kept them in ¾ of an hour, find a great difficulty to get the children to school in time.

Jan. 10th.—Joseph Grant kept without his dinner for playing truant.

Jan. 18th.—David Eldridge sick, having the ends of two of his fingers taken off.

In May 'Rosa Blackman and Harriett Dennis left for the summer months their mothers having to go out into the fields to work', and in early September '102 children hopping' (hop-picking). But the year ended incredibly with an entry on 11 December:'Fanny Cooper admitted 1½ years of age'.

1866 got off to a bad start:

Jan. 16th.—Only 24 children present being a very wet morning, at noon the village was completely inundated.

Jan. 18th.—Very few children present, being unable to pass through the water. 20 sick.

Jan. 19th.—25 sick of scarlatina.

Jan. 24th.—Olive Pike, belonging to the Infant Class died from scarlet fever.

March 7th.—The children attended Divine Service at Church, being a day of humiliation on account of the 'Cattle Plague'.

Visits to the school by 'guest teachers'—ladies from the ranks of the local gentry—commenced in 1868. Mrs. Le Roy Lewis from Westbury House was the pioneer, and over a short period gave 'object lessons' on such diverse subjects as sugar, tea, silk, glass, the eye, paper, salt and money! In June she capped her benevolence by giving the children 'a treat of tea, cake and bread and butter at her own home'. Next term other 'guest teachers' followed her example:

Oct. 13th.—The ladies at Church Villa visited and took 3 Classes to Scripture and Arithmetic.
Oct. 15th.—Mrs. Forbes of Bereleigh visited and took 1st. Class to a Geography lesson.

Since 1861, capitation and pupil teacher grants had depended on H.M. Inspectors' annual reports proving satisfactory. So one can imagine the Forders' relief when writing up the 1869 log-book:

March 8th.—Summary of the Inspector's report on the school and remarks:
'This difficult School is conducted with considerable skill and success. The Room is too full, and it would be very desirable to occupy in addition the large Room which is at present brick floored.'

Later that month 'Annie Willis left because she would not attend the Sunday School and refused to pay the extra fee enforced by the rules of the school'. Which seems to indicate that absence from Sunday School involved a financial penalty, even though disguised as 'the extra fee'. Parading the maximum number of pupils for annual inspection was necessary to obtain full capitation grants, and sick children were some-times wrapped up and brought to school from their beds.[11] So it is understandable when we read:

1870 Jan. 19th.—Frank and Anne Rogers are in the Union at Petersfield for a short time. Are eligible for Inspection. Have sent to ascertain if they can be allowed to attend tomorrow.
Jan. 20th.—Rogers, Frank, Jane and Anne were not permitted to leave the Union.

The severity of Victorian discipline was illustrated when, also in January, John Lintott stole 8d. from another boy, which event was reported to his father 'who wished him to be whipped'. Doubtless this was done, but more was to come.

Jan. 24th.—The Rev. Brodie resolved that John Lintott be excluded from all benefits and presents for the present year as a punishment for theft.
Dec. 8th.—Mrs. Forbes of Bereleigh gave the children tea and cake and each an Xmas present. John Lintott was not allowed to be present, as a punishment for taking money from a boy's basket in the early part of the year.

In the 19th century corporal punishment, nowadays controversial, was taken for granted. Nevertheless, Mr. Forder, after 24 years as master wrote in 1872: 'Have resolved to discontinue corporal punishment for a time.' But a couple of months later: 'Cannot possibly maintain order without occasionally using the cane'.

Reminders that families often lived near subsistence level are frequent: '1872 Dec. 1st. Charles Brewer left; his parents refused to pay the school fee of one penny per week'; and on 21 February 1873, 'Many of the scholars stay away to pick up wood for firing—the high price of coal being the cause chiefly'. (Coal was, in fact, £1 4s. 6d. a ton at that time.) At a meeting of the School Committee later in the year 'Mrs. Forder called the attention of the Managers to the irregular attendance of the children and asked if any remedy could be applied. The Managers quite felt the difficulty but at present could not devise any remedy'.

Frank Rogers disgraced himself in June 1874, the circumstances being recorded at length: 'Mrs. Forder took some of the boys out to play a game of cricket. During the game Frank Rogers would not conform to the rules. The other boys unanimously agreed that he was wrong, but he would not give in, and put himself into a violent passion, and threw the bat with great force, which hit George Collins in the back and prostrated him. Mrs. Forder chastised him'. (He was subsequently suspended from school till after the summer holidays.) At the end of the year we find the entry: 'Dec. 31st. Beer for men removing night soil 1s. 3d.'. Could this have been an annual event? If so, some later health problems are hardly surprising.

After 28 years' employment, the Forders retired at Michaelmas 1876, being succeeded by William S. Tregear, assisted by his daughters, Mary and Elizabeth, the combined annual salary for the three being £90. The new master, a stern, bearded man, was destined to hold the post for 26 years. Throughout that quarter century log-book entries reflect no glimmer of humour, nor compassion, either towards pupils or his family. Yet, to be fair, standards of education, discipline, hygiene and dress all improved markedly under his aegis. Log-book entries within the first few months of Tregear's arrival are informative:

> Oct. 23rd.—Discipline improving. Potato picking kept some away.
> Nov. 20th.—Admit Albert Watts 9 years unable to say letters.
> 1877 Jan. 1st.—Admit George and John Shawyer 9 & 7 to Infants unable to read.
> April 9th.—Many children absent to witness a funeral.
> May 28th.—Admit 2 boys and one girl from the Dame's School in the village.

The 'dame' was undoubtedly Mrs. Elizabeth Kille, listed in *Kelly's* and *White's Directories* as owner of a 'preparatory school'.

The Elementary Education Act of 1876 made school attendance compulsory, subject to certain exemptions, one of which permitted up to six weeks' absence per annum by rural children for agricultural work. Thus: 'Oct. 8th. Commence work after an interval of 8 weeks. The last fortnight, School Attendance Committee, Petersfield, having exempted children from attending during Hop Picking, the School was closed'. A few weeks later, yet another reminder of prevailing poverty: 'Nov. 2nd. The Parish Loan Blankets distributed, causing many to be away', and on 28 November, '170 on Register, about 40 absent'.

1878 entries include:

> Jan 31st. Holiday—The Master having lost the Infant of the family—Buried in East Meon Churchyard.
> Feb. 18th.—Children away now to gather swede greens. Some make a trade of it by picking and selling.
> June 20th.—Fire at Mrs. Attwood's—House burnt. Attendance afternoon small on that account.
> June 24th.—The heat in the room excessive. The closets are far from sweet.
> July 1st.—Master out of school much of Wednesday his youngest child being very ill—also Thursday when she died.
> July 15th.—The Master obliged to call in the Doctor for another daughter—The Doctor ascribes the ailment to the Water & Closets—The Closets being too close to house and school.
> Aug. 5th.—Using Carbolic Powder as a Disinfectant in the offices.

When 1878 ended the master's laconic entry recorded that it had been 'an eventful year for my family'. To describe as 'eventful' a year in which first his 'infant', little Edith, aged six months, and then his 'youngest child', Margaret, aged three years, had died, probably of typhoid fever, shows either a complete lack of human feeling, or else the facade of a stiff upper lip, intended to disguise inward distress. Nevertheless, the battle, conducted in overcrowded conditions, to drum 'the three Rs' into often unreceptive heads continued, sometimes with but little psychological insight: '1880 Mar. 8th. George Edwards 10 minutes over his reading would not speak for class to hear—at last would not utter a syllable. Caned him with 6 stripes'; and on 14 May 1883, 'Agnes Shawyer punished for dirty writing turned sulky and impertinent. Put her on a chair and otherwise punished her. Thursday still refused to obey. Left to stand in front of class morning and afternoon'. Later in the year he noted on 11 December, 'The Assistant E. A. Tregear unwell—Diphtheria'.

For year after year, school life continued much as before. Pupils' unauthorised absences were tolerated provided they were gainfully employed, whether gleaning, picking hops, greens, potatoes or stones, gathering winter fuel, nuts, mushrooms, or wild raspberries, covert beating for pheasant shooting parties, singing at farmhouses on May Day; or even when attracted by Petersfield's annual Taro Fair, Hambledon's Races, military manoeuvres, a meet of foxhounds, steam ploughing, a burning house, a funeral, or the passage of dancing bears through the village. Official holidays, apart from a week at Christmas and Easter and six weeks in summer, were fairly numerous. Seasonal agricultural breaks varied year to year, but single days were awarded on Ascension Day, Coronation Day, The Foresters Friendly Society Fete, August Bank Holiday, for royal weddings and funerals, and, during the South African War, to celebrate the relief of Ladysmith, Mafeking, and the subsequent entry into Johannesburg. The Queen's Golden Jubilee in June 1887 justified a whole week's holiday, and 'the inhabitants were entertained with Dinner & Tea in the meadow in the middle of the village. Races, Bonfire, Torchlight procession wound up a most pleasant day. The School met and walked to Church, thence to the marquee after the band'.

'Treats', usually consisting of tea, with cake and bread and butter, were occasionally provided by Mrs. Forbes, Mrs. Le Roy Lewis or the vicar's wife. Once the vicar entertained the children with a 'magic lantern', another time a conjuror and ventriloquist appeared, and a Sunday School tea was followed by a Punch and Judy show. Involuntary absences regularly resulted from snowbound and impassable lanes, deep floods when the river overflowed, and numerous epidemics, the most common being scarlatina, whooping cough and measles. In the 1888/89 winter some sort of record must have been created when 139 children were stricken with measles. Terribly cold classrooms were stoically endured, as on 2 December 1889 when the master recorded 'Opened school thermometer 36°. Noon 44°'. The Management Committee had increased 'school pence' on a sliding scale in 1880: 'For farmers' and tradesmen's children 6d. weekly for the first child and 3d. for all others. For mechanics' children 3d. for the first and 2d. for all others. For all other parents' children 2d. for the first and 1d. for all others'.[12] A rebate scheme introduced in 1889 encouraged regular attendance, a ticket valued ½d. being presented to each child attending an absence-free week, 12 such tickets being exchangeable for 6d.; this arrangement was ended by the Assisted Education Act 1891, which was adopted by the local committee. On a national level elementary education became virtually free, and no more pence were paid in East Meon.

At last, the School Management Committee began to apply its collective mind to matters of hygiene and cleanliness, as shown by three separate minutes: '5th. July 1886. Ordered, at the urgent request of Mr. Tregear, that the water tank at the school house be cleaned out, this not having been done for ten years'. 'Jan. 5th. 1891. It was decided that the school should be washed once a quarter.' And in October 1892: 'It was agreed that a woman should be hired to sweep the School 4 days a week, clean on Saturdays, and light the fires at 3s. 0d. a week'.

In June 1890, the assistant teacher, Miss Slaughter, had been 'laid up with nervous debility and over-taxed brain', the doctor thinking a fortnight's rest might enable her to resume work; whilst the late summer saw an influx of 10,000 troops for two weeks of cavalry manoeuvres—a matter of great interest to village children. But exceptionally wet weather, which prolonged the harvest, led to the military tented town's premature demise, and the troops' return to Aldershot, doubtless a disappointment for both participants and spectators.

April 1892 saw the school's admission of 'a boy of 10 years who cannot say a letter', and in May 'some mothers out in the fields and keep one at home to look after the house and younger ones'. Less depressingly, the first school cookery lessons commenced in the autumn, and there was a 'Bank Holiday School treat at one of the Chapels'. And in 1895 the 'County Council Dairy School' held a class in the village, attended by 6th standard girls Faith and Daisy Adams, to become 'proficient in butter making'. The young ladies acquitted themselves well, gaining scholarships to spend a month at the Dairy School free of expense.

Good as well as bad weather brought problems; for though the hot, dry summer of 1896 led to 'the machines busy among wheat', the school was without water by 20 July: 'Supply of water from the tank quite gone. All must be fetched from river or wells'. And naughty boys were no less naughty in those days: '1897 Jan. 26th. Caned Gilbert Kille for refusing to obey me, his teacher having sent him out for inattention and laughing when desired to attend. Had 4 or 5 over the seat and then held out his hand'. Clearly unsubdued, he was soon again in the news: 'Feb. 4th. Gilbert Kille again caned for inciting a brother, who had been wilfully disobedient, not to submit. The younger made a rush for the door'.

On a more formal level, the School Committee agreed (Jan. 1899) that Widow Spiers should be asked to attend during the pupil teachers' lessons for 1s. 0d. a week. Doubtless the master provided the seven and a half hours weekly tuition, and contemporary respectability required a chaperon's presence. Widow Spiers may or not have been pleased with her part-time duty, but was almost immediately replaced. 'Miss C. Tregear having offered to be in attendance . . . it was agreed that she be paid 1s. 0d. a week for such attendance.' Clearly, 1s. 0d. a week was not to be despised even by the master's daughter. William Stephens Tregear's mastership ended suddenly on 21 January 1902, when he dropped dead while teaching. The log-book, written up for that day, states: 'He fell in a fainting fit between the desks, and never rallied, although all that could be done to revive him by the usual means was done by his daughters, the Assistants'. He was 63, and his widow, surviving him and the health hazards of the day, lived to the ripe old age of one hundred and two.

The arrival of the new master, Mr. F. Tomlinson, the year after Queen Victoria's death, marked the beginning of a new era in more senses than one. He showed compassion, for example sending home children who arrived in soaking wet clothes; and, on a national level, awareness of school health problems increased, though no sudden and dramatic changes occurred. Indeed, during the master's first year 'Dr. Batten ordered School to be closed until further notice. Outbreak diphtheria', and shortly after: 'Mrs. Tomlinson absent with diphtheria'.

October 1903 saw the County Council take over 'direction of elementary education', and during the following summer holidays the school was 'cleaned and painted'. Overcrowding was a perennial problem, and in 1904, with 171 on the roll, there were recurrent epidemics of mumps, whooping cough, chicken pox and scarlet fever. Yet, when such outbreaks threatened to become serious, the Medical Officer of Health promptly ordered the school's closure. In February 1909 there was 'Medical inspection of children born in 1903. 11 aged 5 examined and 35 special cases'. And the following year: 'Oct. 21. Medical surprise inspection. Dr. Gillespie'.

Further gradual changes included introduction of non-academic instruction in gardening (1912) and, for girls, a few years later, cheese-making. Oddly, catastrophic World War I passed with but one log-book reference, on 1 February 1915: 'Admitted two Belgian Refugees, one placed in the Infants and the other one in Standard V'. The following June, the school was closed for mumps, and in December the M.O. excluded 15 children for impetigo and two for 'nits'.

Peace celebrations in 1919, including a children's tea, a bonfire and sports, preceded by a procession through the village, took place in the same meadow used 32 years earlier for Victoria's Golden Jubilee. Whether or not England had become 'a land fit for heroes', attitudes towards school-children became increasingly enlightened. Epidemics recurred, and the elements did their worst, but regular visits, sometimes unexpected, from the Medical Officer and nurse, often resulted in 'exclusions' of certain children, thus improving standards of health and hygiene. As for 'treats', 8 August 1924 was a red letter day, when 90 children went on the Sunday School outing 'to Bognor by charabanc'. On Empire Day 1926 the vicar gave a flagstaff, Mr. Sam Hardy presented a Union Jack, and a major-general addressed the pupils, who responded 'with suitable songs and a salute'.

The Tomlinsons retired in 1927, when the school's 81 years history had spanned only three masterships. Over that period tremendous improvements had taken place, and perhaps the most welcome was a numerical reduction from 170 to under one hundred. Soon, dental clinics and eyesight testing were organised, a school library established, sports equipment provided, and significantly, Douglas Lambert and Alan Banham won scholarships to Churcher's College, Petersfield, in 1930. At last, secondary education was within reach—just.

During the 1930s a wireless set was bought with funds raised by pupils, a concert was given 'by the scholars at the Court House before a crowded audience', a 'milk scheme' for certain children commenced, and elder girls attended cookery and housewifery classes at the Village Institute. Even inoculation against diphtheria began, and the school seemed to be going from strength to strength; but the log-book brings us down to earth with a jolt::

> 1938 June 13th.—Gwendoline M. Hoyes commenced duties as Head Teacher. The school is in a deplorable condition in every way. There is practically no stock in the school. Many of the textbooks have been mutilated and scribbled on. There seems to be no discipline, and the tone of the school is very poor.

The next year the world was again plunged into war, and with the evacuation of vast numbers of children from air-raid danger areas to the country, East Meon school numbers doubled from 70-odd to one hundred and forty-four. Though it is fashionable for the

British to indulge in self-denigration, we are at least adaptable; a trait strikingly exemplified in schools between 1939 and 1945. What happened here was typical, with teachers facing and overcoming problems of numbers doubling overnight, plus the complications and disruptions of travel difficulties and sleeplessness caused by night-time 'aerial activity'. Gas masks were issued, an air-raid shelter constructed, and, echo from the past, the school closed for two weeks' potato planting. On the credit side, school dinners started in 1944, and, a year later, the European part of the war ended, and V.E. Day was celebrated 'with suitable hymns and prayers', followed by patriotic songs. 'The Union Jack was hoisted in the playground and rousing cheers were given for the King, Prime Minister, Navy, Army, Air Force, Allies etc.'.

Nearly another 40 years have passed, Miss Hoyes has been succeeded by Miss Leach, and she, in 1968, by David Lewis. In 1947 the school which educated village children of all ages for 101 years was reorganised as a Junior School. Seniors were transferred to Petersfield Modern Secondary School, only 72 pupils remaining. The Inspector's 1956 report, immediately before Miss Hoyes's retirement, was yet another reflection of changed attitudes: 'The general behaviour of the children is good: They clearly respond well to the kindly treatment they receive'. Numbers increased to 98 in 1960, the log-book noting: 'Rooms overcrowded'. Other older problems persisted:

> 1961 Dec. 18.—School very cold. Two classrooms were 32° at 9 a.m. rising to 48° at midday. Dec. 20th.—School again very cold—9 a.m. 31°.
> 1962 Jan. 31st.—Impossible conditions this morning. Temperature again only 39° at 9 a.m. in the Infants' Room. By 10 15 a.m. the temperature was only 42°. Children are really cold and jumping and running activities taken regularly throughout the day to keep warm.

By far the most important event in local scholastic history since 1845 was the opening of a completely new school in 1964. Sited off Chapel Street, its bright and spacious classrooms are supplemented by a large multi-purpose entrance hall, a staff room, a medical room, and, equally important, two and a half acres of recreation space that includes a swimming pool. The headmaster is still David Lewis, born in a Welsh village where his early schooling was in the Welsh language. East Meon's children, numbering about 70 these days, are taught by three full-time teachers (including the head). Subjects, apart from 'the three Rs', comprise 'the social studies' such as history and geography, elementary science, handicrafts and music. Other instruction covers cookery, simple woodwork, swimming, and road safety, as well as educational visits to places of historic or other interest. The vicar spends a weekly hour taking each class in religious knowledge. Outdoor recreation includes football and an annual sports day, and indoors is a small gymnasium. The school's strong Parent Teacher Association serves a social function and provides financial help—the swimming pool owes its existence to the P.T.A. David Lewis has the final word:

> During the last decade the pattern of teaching has changed. There is less emphasis upon the teachers being dictators, and more emphasis upon a 'two-way traffic' between teachers and pupils, whereby children are encouraged to find out and to think for themselves. We try to teach children how to become good citizens, by encouraging them to be involved in communal events such as the annual best kept village competition, and to think for themselves how the village and its amenities could be improved.

Chapter Seven

FARMING, 1837–1983

WHEN THE YOUNG VICTORIA became queen in 1837 agriculture had awakened from a lengthy slumber, during which fundamental changes in farming procedures were almost imperceptible. Harvesting was still predominantly manual; and in places a man could be hired for 1s. a day plus his beer. Sixty years earlier bullocks were as commonly used as horses,[1] but parliamentary enclosures, which transformed the face of England and the lifestyle of innumerable country folk, prepared the way for otherwise impossible developments. Nevertheless, in 1837 no farmer could have guessed that within 150 years horses would disappear, that the human labour force, largely displaced by machines, would shrink by three-quarters; and yet output would increase enormously.

By the mid-19th century mechanised harvesting was increasing, and in 1870 something like a quarter of corn was machine-cut,[2] increasing to over three-quarters by 1900. After 1860, first self-delivering reapers, and then self-binders further reduced manual work. As for flail-threshing, which needed a day's work by a strong man to yield 3 cwts. of wheat, horse-driven threshing machines were gaining popularity when, also in the mid-19th century, steam-driven threshers came on the scene, and, by 1870, were replacing both flails and horse-driven machines.

Harvesting, though mechanised, still involved a whole series of successive operations: first, cutting by binders; then stooking—standing sheaves in groups till ripened by sun and air; then carting to yards for building into ricks, subsequently thatched to withstand the elements. Months later, threshing took place, whereupon the grain, in hessian sacks, was sold or stored.

After World War II, combined harvesters suddenly arrived, bringing the greatest ever single harvesting revolution. These self-propelled mechanised giants that cut, thresh, winnow and dress corn in one operation, covering 20 acres daily, numbered 63,000 by 1965.[3] Then there were about as many binders still in use, but today combines have taken over, binders rarely being seen except where wheat-straw has been grown for thatching. Harvesting operations, spread over a period of months since time immemorial, are now completed so quickly that the morning's standing corn becomes, by evening, a grain mountain in barn or silo.

As for the labour force, village populations continued rising until the mid-19th century. In 1851 there were 1.48 million agricultural workers in England and Wales, and, as their numbers shrank, distant events aggravated the situation. The full impact of cultivation of the New World's virgin prairies was delayed by the American Civil War (1861–1865). From 1868–1874 Britain's wheat acreage averaged 3.5–3.6 million, after which the market was flooded with North American grain of a quality and price with which we could not complete. By 1885 wheat acreage had fallen to 2.5 million, and by 1893 to to below 2 million.[4] The great agricultural depression of 1880–1900 resulted.

The decline of the labour force, starting between 1835–1870, has continued ever since. In 1921, British farm workers numbered only a million, with almost as many horses, and a few tractors. Workers were a mere half million by 1965, when there were nearly as many tractors, and horses had almost disappeared. Yet these remarkable trends have since accelerated, and, in 1983, Britain's full-time labour force (excluding farmers, their wives and partners) had dropped to 171,000.[5] But corn yields have improved dramatically through the increased use of artificial fertilisers, chemical sprays and biological breeding of improved plant species, and reduced harvesting losses. In 1850 wheat averaged 15 cwts. an acre, with barley and oats slightly less. By 1982 wheat yields had leapt to 49 cwts.[6] So, in just over 130 years, a dwindling labour force, mechanisation to an unbelievable degree, and vastly improved yields, have resulted in cereal output more than trebling, and *output per man* perhaps increasing forty-fold.

Arable farming necessitates many pre-harvest operations, now carried out by powerful tractors in place of horses, thereby reducing working man-hours enormously. Controlling weeds, and 'singling' root-crops, formerly time-consuming jobs, are achieved by herbicidal sprays and more sophisticated seed-drills; and a comparatively new practice, 'direct drilling' of cereals and brassicas into burnt-off stubble or pasture sprayed with a dessicant, entirely avoids ploughing and cultivating for the particular planned crop.

Livestock farming is more labour-intensive than cereal growing, and here, too, tremendous changes have resulted from selective breeding, higher management standards and mechanisation. Tending and hand-milking 150 cows needed six cowmen; whereas tending and machine-milking them requires one cowman plus a 'back-up man'. Though the dairy cow population of England and Wales remained static at 2.6 million from 1934–1982,[7] herds decreased from 120,000 in 1955 to 44,000 in 1981; and the average milk yield per cow, per lactation, increased from an estimated 440 gallons in 1932 to nearly 1,100 gallons in 1983. As for sheep, shepherding 900 lowground breeding ewes when hurdle-folded over roots required four to five shepherds; now, with electrified fencing, one motorised shepherd does the job.

Great animal health improvements have resulted from co-operation between the Ministry, veterinary profession and farming community. 'Cattle-plague', or rinder pest (referred to in Chapter Six), a highly contagious virus disease, was formerly endemic in Britain, and during 1865, 50,000 cases were reported, most proving fatal.[8] Later in the century the disease was eliminated, and recently great progress has been made towards conquering brucellosis, anthrax, foot-and-mouth disease, and tuberculosis. Indeed, when national attestation was declared in 1981, the country was, for practical purposes, freed from brucellosis; anthrax claimed only 20 known victims in 1982; there has been but one outbreak of foot-and-mouth disease since 1968; and the present-day incidence of tuberculosis occurs mainly in South-West England.[9] Today Britain, with arguably the world's most highly mechanised and efficient agricultural industry, produces 62 per cent. of our food, and 76 per cent. of the temperate foodstuffs which our land and climate enable us to grow.[10] Farming is our largest primary industry, and with 635,000 people directly engaged, and a further 1,500,000 either supplying goods to agriculture, or processing and marketing its output, over 2,000,000 people rely on agriculture for their living.

Having broadly summarised agricultural developments of the last 150 years, and indicated the continuing size and importance of this great and vital industry, let us examine farming progress in the parish, noting especially the significant introduction of 'new blood' into East Meon's farming community. The story of the new blood begins in the 1890s, in the midst of the great depression, when Hampshire tenant farmers, traditionally relying on sheep and corn growing, were in dire financial trouble and, hoping to make ends meet, sold off too many sheep. This caused a chain reaction, for corn-growing land, no longer adequately fertilised, gave lower yields. Soon farms became vacant, and landlords were prepared to attract new tenants by accepting nominal rents of a few shillings an acre, or even offering an initial rent-free period.

At that time landowner William Nicholson of Basing Park, Froxfield, was employing a Cumbrian agent named Hudd Smith; and another Cumbrian, Matthew Williamson, was farm manager at Woodlands, near West Meon. These men passed the word round their home district that tenancies of large farms in Hampshire were available for little or no rent, and, during the next decade, there followed something of a migration of Cumbrians to East Meon and parishes nearby.

The first two migrants, in 1894, were Isaac Wren, former tenant of Low Grove Farm, Keswick, a 60-acre cattle and sheep farm with 50s. an acre rent which was considered high; and his neighbour, Robert Hind. Wren took a tenancy of Riplington Farm from Colonel Le Roy Lewis, and Hind the tenancy of Westbury Manor Farm, West Meon. As the two farms adjoined, the men remained neighbours. They jointly hired a special train to transport their live and dead stock from Keswick to Petersfield station, the line to West Meon having not then been opened. Numerous farm carts and wagons were sent from Riplington and Westbury Manor farms to meet the train at Petersfield, but unfortunately the train was some hours late, by which time the waiting carters had refreshed themselves over liberally at the nearby pub. When the train eventually pulled in, broad Cumbrian and Hampshire accents, mutually unfamiliar, the latter somewhat slurred, resulted in a chaotic situation.

These two farmers, and others who followed from Cumbria, pursued a different farming policy from their Hampshire predecessors, reducing the scale of corn growing, and concentrating on grass and livestock—i.e., sheep and beef cattle. Neither farm had a dairy herd, since Petersfield railway station, eight miles distant, was too far to send milk daily by horse-drawn conveyance. Corn was cut by a reaping machine, followed by workers binding sheaves by hand; and only 10 years earlier Jimmy Blackman had been cutting one and a half acres a day by scythe, with his wife tying the sheaves.

This new policy involved making vast quantities of hay, and where Hampshire farmers had used, and still continued to use, hurdles for folding sheep over roots, the Cumbrians allowed their sheep, newly-introduced Lakeland breeds, to run free in whole fields. These techniques proved so successful that by 1900 Wren was able to take the tenancy of a second farm, Court Farm, West Meon; and shortly afterwards other Cumbrian farmers followed; one to East Tisted, another to West Tisted, and a third, George Atkinson, who had been farming at Skelgill, near Keswick (where his neighbour was Beatrix Potter), came to South Farm, East Meon.

Though a 'foreigner', Isaac Wren, physically a big man, with a booming voice, soon became integrated into local affairs, and, at the first annual meeting of the newly-formed East Meon Parish Council in February 1895, was appointed one of the three parish overseers. Two years later he became vice-chairman of the Council, and, in 1902, chairman, an office he held until his death in 1931. An outstanding man, he was recognised as such. Although already running his own two farms, it was characteristic of Wren also to look after South Farm for Atkinson from Michaelmas 1905, when the tenancy began, till Ladyday 1906, the earliest date at which the new tenant could move in. Atkinson, too, was an exceptional man, as evidenced by the vicar of Keswick's reference supplied to John Bonham Carter's executor, then landlord of South Farm:

Newlands Vicarage,
Keswick,
Cumberland.

Dear Sir,

I have great pleasure in bearing testimony to the high character of Mr. George Atkinson of Skelgill Farm. I have known him well ever since he came to Skelgill and always found him honourable, upright, and straightforward and very pleasant to work with. He has been a Churchwarden, School Manager, and a Parish Councillor for some years and has discharged his duties in these offices faithfully and well. He is an excellent farmer, works his land thoroughly, and keeps the fences in good repair. Indeed, his farming does credit to any estate. I should be pleased to hear that he has succeeded in getting this farm but very much regret his leaving here. I shall be glad to answer any further questions.

Yours faithfully
B. L. Carr.

When carrying on a comparatively small sheep and cattle farm at Skelgill, Atkinson, like his father Joseph, did not confine himself to farming pure and simple. He also undertook haulage work for numerous customers, including 'Skiddow Parish', and acted as a professional valuer, sometimes for both parties, when sheep changed hands. His business ledger, written in a copperplate hand, records many live and dead stock purchases in and around East Meon immediately after Michaelmas 1905, to augment what could be brought with him. Indeed, on the very next day after taking possession he was at Lythe House, East Meon, buying an iron water cart for £7 and a set of chain harrows for £1 15s. 0d. Two days later, over 20 miles away at Herriard, he became the owner of a tip-cart for £9, and the day after, at Oakshott Farm, Hawkley, acquired a nine-tine horse-hoe, a set of harness and a saddle and bridle. The South Farm outgoing tenant's sale was held on 5 October, when 40 lots were knocked down to Atkinson, including a dozen hurdles (10s.), portable fowl-house (10s.), roller (£1), Samuelson reaping machine (£3 5s. 0d.), and a McCormick grass mower (£7). A few weeks later he snapped up five steers at £5 each and another seven at £4 5s. 0d. apiece.

Rent for the 568-acre farm, £293 per annum, represented just over 10s. an acre. One clause in the agreement stipulated that on its expiration the land should be left 'in a four course shift'—meaning a four-year crop rotation; and another provision obliged the tenant to cut three acres of underwood in Hyden Wood annually, as set out by the landlord's agent, though the wood was excluded from the tenancy. Doubtless the capital value of a coppiced hazel plantation would have deteriorated unless kept cut as each section reached maturity. A feature of the farm was its working water-mill, described in contemporary sale particulars (when the freehold was auctioned in 1906) as:

The valuable and recently erected brick and slate turbine water mill, driving a pair of gristing stones, and all the machinery for chaff cutting, cake crushing, winnowing etc., having 3 fine large stores, with hoists to same.

Details of previous cultivations and cropping at South Farm (and at adjoining Lower Farm) exist within a buckram-bound book containing field-by-field records from 1893–99. Crops included leys, wheat, barley, oats, rye, turnips, swedes, mangolds, vetches, clover, mustard, kale, rape, sanfoin, trifolium, peas, potatoes, kohl rabbi and cabbages. Turnips and other root crops had usually been fed off by folded sheep, though superphosphate was a quite widely used fertiliser at 2-4 cwts. per acre. Fields were frequently marked 'fallowed', though seldom for an entire year. Land was sometimes 'couched', and seeds sown 'broadcast', and steam ploughing and cultivating often took place. Ominously, a note recurs, following details of crops sown, simply reading 'failed'. On the other hand, the writer seemed pleased when noting:

> Lower 20 Acres (13a. 3r. 4p.)
> Oct. 1893   Drilled with wheat, ½ bushel seed per acre.
> Sept. 1894   Threshed from field—yield 65 sacks head and tail from machine. 63 lbs. natural weight.

Some of South Farm's uncomplimentary field names, still used today, such as Furzen Field, Spent Hill, Thistle Field, and Hilly Field, were indicative of poor quality land; whilst others were more evocative—Teg Down (grazed by second year sheep since time immemorial); Chapel Field (where once stood the chapel of ease, St Mary's-in-the-Fields); adjoining Fairfield (site of the fair held annually on the Lady Day in Harvest, 19 September); and Furlongs and Partridge Furlong ('furlong' used in either its meaning of the main division of an open field, or of a group of open field cultivated strips—probably the latter).

In his first few years at South Farm George Atkinson's ledger records work done and goods supplied, typifying his threefold business of farmer, wood merchant and miller:

		£	s.	d.
For Landlord's agents (Messrs. Pink and Arnold)				
1905	1 horse and 1 man 1 day carting wheat		7	0
1906	Wheat straw for thatching stables 1½ tons at £2 per ton	3	0	0
1907	Man 2 days breaking stones for Mill Road		5	0
	Man cleaning out ditch side of Mill Road 3 days		7	6
Mr. G. Spencer				
1907	62 bundles of pea sticks		10	4
	1,600 bunts at 5s.	4	0	0
W. W. Waters, Petersfield				
1907	½ ton potatoes	2	0	0
Mr. Singleton				
1907	[Hire of] reaper for 25 acres at 1s. per acre	1	5	0
	[Hire of] corn drill 32 acres at 6d.		16	0
	4 sacks barley ground		4	0
	2 ,, oats ,,		1	6
	5 ,, ,, crushed		2	6
H. Curtis Gallup				
1907	50 hurdles at 10s. per doz.	2	1	8

Already, the mill was busy crushing and grinding oats, barley and wheat for numerous customers, two of the best accounts being those of Isaac Wren and of Mr. Singleton, tenant of adjoining Lower Farm; and George Silk of Frogmore Mill bought oats and barley, doubtless to be crushed or ground for his own customers. The largest single sale at the time was of two ricks of 'mixture hay' to James Marlow of Alton for £215.

A week's army manoeuvres must have taken place in the locality in September 1908, an account of that date being headed 'H.M. Troops':

		£	s.	d.
65	sacks grey winter oats at 21s. per quarter	34	12	6
120	trusses of hay—3½ tons at 80s.	14	0	0
9,031	lbs. hay—80s. ton	16	2	6½
225	bavins at 10s. 6d.	1	3	7½
	Rent of ground	10	0	0
	Use of field for supply depot Sept. 14–21	2	0	0

Also in 1908, the freehold of South Farm, together with much adjoining land, was bought from the Bonham Carter executor by Lord Hotham, whose newly-appointed managing agents were Hall Pain and Goldsmith of Petersfield—some of Goldsmith's exploits will be referred to in Chapter Nine. Shortly after his purchase Hotham embarked on an ambitious water supply scheme involving a pumping station at South Farm, almost adjacent to the springs that constitute the Meon's source, pumping water thence to a reservoir constructed on the top of Hyden Hill, and from there supplying piped water to 'the Estate and the Village'. Atkinson, in consideration of permitting installation of the pumping station, received £5 compensation; also mains water was connected to the farmhouse and a cooling room and 10 extra cowstalls provided.

The following year saw the commencement of wholesale milk production, averaging at first 20–25 gallons a day at 1s. 6d. to 1s. 8d. a gallon. By 1911 (when a quart a day was being supplied to Reginald Burnett at the expense of the 'Guardians of Petersfield Union') daily output climbed to 60–70 gallons, though the price was poor—only 1s. a gallon for months on end. Even worse followed, for in October 1912, 500 gallons a week were going to a Peckham buyer for a mere 8d. a gallon. By April 1918 the price had crept up to 1s. 4d., when a new buyer came on the scene, Trigg and Son of Walton-on-Thames (per West Sussex and Hants Dairy Farmers' Society); but by 1926, with weekly output up to 700 gallons, the price had slipped right back to tenpence.

So much for milk. Other events had occurred between 1906 and 1926, including a ghastly tragedy, when, on 27 December 1912, Atkinson's eight-year-old daughter, Mildred Mary, was accidentally killed through her long hair being caught in an upright shaft of the moving mill machinery, resulting in her being literally scalped. In vain Nurse Micklam rushed to the scene, but nothing could be done for the poor child, whose small coffin was borne to its grave by other village children of her age.

After the war, the Atkinsons, always owners and enthusiastic showers of Shire horses, bought a two-year-old, Southill Yashmate, for 190 guineas at the 1920 London Shire Show. She carried off first prize at each of the Alton and Petersfield shows in that year, and again won firsts at Romsey and Alresford in 1921.

Following George Atkinson's death in May 1922, his sons, George Wilson and Joseph, carried on farming as partners, and, at Michaelmas 1926 expanded by succeeding to Sam Hardy's tenancy of adjoining Lower Farm, then owned, as was South Farm, by Lady Peel. The ingoing valuation came to £856, and the rent for almost 300 acres was £216 per annum. Further expansion took place in 1928 when Lady Peel granted grazing rights over Hockham and Small Downs (159 acres) at only £35 rental, and, as from Ladyday 1942, a grazing tenancy of Wether Down (52 acres) was added at £20 rental. Though these last two tenancies were not full agricultural tenancies, they brought the total area farmed near to 1,080 acres.

In 1953 Lower and South farms, then having an area of 1,178 acres, were wisely bought by the Atkinsons. Their purchase marked a significant stage in the family fortunes, for, after generations as industrious tenant farmers, they had become freeholders. Now, 30 years on, the brothers having departed this world, George's son, Wilson, runs Lower Farm, and Joseph's son, Michael, South Farm, as separate concerns. Wilson says:

'I was born in 1927, married a Cumbrian wife, and have three children, Rosemary, who is married, Susan, a medical student, and George who is carrying on the farming tradition. Before my grandparents left Skelgill, Beatrix Potter was very friendly with my grandmother, who partly inspired the creation of Mrs. Tiggy-Winkle, the hedgehog who was always so busy with her ironing. The book called *The Tale of Mrs. Tiggy-Winkle* is illustrated by one of Beatrix Potter's water-colours showing the hedgehog ironing; and in the background is a large and handsome oak farm dresser which then stood in my grandparents' house, and now stands in mine. I even have one of the plates formerly displayed on the dresser and shown in the illustration.

'There have been enormous changes in farming in the last 80 years, particularly the reduction in the number of farm workers. I now employ only about one man per 100 acres, which is average for a mixed farm, though on an arable farm without livestock, one man to 300 acres could be sufficient. Another change is that far less leguminous crops (e.g., peas, sanfoin, trefoil, turnips, swedes and mangolds) are now grown. But I believe the time could be coming when, due to the high cost of artificial fertilisers, it may be necessary to go back to greater use of dung and so-called "green manure".

'Landscape changes have resulted from a certain amount of hedge-grubbing, partly to reduce the rabbit population, and also to make fields into more suitable sizes and shapes for modern machinery. But I am conscious of the amenity value of trees, and in recent years have re-planted Duncombe Wood, which had been largely ruined as a wood. I have also undertaken a substantial amount of tree planting at the foot of my downland, and have replaced dead elm trees with lime and copper beech.

'In 1952 I took a tenancy of Peak Farm, East Meon, from the late Colonel Humphrey Nicholson, which brought my total farmed land to 1,140 acres. There has been a country-wide trend for sheep numbers to be on the increase, and, on the two farms, I keep about 600 breeding ewes, the annual crop of lambs, at roughly one and a half lambs per ewe, giving me a maximum sheep population of about 1,500 each April/May before I start selling off lambs. The breed I mainly rely on are Border Leicester/Crossed Cheviot (half bred). I also keep some Suffolk Cross ewes, and my rams are Suffolk, Dorset Down and South Down. The shepherd, Malcolm Painter, until recently looked after all my sheep, though he now has some assistance at Peak Farm. Over the years I have managed quite a few showing successes, mainly for fat lamb production. As for cattle, I have two Friesian dairy herds, and a herd of Blue Grey cows for fat cattle production. Bred in the area of Hadrian's Wall, the progeny of Galloway cows by White Shorthorn bulls, they are very hardy and live out on downland all the year. The overall total of my cattle, dairy and beef, is about five hundred.

'Cereal crops average 300 acres, the best yields, in favourable conditions, being two tons to the acre of barley and oats and two-and-a-half to three tons of wheat. I also grow potatoes, but not on a very big scale. I am highly mechanised, and have to keep a large amount of capital employed in equipment. The cost today of buying a new combine, tractor and four-furrow plough such as I use would be nearly £50,000. I also regularly employ aerial top-dressing and spraying contractors to top-dress and fertilise steep hillsides. Otherwise, I could not keep such a large head of livestock. As I have a smooth and level piece of downland suitable for use as a light aircraft runway, I make it available for my cousin Michael and for other farmers.'

Michael Atkinson, 11 years younger than Wilson, has four children: Matthew and Nicholas in their early twenties, and teenage daughters Sarah and Kate:

'I farm approximately 725 acres, the greater part of the original South farm rented by my grandfather, and parts of Oxenbourne Farm (250 acres) which I bought comparatively recently. My Friesian dairy herd numbers roughly one hundred and ten, plus 100 followers, and my beef herds come to about 200, including 34 sucker cows (who produce calves for beef). I use a beef-type bull on my Friesian dairy heifers, and Friesian A.I. subsequently. I also have a Charolais bull. As for sheep, I keep a breeding stock of 300–350 ewes, of which 120 are Scottish half-breds on which I use Suffolk rams to produce Suffolk Cross ewes, which in turn produce butchers' lambs. Lambing is as soon as possible after Christmas to catch the early market, and I average 160–165 per cent. lambs—nearly one and two thirds lambs per ewe. No shepherd is employed, I and my sons looking after the sheep, even doing our own shearing, which is unusual these days. Average cereal crops are 180 acres of barley, 150 of wheat and 30 of oats, totalling about 360 acres. Yields, over the years, come out at roughly two tons to the acre, but in an exceptionally favourable year like 1982, as high as 2.66 tons. I am so mechanised that if I had to buy all my machinery at today's prices it might cost as much as £200,000'.

The three-generation saga of the Atkinsons has been described in some detail for two reasons: first, they now farm over a quarter of the parish's total agricultural land, the greater part owner-occupied; second, they illustrate the effect of new blood being introduced into a community that seemingly lacked adaptability. Not only did the first George Atkinson, like Isaac Wren a decade earlier, bring new and successful farming ideas, but also, like Wren, still found time for concern with local affairs. Within a year of arriving, he became a parish councillor, an office he held from 1907–13 and again from 1919–22, and also shouldered the thankless burden of being one of the three overseers from 1908–10 and 1920–22, when he died. The second George (G. W.) almost immediately stepped into his father's shoes, being a councillor from 1924–48, and was succeeded by *his* son, Wilson, who has served since 1970. Wilson is also a school manager; chairman of the Village Hall; a committee member and past chairman of Petersfield Growmore Club; as well as of the local branch of the National Farmers' Union and of Petersfield Autumn Show. Cousin Michael has recently become a parish councillor, and, lest it appears that they are a family of busybodies, the truth is they work tremendously hard running their own affairs, but still find spare energy for other people's.

However, the Cumbrians were not the only farming 'foreigners' to 'colonise' the area. In 1899, 19-year-old George Jones from Wedmore, near Cheddar, Somerset, arrived at Upper Peake Farm, Exton (not to be confused with Peak Farm, East Meon). The farm, then owned by Colonel Woods and tenanted by Albert Broadway, was a cheese-making farm, with the cattle as well as the land owned by the landlord. Young Jones drove many a wagon-load of cheese to Winchester, 12 miles distant, before the cheese-making expertise he acquired led him into the employment of George Darvill at Court Farm, East Meon.

Also in the 1890s, the Pitman family had moved from Wincanton, Somerset, to Manor Farm, Exton, another of Colonel Woods's cheese-making establishments. In 1905, Jones took two important steps: he married the Pitman's daughter, Edith; and he left East Meon and took a tenancy of a 170-acre mixed farm, Garden Hill Farm, Exton. Four years later, he succeeded Broadway as tenant of Upper Peake Farm, where he lived till 1922, then moving to Hilhampton Farm, Oxenbourne, East Meon, which he had bought earlier. Specialist furniture removers were not employed, the family and all their belongings being transported on farm wagons drawn by their own horses. One of Jones's six children, Stanley, remembers a day in 1919, before the family left Exton:

'My father wanted some heifers driven from Hilhampton Farm to Merryfield Farm, Tisted, about eight or more miles away. So he got out a pony and trap and drove me and a boy named Fred Gibbs, who worked at Garden Hill Farm, from Exton to Oxenbourne. There, the heifers were put in our charge, and father told us to get on and drive them to Tisted, adding that he didn't know how we would get back to Exton afterwards, but he thought we would have to walk. At the time I was 13 and Fred was a year older. We duly got the cattle to their destination, and then set out to walk back to Exton, a further eight miles. It was a hot summer day, and, after a time, feeling thirsty, we called at a pub that no longer exists—*The Wheatsheaf* at Privett. The landlord looked us up and down, since we were only children, and asked what we wanted. Fred spoke up and ordered a pint of bitter, and I asked for a pint of ginger-beer. The accommodating landlord served us, whereupon Fred bought a clay pipe, an ounce of tobacco and a box of matches. Then we resumed our trek back to Exton, during which Fred used most of the box of matches keeping his pipe alight.'

Ownership of 150-acre Hilhampton Farm passed to Stanley Jones on his father's death in the 1950s, and this property, plus about 300 acres of rented land in an adjoining parish, is farmed by Jones and his sons. They keep a Friesian milking herd, and some Longhorn beef cattle—one of the oldest English breeds. Also kept are about 300 breeding ewes, Welsh half-breds (Suffolk Cross), as well as a small lot of pedigree Hampshire Downs. The family's interest in old agricultural implements and tools has resulted in a wide and fascinating collection.

Migration from Cumbria and Somerset may not be so surprising, but the next arrivals came from Normandy, though after a pause on the way by a couple of generations at Botley, Hants. The late Morley John Tosdevine's father was first a coachman and then a small market gardener and strawberry grower there, and Tosdevine Junior with £100 starting capital took a Botley farm tenancy in 1927, moving to East Meon in 1939 when he rented Belmont Farm (100 acres) from Lady Peel. Like the Atkinsons, he seized the opportunity of buying the freehold after Lady Peel's death, and, in the early 1960s, bought adjoining Duncombe Farm (62 acres). Since then, son John has purchased Parsonage Farm, Oxenbourne (158 acres), making the total owned land 320 acres, now farmed by John and grandsons Clive (recent winner of a number of ploughing contests) and Graham, both in their twenties. Apart from casual workers, no labour is employed. Farming is based on beef cattle and cereals, plus some potatoes. The number of cattle has been as high as 65, mainly Aberdeen Angus, Charolais and Hereford Cross. Morley Tosdevine was a member of the parish council for over 20 years and of the former Petersfield R.D.C. for 11 years, and retired after 30 years as a school manager shortly before his recent death.

In the past a dividing line was drawn between so-called 'working farmers' and 'gentleman farmers', now an unacceptable and invidious distinction. Substituting 'dirty-boot farmers' and 'clean-boot farmers' is not much better, so I propose to avoid labelling the owners of two estates who are neither self-important, lazy, snobbish or even 'absentees', but who, by their efficiency and enterprise, have played a full part in the locality's agricultural development of the last 20–30 years. They or their parents also rank as 'colonisers'.

The greater part of the Bereleigh estate (790 acres) was bought by Francis Tyrwhitt-Drake (formerly of Amersham, Bucks) from the Gerald Nicholson executors in 1958, and has been augmented by his son, William, acquiring Lower Bordean Farm (670 acres) from Edgar Wren's executors, Garston Farm (300 acres) from Brian Blacker (Lady Peel's grandson), and Riplington Farm (400 acres) from the Marks brothers. The total estate, now well over 2,000 acres (a small part in Langrish parish) carries a stock of nearly 500 cattle of which about 240 Friesians are milked at any one time, and 1,350 acres of cereals are grown, the balance being oilseed rape, grass and woodland. The farming labour force, excluding the manager, numbers nine, as against 67 on the same land as recently as 1958!

The other estate was until very recently owned by Lynton White of Oxenbourne House, formerly an architect by profession, whose father, the late Sir Dymoke White, bought 4,000 acres in East Meon and adjoining parishes at the 1953 Peel auction. Two hundred acres of farmland and 500 acres of woodland lie in East Meon, immediately south of the Ridgeway; and, of that land, 170 acres comprising part of Oxenbourne Down, Wascoombe Bottom and Hilhampton Down, is let to the Hampshire County Council as a nature reserve—largely unspoilt natural downland, wooded with yew and thorn scrub, and managed by the Hants and Isle of Wight Naturalist Trust. For many years Lynton White served in local government at the modest level of parish councillor, and still serves at the far more exalted level of Hampshire County Councillor—chairman since 1977. Now the land ownership has been spread over other members of the family, farming and forestry reflecting a high standard of efficiency.

Having viewed farming through the eyes of some of the parish's farming families, the picture becomes more balanced by listening to a couple of senior citizens formerly employed on those farms. One, Albert Smith, reminisces at his immaculate pink-washed and thatched Bridge Cottage at Frogmore:

'My father was a self-employed thatcher, hurdle-maker, and sheep shearer. When making hurdles he worked piecework in the woods and copses, the rate being 1s. a hurdle. He also had to cut and sort stakes, poles, etc. When shearing he worked with a gang of half-a-dozen or more—the pay was 6d. a sheep. The shearers wore white corduroy trousers with leather straps buckled below the knee. The trousers soon became filthy and had to be washed several times a week. I learnt the thatching trade from my father, working with him till his death, and then on my own. As a self-employed thatcher, I measured the surface of hay or corn ricks and charged according to the number of 'squares'—that is areas of 100 square feet. For ricks the charge was 1s. a square, with thatching straw provided by the employer. The average farm would have about eight or nine ricks each year. When rick thatching finished each autumn, I used to go on to buildings—barns and houses, in the winter, charging 8s. a square for what was much more of a long-term job.'

The late Jack Cook of Almshouse Cottages was born at Oxenbourne in 1909:

'My father worked as a shepherd for Mr. Henry Berry, who farmed a lot of land in the Oxenbourne area, and employed between 20 and 30 men. After my father died, when I was two, life was very hard for my mother and her children, for there was nothing to live on apart from 'Parish Relief', which I think came to about 8s. a week. But I can't remember being hungry or ragged, though my clothes were certainly patched. I left school at 14 to start work for the Berry family as shepherd boy. The head shepherd was Alfred Merrett, my brother-in-law. My wage was 8s. a week, which I gave to my mother who went on feeding and clothing me. I continued that work for over five years. We looked after over five hundred sheep, a Hampshire Downs flock. They either ran on the downs, or were folded over turnips, vetches, rape, kale or clover. When they were folded, the hurdles, made from hazel, came from the local hurdle-maker, Benny Piper of Clanfield. At lambing time we made lambing pens covering up to two acres in area. These enclosures were made of hurdles with loose straw tied on, and the roofing was also of hurdles thatched with straw. Inside were individual "coops", one hurdle square, and each ewe was put into a coop when due to lamb. The head shepherd and I used a portable hut on wheels at lambing time, having our meals there, and taking it in turns to sleep there too. At night, it was necessary to go out every hour or so with a hurricane lamp to see all was well. For driving and rounding up we used dogs. I used a Scotch collie, and we also had some half-bred collies. The male lambs were castrated at about six to eight weeks old. Alfred Merrett collected the lambs together. He had a special sharp-bladed knife. I held each lamb with its legs apart, whereupon Merrett opened the 'purse' [scrotum], squeezed out the testicles, and then bit them off and spat them out. Often a dog stood by and swallowed them. Sometimes, in severe winter weather, we had to dig out sheep buried by deep snow. By 1928 my wage had risen to about 22s. a week, but I became redundant and had to change my occupation, and, for a time became a rabbit catcher.'

In our competitive society those who deservedly prosper are generally admired, though not necessarily regarded with affection. At the same time, others whose family fortunes have, over the space of generations, declined, are often highly trusted, respected and well liked. The Berry family, now locally represented by John, Dick and Bess Tucker, fall into this category. Bess says:

'The Berrys have lived and farmed at Oxenbourne since my great-grandfather John arrived from the Andover area in the mid 1800s. The Weeks farming family were already established here, and when John's son, Henry (my grandfather), married Mary Weeks the families were united, and by 1900 Henry was farming 1,500 acres. Mary's father, William Weeks Jnr., was a farmer and maltster at Lower House Farm. Prior to 1880 there was a tax or excise duty payable on malt, and there came a day when a malt officer arrived in the village on horseback, intending to call unannounced at Lower House Farm to check the quantity of malt there, and collect the tax due. But he made the mistake of lodging himself and his horse the previous night with blacksmith Jim Hobbs of Ivy House, and, during the evening's conversation, mentioned his destination for the following morning. Hobbs, being a friend of Weeks, plied his visitor with sufficient drink to ensure his sleeping soundly, and, as soon as he was safely in bed, dashed off to warn Weeks. The two then set about moving a great quantity of malt to a hiding place, and, after working most of the night, enabled the maltster to escape liability.

'The Berrys were always sheep farmers, and bred Hampshire Downs. They also bred Shire horses, and had as many as 15 working on Oxenbourne Farm. Usually one or two were sold each October at Petersfield's Taro Fair. Henry Berry's religious convictions led him to say prayers at 5.15 a.m. each morning, and *everyone* in the house had to be present. But a tolerant side to his character is shown by the story of a gypsy who, about a hundred years ago, paid regular visits, ostensibly to ask for casual work. Henry invariably offered him piecework flint-picking, namely collecting the flints that littered the downland into heaps for road metalling. The "traveller" regularly replied: "A man can't work on an empty stomach, Guv'nor", so was given bread and cheese; whereupon he said "A man can't work on a full stomach, Guv'nor", and wandered off, not to reappear for months. Henry's son, Philip, was my father, and he, too, farmed at Oxenbourne. I just remember another gentleman of the road, looking like the traditional tramp, and named Joey, calling on my father for work. He also was offered flint-picking, but always asked for 5s. "on the book", then headed for the village where he got completely drunk on that sum; but without fail, he returned the following day to work off his debt. He was an honest rogue.

'Gypsy horse-drawn caravans were a common sight on the verges of Harvesting Lane or Fishpond Lane in the 1920s and 1930s. They often drew in when the wife was about to "go upstairs"—their expression when a confinement was imminent. The first we knew of their arrival was a call from the district nurse, cadging clean water and old sheets. They were not welcomed by my father and grandfather, for hedges were mutilated to provide wood for their fires, horses were turned out to graze on grass laid up for hay, curses and paper flowers distributed among superstitious cottagers, and mounds of litter left behind.

'By the time the Berry farmland passed to my father, it had shrunk in area, due to my grandfather having provided for his widow and an unmarried daughter. The shrinkage continued during my father's life, mainly because he could not bring himself to abandon traditional farming practices and adapt to changing conditions. He hated the thought of putting a man out of work. Having by 1930 become short of capital during the great slump, he sold the whole farm to Lady Peel, with a lease-back; and over 20 years later, after her death, re-purchased several hundred acres. Once more he was under-capitalised, and, following his own death in 1978, and the departure of my brother Robert, my other brothers, John and Dick, have had to sell most of the family's remaining land.'

Having referred to ebbing family fortunes, what counterbalancing successes apply to the Berrys? If generations of public service, which still remains in full flow, count for anything, therein lies ample evidence of their sterling qualities. Old Henry, one of the original parish councillors in 1895, served the council for 30 years, as well as being an overseer from 1910-20. Philip, after his father's death, put in eight years on the council, succeeded in turn by third generation John, for 12 years; since when Bess, also with 12 years (unfinished) to her credit, has carried on. She capped no less than 62 years of combined family service on the council by being chairman from 1980-1983; whilst Dick is currently a churchwarden, and John a village hall manager. Not such a bad record!

Finally so far as the effects of one and a half centuries of progress in local farming can be summarised in a few words:

(1) Expensive machines and machinery have so largely replaced manual labour that parishioners are no longer, as they were, a predominantly agricultural community.

(2) Due mainly to scientific improvements, output of crops and livestock has increased dramatically.

(3) Farming units have decreased in number as highly efficient farmers have acquired and added to holdings of freehold land, often through buying as 'sitting tenants'.

(4) Though generation after generation of farming families still tend to succeed one another, the 'colonisers' from beyond the parish boundary have significantly strengthened local farming and the local community.

Chapter Eight

VILLAGE LIFE, 1837–1914

IN 1801, WHEN THE POPULATION of England and Wales was 10 million, that of East Meon stood at 1,061. During the following half-century the village populace, in keeping with the general trend, climbed steadily to 1,543, almost a 50 per cent. increase; after which came a levelling out, and the figures hovered around 1,500 for the next 50 years.[1] Child mortality in the United Kingdom was still awful, infant scourges included thrush, convulsions and rickets. Smallpox continued to afflict all ages, though its incidence had been greatly reduced after general acceptance of vaccination. Innumerable folk still lived in squalor, there were but few hospitals, not many antiseptics, and very limited knowledge of hygiene. Impure drinking water led to frequent outbreaks of dysentery, typhoid fever and cholera; and, unsurprisingly, childbirth was dangerous.

East Meon's annual deaths from 1827–36 averaged 23, after which mortality for the next three years rose to 33, 44 and 40 respectively, an unexplained 70 per cent. increase.[2] A clue to the cause is found in a burial register:

Rebecca Ansel, Oxenbourne, 4th Jany. 1839, Infant. Died of the small pox.

A further pointer to a year-long epidemic (probably smallpox) is the sequence of 1838 burials, when 33 out of 44 took place in the last six months, followed by 32 in the first seven months of 1839, a total death-roll of 65 in 13 consecutive months.

During the next 8 years (1840–47), deaths averaged 27, only to soar again to 43 and 57 respectively for 1848–49. In this case a clear explanation, though not necessarily the only one, is at hand, the burial register having a grim footnote: 'Those with an * prefix died of cholera', this symbol appearing opposite the names of 10 persons buried between 10 and 20 August 1849. A terrible outbreak of the malignant, or Asiatic cholera, having begun in India in 1816–17, gradually extended westward, reaching Europe in 1831. The resulting mortality rivalled that of the great pestilence of former ages,[3] and it was doubtless this disease that arrived at East Meon, probably via a south coast seaport, in 1849. Perhaps it was the weaker members of the community who succumbed, for the pendulum promptly swung in the opposite direction, only 15 deaths occurring in 1850, and 19 in 1851, well below previous and subsequent annual averages.

The year 1851, when East Meon's civil and ecclesiastical parishes still included Langrish, and covered 11,601 acres, is a convenient point to turn from disease and death to the affairs of the living; since that is the year of the Tithe Award, and of the first really informative national population census.

The census[4] was carried out on Sunday, 30 March, under the supervision of William Durman, registrar of births and deaths, his four enumerators being John Nathaniel Atkins (postmaster), William Ray and Richard Green (farmers) and 18-year-old Ebenezer Durman, the registrar's son. Their task was a daunting one, for, between them, they had to visit 314 houses scattered over a wide area, and elicit highly personal information from the heads of households, many of whom were incapable of understanding, still less completing, the necessary forms. Nevertheless, the job was efficiently done, showing that 1,543 persons (820 males and 723 females) spent the night in the parish. Three could hardly be termed 'residents', for 64-year-old Abraham Ayling, a travelling tinker, found shelter in 'Gaston Hovel', and 58-year-old William Harris, a chair bottomer, and his more elderly wife, Mary, slept in 'Hoghole Barn'.

The biggest landowner was the Hon. T. W. Gage of Westbury House, a widower described as 'landed proprietor and magistrate', occupying 1,500 acres and employing 25 labourers and 10 boys outside, plus eight indoor servants. Nine farmers cultivated substantial farms varying in area between 392 and 950 acres, these including William Ray of Riplington House (with 15 labourers and nine boys); James Lock of Court Farm (22 labourers and boys); Henry Barnard of Park Farm (18 labourers and eight boys); William Weeks of Upper Farm (20 labourers); and William Lipscombe of Tigwell Farm (13 labourers). Samuel Padwick farmed 580-acre Lower Farm, and employed 13 labourers, his household comprising his young wife, Jane, two-year-old daughter, Jane, seven-month-old Samuel, and an 18-year-old housemaid, a 12-year-old nursemaid and 20-year-old farm servant. Padwick was a successful man, for 16 years later he was farming both Lower and Fairfield Farms, totalling 1,464 acres, a very large area indeed. (Fairfield Farm was known as South Farm both before and after 1851.)

Farmers apart, the largest employer was master-builder Samuel Kille. He ran a sizeable business, employing 14 men and boys; a testimony to his high standard of workmanship being Cross House in the Square at East Meon. His son, another Samuel, described himself as a 'carpenter journeyman', as did kinsman George Kille and Henry Smith (younger son of parish clerk Robert). William Neal, the High Street shoemaker, employed two men, but his 30-year-old son was a 'journeyman shoemaker'. It seems to have been customary for younger members of a family business to assume a mobile role outside the village, though there were doubtless instances where a son preferred not to work under his father's supervision, but to tread an independent path.

Other inhabitants included Henry Green (land surveyor), John Smith, the 29-year-old police constable, three ladies each described as 'proprietor of houses', William Sims (publican at *The George*), Henry Sims (sieve-maker), 62-year-old George Lock (gardener and schoolmaster) and his wife, Elizabeth (schoolmistress). The Locks lived in Halley Street, subsequently corrupted to 'the Alley', now Chapel Street, and must have had a dame-school there, for neither taught at the village school; the few pence per week paid by their pupils' parents being supplemented by the master's gardening work. Sarah Norris, also a widow in her sixties, had fallen on hard times, possibly having been put out of business by the Locks, her description being 'Pauper schoolmistress or dame'. Other tradesmen or artisans were William Love (master-blacksmith), James Lock of Farm Lane (another master-blacksmith, employing two), and Edward Allen (master-butcher, employing two). The *New Inn's* publican, John Dear, spent the census night outside the parish, leaving the premises in charge of his wife (victualler) and 32-year-old son, William, whose occupation (brewer to his father) showed the pub sold its own brew of real ale. The 'learned professions' were represented by the elderly vicar, Thomas Kemp, living at Vicarage House with his wife and three daughters, and the surgeon, George Pink, a widower. Of the hundreds of other inhabitants, by far the most common description was 'agricultural labourer' or 'scholar', the latter applied to virtually all children of about 5–11 years, though one two-year-old was so described!

Approximately 80 individuals were labelled 'pauper', or, by one sensitive enumerator 'In receipt of poor-law relief'. Amongst child workers were Eli Earwaker, aged 13, a 'bird keeper', and three shepherd boys, William Spiers, 11, and brothers James and John Greentree of Park Cottages, 12 and 10 respectively. Middle-aged widow, Elizabeth Merrett ('works in coppice'), may have been a hurdle-maker, helped by her son, James, 15; and, to round off these extracts on a cheerless note, there was a 32-year-old woman lodger living at 'Bereley Lodge' ('receiving parish relief owing to being idiott'), a nine-year-old ('pauper, scholar and orphan'), and a nameless four-year-old 'visitor' ('illegitimate, father unknown').

A few years later, in 1855,[5] there were eight families of gentry, and 56 'traders' in the parish; and if one trader to every 30 men, women and children seems a high ratio, the explanation is simple: 27 farmers, two farm bailiffs, two innkeepers, a drillman, a carrier, a brick and tile maker, the registrar of births and deaths, and even the surgeon were included in that all-embracing term! Then, and for the next 40 years or so, many individuals followed multiple occupations. Thus, farmer George Berry of Langrish (unrelated to the Berrys of nearby Oxenbourne) was a lime-burner too, farmer Richard Green of Ramsdean doubled as a 'shopkeeper', and John Dear of *The New Inn* also farmed. Langrish postmaster, James Carter, was a blacksmith, whilst his East Meon opposite number, postmaster John Nathaniel Atkins, managed to be a grocer, draper and miller—apparently with success, for he owned and occupied the imposing 'Glenthorne' described in Chapter Five.[6]

Other millers were John Lillywhite of both South Mill and Frogmore Mill, who, being a baker too, doubtless baked the flour he ground, and William Porter of Bordean, content to be just a miller. Parish clerk, Robert Smith, and his elder son, Robert junior, were wheelwrights, carrying on business where 'Westbrook Cottages' stand, then described as 'Wheeler shop and orchard'.[7] The father owned that property as well as those adjoining now known as 'Farriers' and 'Wheelwright Cottage', part of the latter, then two cottages, being occupied by the son. Robert senior, was also village sexton, receiving fees that included 6d. on publication of marriage banns, 2s. 6d. at each marriage after banns, 1s. 0d. for each knell, 3s. 6d. for a child's grave, and 6s. 0d. for an adult's, though graves were subject to a sliding scale of additional fees if over five feet deep; and all fees were doubled for non-parishioners.

Some other traders[8] were Thomas Bricknell (harness maker), Messrs. Gale and Beagley (grocers and drapers); John Greentree (shopkeeper, though a few years later, 'clock and watch maker'); William Suter (beer retailer—almost certainly at the former *Ploughman's Joy* beerhouse adjacent to Church Farm, Langrish); John Pearson (carrier); Henry Vokes (drillman); Uriah Shole (wheelwright); William Hill (millwright); a second grocer and draper; and, finally, five boot and shoemakers, one of whom was George Attwood.

Significantly, traders included a brick and tile *maker,* harness *maker,* clock and watch *maker,* and five boot and *shoemakers.* Although no brewer is listed, beer was brewed in most farmhouses, as well as in plenty of other homes, and at one of the inns. Thus, the village was largely self-contained, mainly due to communication and transport problems. Petersfield was but five miles distant, Winchester 15 miles, and Portsmouth 17 miles; but those miles were not swiftly or easily travelled in a horse-drawn vehicle, or, much more likely, on foot, by hard-working breadwinners, or womenfolk fully occupied rearing large families. Certainly, people were not afraid of walking, a fact borne out by the number of boot and shoemakers!

In January 1863, the squire of Bereleigh, George Forbes, died, aged fifty-seven. His widow, Johanna Agnes Forbes, whose benevolence towards local children has been noticed, wasted no time in perpetuating her husband's memory in a practical way. Before the year was out she had purchased a cottage and land in Church Street, demolished the cottage, erected five almshouses on the site, and executed a trust deed creating 'The Forbes Almshouses Charity', endowed with £1,100 of Government 3 per cent. Stock. Each 'inmate' had to be 'above 65 years of age and a parishioner of this parish or irremovable from the same, of good character and reputation but in indigent circumstances'. Occupancy was free of charge, and every single inmate was to receive 5s. 0d. per week, and married couples 7s. 6d. Mrs. Forbes survived till 1898; the almshouses are still in full use, and an important village feature.

Changes still occurred gradually, and by 1865 a directory[9] listed 10 non-commercial residents, no longer labelled 'gentry'; and 22 farmers as against 27 a few years before; the early stages of mechanisation having already led to fewer but larger farming units. Yet one of the farmers was also a grocer, draper, and postmaster; and others were respectively lime-burner and brickmaker, brick and tile maker, grocer and land surveyor, and baker and miller. Village traders included a licensed hawker, a combined bookseller, stationer, newsagent and stamp office (Messrs. J. M. and E. Barnard), an agricultural implement maker, and Sims, the sieve-maker, a reminder that sieves were still widely used for winnowing grain. Noah Beagley had become a grocer and tailor, Messrs. Gale and Beagley grocers and *linendrapers,* and the carrier to Portsmouth, James Restall, undertook the return journey on Tuesdays and Saturdays. Though they would not be called 'tradesmen' today, three gamekeepers were listed as such. 'Previously gentlemen had walked through woods and shot pheasants as they flew away. Now it was the estate workers who did the walking, driving the pheasants towards the gentlemen, who stood the other end'.[10] The invention of breach-loading shotguns led to game-shooting becoming a highly organised and sociable sport for owners of estates with favourable woods and terrain. Westbury and Bereleigh estates were such, and Leydene, too, in later years. Foxhunting remained another popular field sport, East Meon falling within the territory of the Hambledon Hunt, officially founded in 1800. During the Mastership of Captain (afterwards Earl) Powlett from 1859-68 hounds were hunted six days a week, and frequently master and huntsman were out with different packs on the same day on opposite sides of the country.[11] Earlier, in the 1840s, there were times when 'foxes were not too plentiful; but that the master had a few good supporters is shown by the fact that in one small covert on the farm of Mr. Henry Barnard of East Meon no fewer than eight foxes were found during one season, and every one of them gave a good run'.[12] Barnard, who farmed at Park Farm, was not content with supporting the Hambledon Hunt, but also kept his own pack of harriers at one time.

The years 1869-70 were important for All Saints' Church, whose extensive restoration included the replacement of spire timbers, the re-roofing of both church and spire with lead; and the reclamation of the north transept from its former scholastic use; the cost being the then substantial sum of £4,000, 'exclusive of gifts'. In 1872, the year Langrish became a separate ecclesiastical parish, the Rev. W. Brodie planted a row of lime trees in the churchyard parallel to Church Road. This act, perhaps thought unimportant at the time, has, well over 100 years later resulted in mature trees that considerably enhance what town planners call 'the streetscape'.

Meanwhile, how was 'commercial' life developing? In 1875[13] farmers' numbers were down to 20, including Henry Vokes of Ramsdean, also a threshing-machine proprietor, corn and seed merchant. The Kille family were strongly represented by Benjamin senior (carpenter, joiner and cabinet maker, *and* assessor and collector of taxes); Benjamin junior (relieving officer and registrar of births and deaths); Mrs. Elizabeth (preparatory school owner); George (grocer and draper); Samuel (still carpenter and builder); and Mrs. Sarah senior (also listed as carpenter and builder). No startling changes had occurred in the occupational pattern, though the five boot and shoemakers of 20 years earlier had shrunk to three, and the millwright had become 'millwright and machinist'.

By 1889 Thomas Adam Adams, grocer, baker, clothier and coal merchant, was carrying on his substantial retail business in the High Street, opposite the *New Inn*. The shop, house and delivery vehicles, as depicted by billheads, were impressively smart, and in addition to plying the above trades, he stocked a wide selection of wines, hardware and ironmongery, plus malt and hops. Plates cost 2s. 4d. a dozen, frying-pans 10d., brooms 2½d., candlesticks 7d., and baths 2s. 9d. Following his premature death, aged 45, in 1896, the business passed to the Savage and Parsons partnership—Albert Savage of Gosport being the senior ('sleeping') partner, and his nephew by marriage, Stephen John Parsons (who previously ran a grocery shop in West Street, Chichester) being the working partner. His daughter, Elizabeth, born in 1900 ('Nurse Micklam brought me into the world'), recalls the shop being open from 7 a.m. until 10 p.m. The bakery, operated by three bakers, Messrs. Lunn, Crockford and Chris Budd, was a detached building at the rear, always known as 'the brewhouse', with a great stack of bunts nearby. These were burnt inside the ovens, making the brick linings very hot indeed; whereupon the ashes were raked away, the ovens roughly swabbed out with a sack tied to the end of a pole and dipped in the river, whereupon the ovens were ready to receive the dough (also made with river water) or cake mixture.

Another Adams, Alfred, originally also a baker, had become publican at *The George* about 1880, thereafter combining both businesses. His family had good reason to fear him, for he was a man of violent temper, aggravated by heavy drinking. Once his son, George, then aged about 16, was delivering bread by pony and trap in a remote part of the parish, when the trap accidentally overturned and the load of bread was wasted. The boy, terrified of facing his father's wrath, ran away from home and joined the army, by putting his age on; and remained a soldier for life, eventually retiring as a regimental sergeant major. After Alfred Adams died of 'galloping consumption' and alcoholism, his widow Mary took over the licence of *The George,* married a Mr. Damen, and, when widowed a second time in 1906, retired from the pub and ran a fish and chip shop at the back of the post office, from which she supplied many a labourer with 2d. worth of fish and chips for his midday meal.

In 1895, the year after Langrish became a separate civil parish, only 12 farmers were listed,[14] mainly due to the secession of Langrish, but perhaps also partly resulting from the great agricultural depression. The almost immortal George Attwood still made boots and shoes, and other traders included a builder and undertaker (Henry Coles); a physician and surgeon, medical officer of health and public vaccinator (Dr. H. A. W. Batten), blacksmiths (Messrs. Lock and Hobbs); a licensed hawker (Edgar Potter); and a librarian (Harry Leach) at The Working Men's Reading Room and Library—later to be known successively as The Institute and The Village Hall.

The same year saw the birth of East Meon Parish Council, a considerable step towards 'grass-roots democracy'. Original councillors included the vicar, doctor, cattle dealer, licensed hawker, undertaker, and two farmers, the curate being appointed clerk at an annual salary of £5.[15] They plunged enthusiastically into their duties, resolving to acquire land for allotments, asking the Local Government Board for advice regarding recurrent house flooding (a problem destined to endure for another 60 years), and tackling necessary footpath repairs. One such path, leading from Frogmore to the school was 'made up with chalk, flints and gravel, as follows:

									£	s.	d.
13 yards of flints at 3s. 6d. per yard	..	..	..	..	..	..	..		2	5	6
15 yards of gravel at 2s. 0d. per yard	..	..	..	..	..	..	..		1	10	0
Carting of gravel at 3s. 0d. per yard ..	..	..	..	..	..	..	..		2	5	0
Stout iron pipe, for drainage ..	..	..	..	..	..	..	..			6	0
Two men for 5 days (2s. 0d. per day)	..	..	..	..	..	..	..		1	0	0
									£7	6	6

The following year the council 'guaranteed £28 a year to the Postmaster General for introducing the telegraph into the village, a sum being guaranteed to the Parish Council by several inhabitants and owners of property in the Parish'. The Lighting Sub-committee proposed that 11 street lamps be purchased, the cost to be met by levying a rate of 1d. per acre of land and 3d. on each house. Walter Kille was appointed to 'light, clean and turn out if necessary all lamps', but was dismissed the following year and replaced in fairly quick succession by Edgar Moor, Albert Luff, James Pollard and W. Hockley; perhaps not surprisingly, as the lamplighter's weekly reward was 5s. 0d., out of which he supplied the oil! The council was clearly not over-generous towards its employees, for when the Rev. J. Hindle retired as clerk in 1899, to be succeeded by Henry Steele, the clerk's salary was reduced from £5 per annum to £3 per annum.

In 1903 the G.P.O. 'offered to open the Telegraph Office in East Meon at night, in case of emergency, at a small extra cost to the Council', an offer that was declined. In succeeding years, the G.P.O. were asked for a second delivery of letters to Frogmore, the county council were requested to set up a weights, measures and stamping centre at West Meon, and the London and South Western Railway were petitioned not to discontinue the Sunday service on the Meon Valley line.

The vicar, the Rev. T. H. Masters, occasionally recorded events of local interest, and ensured that his notes would be available to posterity by writing them in the then current Churchyard Burial Register! One such note[16] describes the 1904 consecration of a church enlargement, following previous purchases of land to the south 'having a cottage upon it', and further land to the east 'having three cottages upon it'. The cottages, picturesque Tudor ones, were demolished, the 'improvement' being largely financed through the munificence of William Nicholson of Basing Park and John Bonham Carter of Adhurst St Mary, whilst Colonel Hudson, 'the new owner of Bereleigh', generously relinquished his right to use the well on one of the plots.

Religion played an important part in the daily lives of many people, as illustrated by a local newspaper report: 'May 26th. 1905,—Members of the International Bible Reading Association, East Meon, held a service at 6.30 a.m. before leaving for their annual outing. This year the trip was to Southsea and 57 members made the journey. They travelled by van to Horndean and then took the electric car to Southsea'.

Also in 1905, ownership of the Bereleigh Estate passed to Henry Curtis Gallup, a well-to-do man of leisure and former Master of the Wilton Hunt. An improvement carried out to his newly-acquired property was creation of a 'water garden', whose striking feature was, and still is, a number of sarsen stones, some weighing several tons. They were hauled by a steam traction engine from War Hill, Tigwell, a part of the Bereleigh estate—their original use was possibly related to an ancient pagan site of worship. Paving of the water garden consisted of tombstones removed from the graveyard of Winchester Cathedral as part of a tidying-up operation. More shall be heard of Mr. Gallup in Chapter Ten. ·

The same year saw an extension of Forbes Almshouses, when a further two (bungalow) dwellings were erected opposite the original five, their cost being defrayed from accumulated income. An amended scheme for regulation of the charity was drawn up by the Charity Commissioners, increasing the 'stipends' payable to existing almspeople to 10s. 0d. a week for married couples and 7s. 0d. for single persons. After the expiration of a three-year interim period, prospective almspeople, although otherwise qualified, were to be debarred if they had received poor-law relief in the preceding two years (showing that receipt of relief was still considered a disgrace, or, at least, a serious blot on one's character). However, those fortunate enough to be appointed were still bound by regulations that forbade them to entertain visitors except 'such as are of good repute', obliged them to repair broken windows and damage to walls, hearth stones, locks or other fixtures at their own expense, forbade them to be absent for seven consecutive days without written permission, and made regular attendance at divine service on Sundays compulsory.

Before leaving 1906, one small incident—indeed 'a driving offence'—speaks volumes for the tempo of life and of road transport. On a February day, John Pile, an East Meon carter, was summoned to appear at Petersfield Petty Sessions for being asleep in charge of a horse and cart on the highway, though his prosecution involved an element of ill-luck. For, as his wagon and two horses, returning to East Meon, plodded round the sharp bend on the main Petersfield to Winchester road near *The Red House* at Stroud, who should be travelling in the opposite direction but Police Superintendent King. The result was a fine of 5s. 0d. and 4s. 0d. costs. Then, a portent for the future:

> December 10th. 1907. Vandalism: As a result of certain notices disappearing from the notice board, the Parish Council resolved that a small wire door with padlock, should be provided for the front of the notice board to prevent this trouble happening again.

Lord Hotham's provision of a public water supply in 1909 was of immediate and far-reaching importance, and for the first time, piped water became available. This was a tremendous convenience to villagers who had relied previously on wells, rain-water tanks and the river; and an equally significant step towards improved public health. Yet the piped supply remained unconnected to the vast majority of individual houses, 17 stand-pipes being shared by groups of householders, each of whom had a key to operate the nearest standpipe, from which water was drawn and carried home in pails or other containers. In spite of this limitation, the parish council had, during its first 15 years, obtained both public street lighting and a public water supply. Major problems remained, including lack of both main drainage and electricity, and prevention of flooding. But at this stage I propose to take a breather from 'parish pump politics' and the recital of statistics and other information culled from trade directories, hoping that first-hand reminiscences of septuagenarian, octogenarian and even nonagenarian villagers may add colour to the picture, and even touch on minutiae seldom committed to writing.

Clara Fisher, East Meon born and bred, talks about the old days in a simple, unaffected yet vivid manner that brings to life her childhood in this century's first decade:

'I was born at "Vicarage Lodge", The Cross, in 1902. My father, Robert Fisher, born near Midhurst in 1866, became a carpenter and joiner after starting work as an 11-year-old in racing stables and becoming a farm carter three years later. He also worked with sheep at one time, and, earlier than my own memory, sometimes worked in the harvest-fields cutting corn with a scythe. During my childhood most cottagers were farm workers, and at times people not normally employed in agriculture became part-time workers—for example during hay-making, corn harvesting and hop-picking. In fact, school children were allowed an extended summer holiday for hop-picking, mainly at Buriton, about four miles away. My mother, with other village women, walked there and back daily, taking me and my sister with her. At sheep-shearing time a gang of half a dozen men would leave the village at 2 or 3 o'clock in the morning and walk to farms up to seven miles away. Using hand shears, they each sheared 20 sheep a day. They wore white corduroy trousers, which had to be washed several times a week. The shears were taken great care of, and never used for any other purpose.

'My father was always interested in music, and in his younger days led a stringed band in which he played the violin, and his brother the cello. The band performed at dances, and at one such dance my father met my mother. Later, he followed in his father's footsteps by becoming leader of a brass band, and he also led a fife and drum band. Another 'rival' band in the village was known as the Chapel, or Methodist band. My father was in the church choir and also a bell-ringer for 70 years. He tolled the bell when Queen Victoria died, and had been bell-ringing at East Meon Church on the day he died in 1964, in his 98th year.

'Wages were low, but provided families were thrifty, there was no hunger, and life was enjoyable. Music and singing played a big part in our lives. My sister and I belonged to the glee class, mainly adults, though children were allowed from about 12 years old. We met for practice at Arthur Warren's house, called 'The Square Grocery' (now 'The Tudor House'), and the conductor was Albert Legg, registrar of births. Concerts were given from time to time.

'Travel outside the village by those not prepared to walk or cycle meant cadging a lift in a horse-drawn vehicle, paying for a seat on a carrier's cart (which undertook regular journeys), or hiring a wagonette or dogcart. One carrier, George Noble White, lived at 'The White Cottage', High Street, and every Tuesday, Thursday and Saturday did the return journey from East Meon to Portsmouth, about 17 miles each way. If full up with goods, he could only carry one passenger, who sat with him on the front seat, open to the elements. In 1921 my sister Dorothy, then 15, travelled to Portsmouth by carrier for a holiday with our aunt. The wagon left at 5.30 a.m., arriving at its destination, the Gosport Ferry, at 12.30. It was a cold October day, and on arrival my sister was so cold and stiff she had difficulty in moving. William Luff, licensee of *The George Inn* from 1906 to about 1919, owned a wagonette and dogcart, available for journeys to places like Petersfield and West Meon, especially to meet trains.

'During summertime we occasionally met a strange horse-drawn contraption for tarring the roads, which suffocated one with fumes and dust. A barrel of tar was hoisted up over the centre frame of a tank, the bung was released and thick black tar poured into the tank which was heated by a fire underneath, a big tap was turned on, and the hot tar sprayed on to the road. With long-handled brushes it was spread over the surface and then sand thrown on it. The workmen tied sacking over their boots for protection.

'One often met herds of cows, followed by a man with a bull attached to a pole by a ring through its nose, and flocks of sheep being driven to market or fairs, all looking very tired and dirty. Several farmers kept Shire horses which were taken for long exercise walks on the roads. They were beautifully groomed and their manes and tails plaited and tied with coloured braids.

'Children's parties took place at Christmas and in summer. At the Christmas party there was a tree, and games, tea and a bun, and an orange and cracker to take home. At the summer party in the Vicarage garden we had games, races, and scrambles for sweets, and finally a large paper balloon, warmed by methylated spirit lighted in a saucer, was sent soaring into the sky. On each Christmas morning one of the bands went round playing carols at about 7 a.m., and the Church bells would ring out, and we always had a great gathering of the family at Granny's.

'The village had four bakers, three grocers, a paraffin and hardware store, a saddler, two butchers, two mills, wheelwrights, farriers, a post office and even a fish and chip shop, as well as visits from "travelling shops" selling fish and meat. Clothes, boots and shoes could be bought at one grocery shop.

'There was a "dame's school" at 4 "Westbrook Cottages", where the Misses Attwood taught a few children whose parents could afford small payments. "Sooty" Hurst, the chimney-sweep, had a donkey to pull his cart. He was always very black and rather frightened us children. He made what was called "Poor Boy's Ointment", useful for man and beast, which he sold and often gave away. It was made from a plant or creeper which grew in his garden and spread all over his thatched cottage in Workhouse Lane. His son had to climb up the inside of chimneys, and once got stuck for some hours in the kitchen chimney at Up Park House, near Harting. Another character was Jack Daughtry, rag-and-bone-man, who came every week from Petersfield with a pony and cart. We saved bones for him and kept them dry, but he told us they would weigh heavier if wet, and the price would be more! Then there was old Mr. Norman who spent his days breaking stones for road mending. He was paid by the cubic yard of broken stones.

'Oil lamps and candles lit our houses, and each evening the lamplighter did his round of the street lamps, carrying a ladder and can of oil. The church also had oil lamps which were trimmed by Mrs. Sam Kille, who, for 40 years, washed the choir surplices of 10 men and 10 boys and did the caretaking as well for 2s. 6d. a week. Five farmers had small dairies, selling, milk, butter and cream, some of which they took to market. John Scott of Belmont Farm carried pails of milk suspended from a wooden yoke on his shoulders, and poured out pints and half pints at your door with measures that hung from the rims of the pails. At Court Farm there was a cheese factory. Many people baked their own bread.

'The Aburrow family carried on their wheelwrights' business where East Meon Stores now stands, and at Pound Meadow, the old parish pound. Horse-drawn vehicles were taken there to be repaired or have wheels replaced, and new wagons were built. The family owned a traction engine, used to draw timber from the woods, and, when stationary, to operate a belt-driven circular saw. The saddler's shop was in the High Street at "Old Bell Cottage", Mr. Banham coming daily from West Meon to run it. The great collars worn by cart-horses, and other large pieces of harness hung outside the shop. Across the road, in the heart of the village, where the motor garage is now, was a farmyard belonging to David Coles (brother of Henry Coles the builder and father of Cyril Coles the author). He kept a retail shop at what is now "The Gatehouse", and sold sweets, milk, butter and, when he killed a pig, faggots and offal. He had about six to eight cows that grazed on the present Glenthorn Meadow housing estate.

'The smithy stood, as it still does, at the junction of High Street and Frogmore Lane, a hive of activity, with many horses queuing up for shoeing. Three or four farriers worked there including Jim Hobbs the boss. It was thrilling to watch horses shod, and iron tyres put on wagon wheels, with sparks flying from the fire, and more from the anvil as shoes were hammered into shape. There were two working water mills, one at South Farm, where Mildred Atkinson was accidentally killed. My sister was one of six children, all dressed in white, who bore the coffin. The other working mill, at Frogmore, belonged to George Silk. Boot and shoe repairs were carried out by Ernie Blackman at "The Cross", adjoining our home. But many people did their own repairs. A large sheet of leather was bought in Petersfield from time to time, and my father would repair the family's footwear on his last.

'Most people kept fowls, a pig or two, and, in some cases, goats. We always had a pig in a sty in the garden, fed on household scraps and barley-meal bought quite cheaply from Frogmore Mill. My father was his own slaughterman, and my parents undertook the curing or salting. Smoking was carried out by burning oak. People who didn't like to slaughter their own pig took it to Dick Norgett, the butcher at what is now "Riverside", High Street, He had a tame pigeon that had been rescued when a squab, and brought up as a pet. The pigeon, named Charlie, accompanied Dick on his delivery rounds, flying beside the pony and trap. It even sat on the doorstep of the pub when he went there at the day's end, and everyone knew where Dick was. Fresh fish was brought, I believe once a week, from Portsmouth by horse and cart, and, every Friday, from Petersfield.

'Many more houses were thatched than now, and, of course, countless hay, corn and straw ricks. Nurse Micklam was the village nurse and midwife and always wore a grey uniform. There were also several amateur midwives. The doctor was Dr. Jones. Until he acquired the first car in the village in about 1910, he drove a gig or rode a bicycle to visit patients. On one occasion, when urgently called out at night to a confinement, he went in bedroom slippers and lost one on the way, but was in time to deliver the baby. He removed my tonsils at his house when I was about six. A Petersfield doctor administered the anaesthetic. Doctor was dentist too. You just sat in the chair and your tooth was yanked out without any pain-killer. When people were very ill straw was laid on the road outside their house to deaden the sound of horses and carts.

'Each year a fair visited the village for about a week, and often the gypsies who came with it stayed on to work in the fields, and their children temporarily attended our school. We had a really good cricket team. Horse brakes would bring opposing teams from Privett and other villages, and a grand tea was provided by the womenfolk. Men also played quoits and skittles. There was no proper sanitation. The "privy" in the garden was still used, and the rumble of the horse-drawn cart was heard in the evenings as the cleansing team were about their work while we children enjoyed our bath by the kitchen fire.

'On Sundays, dressed in our best, we went first to 10 o'clock Sunday School, then marched two by two to Church at 11 o'clock. We sat through quite a long sermon, then home to dinner; next to Children's Service at 3, then a walk with parents, and Church again at 6.30. All farmers and their families attended Church on Sundays. The Coral League met on Fridays, where we sewed and made articles for missionary sales. We had much fun acting in pageants and plays which were held. Boys had carving and carpentry classes. Games of hopscotch, marbles, buckle, tops, skipping and hoops all came in their season. I mind once the snow being so heavy it topped the hedges—we could walk on them. One of the grocers filled a sledge with bread and other food for people at Bereleigh and Old Down, and coal was brought from West Meon by sledge.

'On Ash Wednesday we always wore a sprig of ash to school—if not we had our toes trodden on. Sweets were cheap in the shops, and were kept in large tins or rows of glass jars, and sold in cone-shaped paper bags made from square of paper rolled round the hand, about ¼lb. for 1d.; sherbert ½d. a bag, and a yard of "braid" or "bootlaces" (really liquorice) for 1d. "Robin Redbreast" tobacco was 3d. an ounce, coal 1s. 0d. a cwt., a bunt of wood cost 1d. or 2d., and matches were ½d. a box. There was great excitement when army manoeuvres took place—soldiers with gun carriages and horse-driven wagons rumbled and rattled through the village, and sometimes there were hundreds of marching soldiers in red coats, headed by a brass band, and even a Highland regiment in kilts, with pipers. Often they camped here several days.

'Many people kept bees, and in summer one heard the rattle of fire irons and shovels as a neighbour rushed off to pursue and claim his precious swarm. When the honey was taken and surplus bees had to be killed, a hole was dug in the ground and a sulphur match (home-made from corrugated paper dipped in melted sulphur) stuck in and lighted. The skep was then put over the hole and sealed round so the bees were asphyxiated. Next day the honey was cleared and put into a warecloth bag, suspended from the kitchen ceiling, and allowed to drip into jars, or eaten from the comb in chunks.'

John Macdonald, a cousin of Clara Fisher, lives alone at 3 Westbrook Cottages. A man of military bearing, always immaculately tidy in dress, he looks and acts like a healthy 60-year-old. Unbelievably, he was born in the village in August 1894.

'My childhood was spent at "Copse House" (now "Copse Cottages"), which was my mother's parents' home. My father, a regular soldier in the Cameron Highlanders, was away much of the time. I went to the village school from five to thirteen. There were about 120–150 pupils, and the school was divided into sections labelled "Boys", "Girls" and "Infants". Discipline was strict compared with the present day, and I was caned plenty of times. But standards were high. I remember a mental arithmetic lesson when a question to be answered without pencil or paper was: "It is four miles to Petersfield. There is a telegraph pole every 60 yards. How many posts are there between here and Petersfield?" Sometimes a class went out of school for a lesson. Once we were taken high up on Park Hill, from which there is a birds'-eye view of the village and surrounding countryside, and the master gave a geography lesson, illustrated by the features of the hills, rivers, etc., we could see spread out below. I was at school in 1902 when the master,

Mr. Tregear, collapsed and died while teaching, although at the time we didn't know he was dead. All the children were hustled out and sent home.

'In summer I sometimes worked for George Darvill of Court Farm, hay-making. I used to lead a horse pulling a hay-rake, and was paid about 6d. a day. Other children, and many women worked at hay-making time, turning and scattering the hay with long-handled prongs. The Court House was used as an ordinary farmhouse, surrounded by cowsheds, a farmyard, a midden and a pond. When the pond froze in winter we boys used to slide there on our way to and from school. Later, the Court Hall was divided into three floors to make living space for several families of farm workers. I sang in the church choir on Sundays. Choirboys were called "penny boys" and "half-penny boys", the older ones being paid a penny for each service, and younger ones a half-penny. Afterwards, we went to Mr. Potter's shop to buy sweets. When I was about nine or 10 I used to help catch roosting sparrows in a net stretched between two long thin poles like bean-rods. Their favourite roosts were under the eaves of thatched houses and corn ricks, and on ivy-covered walls. The village rat and sparrow club paid a bounty for rats' tails and sparrows' heads. We took them to the Forge, produced our member's cards to old Jimmy Lock who counted them before throwing them on the blacksmith's fire so they couldn't be brought along a second time.

'The Bonham Carter family were very big landlords in the parish. They built at least two houses as retirement homes for employees. One was Duncombe Farm (nicknamed "Spyglass") for John Lambert, a gamekeeper, and another, "Pastures" for George Spencer, a farm bailiff. Each house had a few acres of land with it, so that one or two pigs and a cow could be kept.

'I left school at 13, and worked as stable-boy for Bert Warren, a general carrier, who lived at what is now "Heycroft House". Among the goods he carried were consignments of pheasant eggs from Messrs. Robb and Martin's game farm at Coombe. Mrs. Grace Matier, a music teacher lived next-door, in a small house since burnt down. Before my 14th birthday I was apprenticed to Henry Coles as painter and decorator. He carried on his building business at what is now "Chalk Dell", where he also lived. Sometimes I drove a horse and cart to Petersfield, and, before returning, called at the Petersfield Workhouse to pick up a load of small stones. They had been finely broken down from bigger stones by destitute men as payment for a night's lodging. At that time I was working on the renovation of "Eames Cottages" at Frogmore. The front walls were rebuilt in brick, finished with a roughcast made from the work-house stones. Just upstream from the cottages were several old, disused, primitive mud and wattle houses. In 1912, when I was 17½, a disagreement arose with an older fellow employee who clipped me over the ear. That decided me to run away and join the army, which had always been my ambition. Another lad, Percy Blackman, had the same idea, so the next morning, without telling our families or employers, we cycled to Winchester and enlisted in the Hampshire Regiment. A day later, my mother and grandmother, who had somehow found out where I'd gone, came to the barracks, and were sitting crying when I was brought to face them. I remember the sergeant in charge saying to my mother: "Don't worry mam, we'll make a man of him".'

Winifred Kate Lambert, one of John Macdonald's schoolmates, seems equally well-preserved:

'I was born at "Fern Cottage", East Meon, in July 1894. My mother, whose maiden name was Kate Quennell, had been trained as a nurse at St Thomas's Hospital. Later she became East Meon's village nurse living at Vicarage Lodge. My father, William Micklam, already lived in the village, being employed as a baker and delivery man at Savage and Parsons' shop. His first wife had died, and when his second wife died in childbirth, leaving him with seven children, all under school-leaving age, my mother married him. I think she must have been mad; or perhaps she felt sorry for him.

'After I and my younger sister were born, my mother resumed working as village nurse. When patients came to our house, I had to make myself scarce. Often, in the middle of the night, she received a call that involved her cycling to some outlandish place, but I don't think she was ever afraid. When she finally retired in 1918 she was handed a scroll naming a vast number of parishioners who gave a cheque "as a token of their grateful and affectionate remembrance of . . . twenty years of labour as Parish Nurse". At the village school many children were verminous, and my mother inspected our own heads daily in case we had picked up nits.

'Lots of people took their Sunday dinners to one of the bakeries to be cooked because they had no ovens—home cooking was done in a pot suspended over an open fire. Each Christmas Day the Methodist Band started playing in the middle of the village about 6 a.m. as children were opening their parcels. The village doctor was Dr. Batten, who travelled around in a pony and trap. He was a good doctor, and kind, waiving fees for those who were hard-up. There was an orchard and sawmill, belonging to Henry Smith, where 1–4 Westbrook Cottages now stand. Three old thatched cottages stood on what is now Washer's Triangle, and, a few yards away, Granny Luff took in washing. The two pubs were open all day.

'When I was about two or three years old, my parents moved to what is now "Barnards", in the High Street. The tiny cottage next-door (only a part of "Middle Barnards") was occupied by the Nicholsons, who had about 13 children; and in the equally tiny cottage next-door but one (being the remainder of "Middle Barnards"), Mr. and Mrs. Albert Luff had seven children. So, at the turn of the century, even allowing for some of the elder children having gone out into the world, there could have been between 15 and 20 human beings squeezed into what is now one house of average size occupied by Captain and Mrs. Ross.

'Mail was brought from Petersfield twice a day by horse-drawn van, and then delivered by local postmen. Our milk came from a small dairy at "Brooklyn", High Street, the milk-round later being taken over by Jim Hobbs, operating from "Ivy House". Other childhood memories include the dusty roads in summer, the annual fair held in Pound Meadow, and also two old men, one named Underwood and the other Bob Chivers, who still wore old-fashioned country smocks of coarse white linen.

'When I left school, domestic service was almost the only employment for village girls, and I took jobs at Haslemere, London, Bournemouth, and near Bridport. Eventually, during World War I, I married John Lambert of Duncombe Farm, who had been born in the cottage in the valley at Gravel Hill which was the "road-side inn" where Nicholas Nickleby spent a night when walking from London to Portsmouth, and there met Mr. Vincent Crummles.'

Ethel Gladys Lambert, late of No. 7 'Almshouse Cottages' (who married Winifred's husband's brother) was born in 1892:

'My father was a blacksmith employed in the Clarence Victualling Yard at Gosport. When Queen Victoria travelled to Osborne House, I.o.W., she used to arrive at Gosport railway station, and proceed to the pinnace which took her out to the Royal Yacht by means of a phaeton (a large Bath-chair type of vehicle) drawn by a pony. My father, dressed in his best clothes, with a bowler hat in his hand, always led the pony. I watched this procedure on several occasions, and, with other children, sang the national anthem when the royal train drew in at the platform. When my father retired in 1915, we moved to East Meon where my father, a trained farrier, became employed at the Forge. We lived at "Westbrook Cottages", just down the road. After working at the Forge for three years, my father became village postman, walking 10 miles a day.

'I knew East Meon before we moved there, having become friendly with Herbert Lambert. On one visit to the village, in 1911, I travelled in the carrier's cart, though I could have gone by train from Gosport to West Meon, to be met there with a pony and trap. The carrier, Noble White, left Commercial Road, Portsmouth, about 6 p.m. with several other passengers, a goat and a varied assortment of goods including a cycle, a perambulator and a mangle. By about 11.30 we had arrived at the foot of the long hill leading up through Hyden Wood. There Mr. White hitched the reins of the two horses to a hook, climbed into the interior of the wagon and immediately fell asleep. The horses, accustomed to this procedure, plodded steadily up the hill with no one in charge, their way being lit by thousands of glow-worms. At the top they halted, whereupon Mr. White woke up, resumed his seat, and produced a bugle which he blew loudly to announce his approach to the village. This proved to be the signal for lights to appear in windows of homes awaiting delivery of goods, and I remember the cycle being dropped off at South Farm cottages. The bugle was blown again at the Forge. As we eventually pulled up in the village, lit by a beautiful harvest moon, the church clock struck midnight.

'I married Herbert Lambert in East Meon Church in 1916, one week before he was called up for military service. We lived at "Westbrook Cottages" with my parents, who shortly moved across the way to "Brook Cottages", leaving my husband and me on our own. In 1916, "Washers Cottages" were still standing, though unoccupied. They were devoid of sanitation, and "everything" went in the river! Henry Luff, who lived at "Templars' Brow Cottages", was the lamplighter, and also a chimney sweep. Often the wind blew the lamps out. Mr. Potter, who kept the shop in the centre of the village which is now "Corner Cottage" sold sweets, tea, tobacco and, afterwards, groceries; but he was a dreadfully bad tempered man.

'I well remember Nurse Micklam, a very good nurse, and highly regarded. She acted as midwife when my daughter was born on Easter Sunday 1917. While I was in labour she encouraged me by saying "Come on now, your husband is at the top of Park Hill playing in the Chapel Band; have a baby to show him when he comes back".'

*   *   *   *   *   *

One facet of life around the turn of the century was the courage with which simple villagers, who may never have previously travelled beyond the next parish, ventured into the unknown, either emigrating to 'the Colonies', or taking less permanent employment overseas. Frank Fosberry, born in East Meon in 1878, went to the village school, and later became a bricklayer. Aged 25 and with but limited horizons, he heard of the need for bricklayers in South Africa (where the war had ended three years before). In October 1903, a letter arrived for him from J. Osman and Son, Kiln Builders and Contractors, of Arundel Street, London:

> We have today received a cable from S. Africa requesting us to send out good, industrious men, and we propose sending them out from Southampton on the 17th inst.
>
> The terms we offer in this case are out passage money advanced, to be repaid at £3 per month. Wages 14s. 0d. per day of 10 hours, no lost time. Free lodgings, and 6 months engagement if you do well. The men are to be sent to Grahamstown which is about 100 miles inland from Port Elizabeth, in South Africa.
>
> You should understand that those who go there will have to rough it somewhat, as the country is in an unsettled state as yet, but one gets used to that sort of thing. Two of the writer's sons are near Cape Town and they rather enjoy roughing it—kiln building too is not like house building. The men we are sending out will all be steady fellows, and by clubbing together you will, we think, be able to live very well for £1 per week.
>
> We have to be very careful in selecting men, because some that we have previously sent out have given way to drink and got very slack with their work, and this we must avoid in the future.
>
> You will please well consider what we say and let us know if you are willing to accept the terms if we should select you as one of the party.
>
> Yours faithfully,
Jas. Osman
Manager.

Following an interview in London, Frank, doubtless dazzled by the splendid prospect of earning 14s. 0d. for a 10-hour day, sailed from Blackwall, London, in the *Arundel Castle* on 6 November. His experiences at Grahamstown are not part of the history of East Meon, but by 1908 he had returned to his native village and married Frida Kille who taught in the school. By now he had graduated from bricklayer to 'builder', had saved from his overseas earnings, and was soon building a terrace of cottages in the High Street for a Mr. Westbrook. They were, and still are, known as 'Westbrook Cottages', and although not architectural gems, their brickwork is still perfect—a tribute to Edwardian standards and to Frank.

The first decade of the 20th century drew to a close, and with it the life of Edward VII. It was a time of great change, almost everyone's life being affected, or even revolutionised, by new inventions and an increasingly compassionate attitude towards the less fortunate. Class distinctions remained rigid, but Britain was still great, and, with the support of her world-wide Empire, tremendously powerful. At times during the previous 100 years, wars, usually minor ones, had broken out, always ending in victory. Patriotism was taken for granted. Yet Britain was approaching the abyss of World War I, the terrible and bloody conflict destined to last for over four years, to destroy the flower of her manhood, and leave her economically crippled.

Chapter Nine

FIRE, FLOOD AND FELONY

DISASTERS AND TRAGEDIES have always been, and doubtless always will be 'news-worthy'. Though we dread personal involvement in such events, most of us find a compulsive, possibly morbid interest, in reading subsequent newspaper reports. Disasters entailing fire or flood must, by their very nature, be dramatic; and, amongst crimes, murder has a macabre fascination all of its own. Perhaps the majority of people, leading comparatively humdrum lives, can be excused for experiencing a degree of vicarious excitement when reading of the horror, and maybe heroism too, in which others have been involved.

Any one of East Meon's native octogenarians, if asked to name the most dramatic or vivid recollection of his or her childhood, would probably answer 'the great fire of 1910'. The early summer of that year had been hot and dry, with clear blue skies day after day. Monday, 20 June, was yet another such day, and, early in the morning, hay-making was well under way in the fields. But every Monday, traditionally 'washing day', saw housewives equally busy in their homes. By 8 a.m. coppers had been lit in many a cottage, and industrious activity proceeded in field and home, with no reason to expect anything unusual. Then, at about 8.30, things started to go wrong. Reference has previously been made to Petersfield's former weekly newspaper, *The Squeaker,* and its issue of 22 June represents a reasonably accurate contemporary account of what took place, and captures the very 'flavour' and atmosphere of life in a country community at that time, though some of the descriptive expressions chosen by the paper's 'man on the spot' seem hardly appropriate:

BIG BLAZE AT EAST MEON

SIX DWELLING HOUSES BURNT DOWN

EXCITING SCENES

The people of East Meon had the very unpleasant experience on Monday morning of a most destructive fire occurring right in the centre of the village and rendering a number of the villagers homeless. It was by far the most serious fire which has taken place in the village within living memory and was of such a character that great alarm was occasioned and there was fear lest the disastrous effects might be much more extensive than they ultimately proved to be.

The journalist, whose editor had evidently allowed him ample space, then described the terrace of six ancient thatched High Street cottages adjacent to the Village Institute, adding, unflatteringly, that they were outwardly picturesque, 'but inside not . . . the most sanitary or convenient dwelling-houses'. It appeared that Mrs. G. Smith, living in one of the middle cottages, had lit her copper fire as usual, whereupon the chimney caught alight, ignited the thatch, 'and the flames, fanned by a breeze from the north-east, spread with alarming rapidity'. Everyone within reach, including men who came running from nearby hayfields, helped rescue furniture from the doomed houses, and did all they could to prevent other buildings being involved. The Institute and caretaker's cottage were in danger, as were properties opposite, including Mr. Potter's thatched house, his stables full of hay and oil-store containing 'tanks of petroleum'. Both the stables and oil-store were burnt to the ground—'the oil blazed furiously and added to the picturesque effects of the fire and now and again an explosion occurred sending big masses of smoke rolling away over the village'. Mr. Potter's house, now 'Corner Cottage' and no longer thatched, was saved by countless buckets of water being thrown on its roof by means of a human chain of volunteers linking the nearby river to the roof via ladders; and several other properties narrowly escaped destruction after their contents had been moved into the street. Now let *The Squeaker* continue:

Soon after the fire broke out a telegraphic summons was sent to the Petersfield Fire Brigade, who received the message about 9 o'clock. With all speed practicable the steamer was got out and three or four firemen started off with the engine in charge of Captain Tew. The road to Eastmeon [*sic*] is a hard one to traverse because of the very steep gradients at two or three places, but the brigade reached the scene of the fire just before 10 o'clock and lost no time in setting to work to try and put the fire out. Before their arrival many of the residents of the village had been exerting themselves untiringly endeavouring to stop the spread of the fire to other places in the neighbourhood by throwing buckets of water upon the adjacent buildings and they are to be warmly commended upon the manner in which they rose to the occasion. The water supply which has lately been laid on to the village could not be used in coping with such an outbreak as this, but there was a plentiful supply from the River Meon hard by, though the only means of lifting it was by buckets. The stream was dammed up by the bridge. Those who lent a hand where their services were wanted were P S. Telling, who cycled from Petersfield, P.C. Steel, the Vicar (the Rev. T. H. Masters), the Rev. G. L. May, Dr. Ross Barker, Mr. Curtis Gallup, Mr. Tomlinson (the school-master), Mr. Gordon, Mr. R. Dunn, Mr. Williams and many another who equally deserve mention for the manful work that they did. The newly formed Boy Scouts under the direction of their scoutmaster (Mr. Dunn) were pressed into service in passing buckets of water along from the stream and afterwards in clearing the schools for the reception of the homeless people who made that their temporary habitation.

The firemen, who were soon joined by other comrades who had followed them, had a hard task in front of them in getting the fire under, but after about half-an-hour's pumping they succeeded in subduing the flames and practically getting the upper hand. By eleven o'clock the cottages were only a smouldering heap of ruins, the outer walls and one or two chimneys being all that was left standing. The sun shone brilliantly in a cloudless sky all the morning and seemed only to heighten the calamity. The streets in the neighbourhood of the fire were piled up with furniture and the owners sitting in the midst sadly surveying the ruins of their homes. The utmost sympathy was shown to them by their neighbours who did all they possibly could to alleviate their misfortunes. Later in the day the furniture was stored in the Institute and the school was got ready for the people to occupy as a sleeping place for the night.

The cottages which were destroyed were the property of Mrs. Rutter, of Oxenbourne, and were insured. Mr. Potter, we understand, sustained a loss estimated at nearly £40, as the contents of the premises which were burnt had not been insured. Messrs. Aburrow, we believe, have sustained some damage. Mr. Potter was away from the village at the time the fire was raging.

Only limited further comments are called for:

(1) The site of the burnt cottages was on the south side of the High Street just before it terminates in The Square.

(2) Getting the Petersfield brigade into action was inevitably a lengthy affair—frighteningly so. The telegram led to an alarm-bell ringing at the fire station (then sited behind the *Market Inn*) which summoned voluntary 'engineers' from their places of work; whereupon they donned uniforms, harnessed two horses to the large mobile fire-engine (the 'steamer'), and set off on the five-mile hilly journey to East Meon. Even on arrival, nearly one and a half hours after the outbreak, it was still necessary to raise sufficient steam to activate the pump.

(3) Though the newly-installed mains water was available, via stand-pipes, for domestic purposes, there were no fire-hydrants. Accordingly, the river had to be dammed, that supply being further augmented by opening the Frogmore Mill hatches. Fortunately, the distance from the river to the fire was but a few yards.

(4) Because of the inflammable nature of tinder-dry thatched Tudor cottages, local action was inevitably confined, first to evacuation of people and possessions from the burning and other endangered premises, and, secondly, to preventing the conflagration spreading.

(5) Numerous photographs (some printed as postcards, being the current fashion!) show men and youths in shirt-sleeves, women with white aprons, Eton-collared boys and pinafored girls. Judged by the direction of billowing smoke, the breeze blew more from the south or south-east than from the north-east; which explains the particular danger to Mr. Potter's premises on the opposite side of the narrow road.

(6) Mrs. G. Smith, who unwittingly caused the fire, was the mother of Albert Smith (already encountered in Chapter Seven), then aged 11, and of a daughter two years older. Albert remembers sitting on the railing by the river while his sister stood nearby with a lady who held a parasol, the two children impassively watching their home completely destroyed. The family were temporarily housed by Albert's grandparents, until, shortly afterwards, a tenancy became available (at 4s. a week) of 'Bridge Cottage', Frogmore. A few years later the Smiths wisely bought the cottage, together with 'Frogmore Cottage' next door, for £100. Albert duly inherited 'Bridge Cottage' from his parents, still lives there with his daughter, and can hardly believe the present-day vacant possession value of the two cottages which cost his father £100 could be approaching £100,000.

Another spectacular fire had occurred on a bitterly cold night in November 1904, when the brigade was called to the extreme west of the parish, some eight miles from Petersfield. One house only was involved, though a very special one, the Palladian mansion, Westbury House. The *Portsmouth Evening News* had this to say:

Col. Lewis's heroism.

He saved forty lives.

Family's great losses.

Sterling deeds of bravery, carried out with conspicuous coolness and courage, were performed early on Wednesday morning by Colonel Le Roy Lewis during a disastrous fire, which resulted in the almost total destruction of his beautiful mansion near Petersfield, Hampshire.

The Colonel was instrumental in effecting the rescue of all but one of his household. Unfortunately the housekeeper, Jane Harfley, who was about 69 years of age, who had been in the service of the family for many years, died from shock and fright on the roof before she could be brought down, while other servants received injuries necessitating removal to Hospital.

Colonel Lewis had already exhibited bravery on the battlefield, having won the D.S.O. while commanding a battalion of Imperial Yeomanry in South Africa . . .

. . . At 3 o'clock in the morning the French governess awoke to find her room filled with smoke. She rushed to the door, but her passage was barred by smoke and fire. Then she ran to her window and screamed loudly for help. Colonel Lewis, whose bedroom was not far distant, was roused by her piercing cries. He too, tried to get along the landing, and failed. There was no hope of escape by the staircase.

The account then relates how the Colonel made his way from his bedroom window along a narrow external ledge, descended a stack-pipe to the lawn 40 feet below, and dashed to the stable block, roused three stable-men, and, armed with a long ladder, returned to rescue the governess. The flames had reached her room, but, just as the ladder was put in position, it fell and broke. Fortunately, another ladder was quickly found, and the girl was saved.

Attention was next directed to the bedroom of the German governess on the other side of the doorway, and she was also rescued. The other servants, who were sleeping on the other side of the house and who by this time had been roused, had obtained access to the roof of the children's wing, the point furthest from the fire. One of the servants who did not reach the roof attempted to clamber down the ivy at the end of the house. The ivy gave way, but, falling among some bushes, she reached the ground without any injuries.

The cook, named Hale, who was on the roof with the other servants, jumped to the ground, and sustained a broken wrist. She was removed to Winchester Hospital. The footman and hall boy also received injuries, and they were also removed to hospital. All the other servants, who were clad only in their night attire, were taken from the roof by ladders. Mrs. Le Roy Lewis had her face burnt, and Colonel Le Roy Lewis had his hand burnt, but neither of them was seriously injured.

The building, described as being 'in the style of Queen Anne', was completely gutted, apart from the recently-built school wing, the destroyed contents including fine pictures and a valuable library. The Colonel, wearing his night clothes plus a khaki coat, 'had to borrow a pair of trousers from the butler, and a pair of boots from a local clergyman'. Though the Petersfield fire-brigade had been summoned, by the time they arrived there was little they could do but pump water on the blackened ruins.

The gallant Colonel lost no time in rebuilding the mansion, regardless of cost. Ground-floor rooms included a 'saloon or lounge' (45ft. by 27ft.), with oak-panelled walls and housing a 'three-manual organ, electrically blown', an elegant drawing-room (72ft. by 21ft.), fitted with mahogany glazed bookcases of Chippendale design, a dining-room (32ft. by 21ft.), with painted panel walls; plus a study, boudoir and billiards room. Approached by a massive carved oak staircase, the first floor comprised three suites, each having two large bedrooms and bathroom, and three more large bedrooms. These nine rooms were doubtless for use by the owners and their guests, for there were seven more bedrooms and a bathroom on the second floor for female domestic staff, a nursery wing with yet another seven bedrooms and a bathroom, and a school wing containing a schoolroom, and two more bedrooms. The second floor also included a squash court, whilst the 'domestic offices and servants' accommodation' consisted of a butler's pantry, housekeeper's room, box-room, wine cellar, huge kitchen, scullery, boiler room, and coke store, with five bedrooms and a bathroom above for men servants.

The house had an electric passenger lift, a dinner lift from the kitchen, and electric light throughout, electricity being generated by two 25 h.p. Hornsby Stockport engines. Heating of the whole building was by radiators, two reservoirs held 80,000 gallons of water pumped from a deep well, and (predictably) there was 'an elaborate system of fire-alarms and well planned fire-escapes'. Apart from the mansion, detached buildings included 'commodious stabling', with grooms' rooms above, a coachman's house, an estate office and steward's house, an elaborate cricket pavilion, and numerous 'estate buildings'. The gardens and grounds covered 21 acres.

This information, and much more, was contained in the auction catalogue when, in July 1918, the mansion and Westbury Estate of nearly 5,000 acres was offered for sale in 10 lots. Although several outlying farms duly sold, the main property and the large adjacent farms failed to reach their reserves; and the estate was not finally broken up until 1924, following a second auction sale, this time conducted by Knight, Frank and Rutley. Thereafter, Westbury House became a well-known and successful boys' preparatory school, a use that continued for many years, until comparatively recently when it was converted into a nursing home.

Though only two fires have been described in detail, there have been many others, both before and since. Repeatedly, the river was man's natural ally in fire-fighting, whether for on-the-spot self-help, or of the more professional kind. This use could be regarded as a sort of bonus over and above the river's original function of providing drinking water for man and beast, and its secondary use of driving mills. But there were also times when, following exceptionally prolonged and heavy rainfall, the river ceased to be a friend, and, overflowing and invading many a home, caused great damage and distress, and the resulting ill-health was quite immeasurable.

As the village lacked main drainage until 1959, it follows that 'sanitary arrangements' consisted of an earth-closet in most gardens; or, for the lucky ones, an indoor water-closet connected to a cesspool or septic tank. Accordingly, the mind recoils from the thought of vast quantities of flood water swirling through the village, carrying sewage into the river, and, far worse, into shops and dwellings. Even if the river were not in flood, the situation was shocking, as evidenced by a parish council minute in March 1957, when it was 'resolved that a letter be written to the R.D.C., stating that East Meon was the most insanitary for many miles, sewage and waste actually flowing along the sides of the roads, apart from that which flows directly into the river'.

Floods had been a perennial problem for at least the previous 100 years, as is clear from entries in the school log-book (in addition to those quoted in Chapter Six):

1863 Dec. 2 Weather so exceedingly boisterous, obliged to send home all the children from a distance at noon, the lower districts being inundated.

1903 Oct. 28 Rain having fallen for some hours, roads are impassable.

1921 Jan. 7 Floods kept children away this afternoon. Only 50 out of 150 on the Roll were present. 6 of these 50 were fetched home in a cart at 1.45 p.m.

1935 Nov. 13 Owing to many roads being flooded the attendance is low.

1954 Dec. 8 Afternoon session cancelled and the children sent home on account of severe flooding in the village.

By 1925 the parish council had become increasingly concerned with the situation, and sought a solution, as appears from the minutes: 'Flooding problems. It was reported that Petersfield R.D.C. was trying to remedy this, and the Parish Council generally agreed that if a small bridge over the river at Portsea Co-op. Meadow was enlarged, and the ditches nearby cleared, and the obstruction between The Cross and the bridge removed, there would be a considerable improvement'. But 26 years later, in November 1951, it was recorded that 'a vote of thanks was passed to Mr. Mott for his trouble taken in the recent flood to visit the flood victims personally and also obtained for them two cwt. of coal for the drying of their homes'.

At last, on 10 Nov. 1953, definite action was decided on:

> Mr. J. Steer (Chairman) presided over a meeting of the Council attended by approximately 150 members of the public. Sir Dymoke White, Chairman of the River Board, addressed the meeting concerning recent floods and expressed sympathy with the victims. He went on to say that whatever scheme was agreed would be given top priority by the River Board when it met in February 1954.

By midsummer 1955 an imaginative and comprehensive scheme was well under way, the main ingredients being:

(1) Excavation of a completely new river course from The Cross to the western extremity of Workhouse Lane, which by-passed and shortened the old devious course.

(2) Re-building of six bridges to allow a far greater volume of water to pass beneath.

(3) Deepening and widening the river and concreting its bed along the length of the High Street and as far as Frogmore.

Before these works were completed, the River Board's engineer, when interviewed by a local paper, estimated that 'the flood discharge of the river in November 1953 (when flooding was the worst for 40 years) had been at least 160 cubic feet per second, and may have been as much as 250 cubic feet per second'; and Mr. Steer said the start on the improvement scheme had brought considerable relief to all the villagers, adding: 'We shall not need to paddle down the village streets any more'. His confidence was justified, there having been no semblance of subsequence flooding in the village, though a tiresome but comparatively minor problem persists at Frogmore, where surface water fails to reach the river, rather than the river overflowing. The total cost of the scheme, £26,000, looks ridiculously cheap today.

At the commencement of this chapter I said the crime of murder has a macabre fascination. Yet, disappointingly, few details are known about a double murder in 1600, another murder the following year, and yet a further murder in 1667. The only record I have found of the double murder is tucked away in East Meon's Burial Register:

> 12th. November 1600 Gregorie Johnson and Anne his weife which were both slane on sundaie night the 9th. November.

Perhaps we shall never know whether the hapless couple were killed out of vengeance, or by robbers, or even by a deranged maniac. Similarly, another burial register, that of Harting, records the murder of an East Meon man, coincidentally in the following year:

> 1601. Item this yeare about the Feast day of St. Michaell the Arkangell or shortly after, the bones and apparell of John Roche of Eastmeane was founde

in Hale Wood, within the Parishe of Hartinge, which John Roche was suspected to have been kylled there by William Torner, who was hanged at the next Assyse at Estgrinstead for the same facte, and other roberyes. Also the sayd bones weare buryed in the place where they were founde by appoyntment of the Crowner.

So, though it seems the motive for Roche's murder was robbery, one is left wondering what valuables (if any) he carried, and why he was passing through Hale Wood, if, in fact, he was killed there, some 9–10 miles from home. As for the other foul deed, again it is the East Meon Burial Register that provides minimal information, simply recording, '1667 July 1. Charles Cranly gent. was murthered att Pettersfield'

By contrast, a murder committed in August 1906 took place in full view of witnesses, and the circumstances justified 'full treatment' by the press. Peak Farm, still part of the Westbury Estate, was the home of estate bailiff Thomas Treble, himself a man of some local status, having served as parish councillor and churchwarden. His second son, Robert, lived and carried on his own saddler's business in Lymington; and, as he and his wife Margaret and little three-year-old daughter travelled from Lymington to Peak Farm for their annual summer holiday, they were doubtless full of happy anticipation. On 17 August, part way through the week, the three holiday-makers, accompanied by Robert's sister, Amelia, drove into Petersfield for the afternoon, leaving their pony and trap at the *Railway Hotel* stables. It was arranged that the ladies and child should go on a shopping expedition, and meet Robert at 4.30 for the return trip; all of which seemed perfectly straightforward and unadventurous. But fate was to decree otherwise, as will be seen when the *Hampshire Telegraph* picks up the story:

AWFUL AFFAIR AT PETERSFIELD

MAD SAILOR HOLDS THE TOWN IN TERROR

WILD RIFLE SHOTS

A WOMAN KILLED

CHARGE OF MURDER

A terrible crime under circumstances of a most sensational character was committed at Petersfield on Friday evening. Just before four o'clock a sailor in uniform and leggings, but without a cap, and carrying a magazine rifle with bayonet fixed, came along the Portsmouth Road towards the town, and when about half a mile from the town fired the rifle at some cottages, bullets going through one of the doors and a window.

Then a soldier, Lance-Corpl. White, of the 2nd S. Lancashire Regiment, who was cycling along on pass, saw him lying in the hedge, and a few minutes later a bullet struck his machine, going right through the rim and puncturing the tire. The soldier had to dismount, and he asked the sailor what was the matter.

The latter replied that he had better get on as fast as he could and again pointed the rifle at him. White, not liking the attitude of the man, hurried off into the town, and the sailor apparently followed him, but before reaching the town the latter met Mr. Fleet Goldsmith on horseback, and threatened him with a rifle. Mr. Goldsmith went back and gave information to the police.

The sailor proceeded through the town at a fast walk, repeatedly pointing his weapon at people, and several times discharging it. A police sergeant and two constables who 'set out to capture him', were kept at bay as the man pursued his course along Dragon Street, High Street, Chapel Street and Station Road. The *Hampshire Telegraph* continued:

TRAGIC CLIMAX

Mrs. Treble, the wife of Mr. Treble, a harness maker living at Lymington, who had been staying with some relations at Westmeon, was, however, walking on the pavement near the 'Railway Hotel' stables in Station Road with her little girl, when the sailor catching sight of her dropped on one knee and fired at her at a distance of some 20 or 30 yards. The bullet went through her right thigh, and she dropped to the ground blood flowing fast from the wound.

The sailor passed on over the level crossing at the same quick pace as he had marched through the town, and was pursued for about a mile on the Winchester Road by the police, and others on bicycles and on foot, but he kept them at bay and fired three or four times, narrowly missing some of his pursuers.

RUN DOWN AT LAST

Meanwhile, Mr. Fleet Goldsmith had procured a shotgun, and going across the meadows came within range of the man near the 'Seven Stars' Inn. The sailor was still marching along, and taking aim from behind a gate Mr. Goldsmith fired and hit him. He at once turned round with the rifle in a menacing attitude, but Mr. Goldsmith fired again and gave him such a peppering that he fell and rolled over on the ground.

Mr. Goldsmith and P.C.s Stockwell and Cooper, who were following behind with the others, at once rushed to him and seized him. The rifle had fallen out of his hands. Handcuffs were quickly clapped on and the man lifted into a passing van, and, followed by quite a crowd of cyclists and others who had come up on hearing that the man was captured, was conveyed to the Police Station. There he was seen by Dr. Cross, who had been summoned from the Cottage Hospital (where Mrs. Treble had been carried on a stretcher from the 'Railway Hotel' stables in which she had been temporarily placed), and it was found that the man's injuries were in no way serious. He was placed in a cell and watched during the night.

The account then concluded with the information that the man's name was Joseph Burbage [*sic*], a stoker on H.M.S. *Nelson*, who had been at musketry practice at Tipnor earlier in the day; and that Mrs. Treble had died from loss of blood an hour and a half after being shot, her femoral artery having been severed.

Apart from the erroneous reference to West Meon instead of East Meon, the newspaper report was substantially accurate. The subsequent inquest, committal proceedings in the magistrates' court, and trial at Winchester Assizes, revealed a remarkable explanation of what had seemed inexplicable. The killer, whose true name was Herbert John Cyril Mitchell, had apparently suffered severe sunstroke in a foreign clime some years previously, had later joined the Royal Navy, attacked one of his mates with a spanner when on board H.M.S. *Hannibal* in the port of Vigo, and, in consequence been courtmartialled, sentenced to two years hard labour, and dismissed the Service. Unfortunately, this was not the end of his naval career, for, having served his sentence, he proceeded to re-enlist under the false name of Joseph Burbidge [*sic*], after which history repeated itself when he 'went for one of his mates in H.M.S. *Nelson* with a razor', this behaviour leading to his spending two or three weeks in Haslar Hospital under observation. Tragically, he was then discharged from hospital as fit for duty, and shortly afterwards spent several days at Tipnor rifle range receiving musketry instruction.

On Friday, 17 August, Mitchell was missing when the firing party mustered at Tipnor, by which time, unknown to the naval authorities, he was heading up the London road, complete with rifle, bayonet and ammunition that he must have secreted during previous days. As for subsequent events in and near Petersfield, it is hard to understand how onlookers were sufficiently foolish to follow 'at a safe distance', as the paper put it, since a service rifle is lethal at ranges of a mile and more. Even more remarkable was the courage, almost tantamount to madness, that led Fleet Goldsmith to tackle the rifleman with a shot-gun whose effective range as a 'man stopper' was probably no more than 60 yards. The very fact of a member of the public arming himself and acting as a one-man sheriff's posse in the year 1906 is pretty startling; and, not surprisingly, the coroner had something to say on the subject:

> While congratulating Mr. Goldsmith, who shot down the man, and having stopped his mad career, he reminded him that it was not a legal method, and that had the man been killed Mr. Goldsmith's position would have been serious.

At Winchester Assizes in November Mitchell was tried for murder, found guilty but insane (due to post-epileptic mania), and ordered to be detained as a criminal lunatic during His Majesty's pleasure. Ironically, Fleet Goldsmith was, in later years, also certified insane, escaped from the asylum to which he was committed, and after seeking refuge in Ireland, returned to end his days (at liberty) not far from Petersfield. The widower, Robert Treble, later remarried, his second wife being Dora Jenkins, a governess employed by Mrs. Curtis Gallup at Bereleigh.

Finally, in 1920 there was the apparent murder that never was a murder (according to the coroner), or was it? Curiously, Peak Farm again comes into the picture, as reported by the *Hampshire Chronicle* in their 28 February issue:

Gruesome find at East Meon

> One of the most mysterious cases of tragedy recorded in Hampshire was discovered on Saturday morning in an open field adjoining the Petersfield–Winchester main road at East-meon, not far from the railway viaduct,* half a mile or so beyond the side road that leads to Privett.
>
> About half past eight, Mr. Harry Silvester, of Peak Farm, of which the field forms part, happened to be in that vicinity, when he came across the dead body of a man, absolutely nude, lying in a furrow, in a ploughed field, some 60 yards south of the highway. He at once reported the discovery to P.C. Steele, at Eastmeon, who made investigations about the spot, but failed to find any trace of the man's clothes. The body was seen by Dr. Stafford, and removed to the 'New Inn', Eastmeon. Every possible means have been taken since to establish the identity of the deceased, but so far without success.
>
> (*the word 'viaduct' is erroneous, and should read 'tunnel'.)

The official description of the man put his age at between 30 and 35 years, height 5ft. 8ins., blue eyes, auburn hair brushed back, pale complexion, clean shaven and apparently a non-manual worker. At the inquest Dr. Stafford said the deceased's body was well nourished, of slim build, and had apparently been dead seven or eight hours when first seen by the doctor at about 1 p.m. There were many cuts and deep scratches on both arms, and a deep lacerated tear on the right hand, as well as abrasions on the chest, abdomen and legs, and a bad tear on the sole of the left foot. No bones were broken, there was no evidence of any punctured wound from firearms or stabbing, nor indication of poisoning of a corrosive nature. The witness's conclusion was that death resulted from syncope, due to exposure and shock from the injuries described, which might have been caused by the man struggling through hedges and bushes and treading on thorns. The wound on the hand might have been caused by barbed wire. Other evidence described the prints of bare feet having been traced from the road along the field to where the body was found. Ultimately, the coroner, sitting without a jury, said it seemed that the man's death had been caused by exposure, and not by foul play, and possibly he might have been suffering from light-headedness, neurasthenia, or shell-shock; the verdict being 'Death from syncope due to exposure'.

To my rather unimaginative mind, the reported facts do not satisfactorily 'add up', and so many questions are left unanswered. There must surely be a suspicion of more than meets the eye; possibly the deceased was a lover, who had been caught in *flagrante delicto,* and chased by an outraged husband; or the victim of some kind of gang-warfare or vendetta, which left him deprived of his clothes, and pursued through the night till he died of a heart attack. Apparently the man was not a tramp, for the body was 'well-nourished', and there was no mention of its being unkempt; and surely neither those suffering from 'light-headedness, neurasthenia, or shell-shock' carefully hide or destroy their clothes before struggling through hedges and bushes, and perhaps barbed wire and then facing, and meeting death by exposure. I am left wondering.

Chapter Ten

THE GREAT WARS

THE FOURTH OF AUGUST 1914 happened to be the occasion of East Meon's annual flower show, a festive event eagerly anticipated by the local populace, though by this time distant events had cast their sobering shadow. Yet it was unthinkable that sabre-rattling Germany would challenge the whole world, and that we would be directly involved. Suddenly the holiday atmosphere melted away, and spines chilled as Colonel Le Roy Lewis, having driven over from Westbury, made the dreaded announcement: Britain had declared war on Germany and Austria. All thoughts were with men in the armed forces as reservists reported to their depots, the local Territorial Cycle Company mustered at West Meon, and the advance guard of Britain's professional army embarked for Europe.

Squire Gallup, without previous military experience and no longer in the first flush of youth, knew where his duty lay. Volunteering for army service, and persuading his gardener, Mark Neil, and his chauffeur, George Knight, to do likewise, they headed for Larkhill on Salisbury Plain to be trained as gunners. Gallup also took his favourite hunter, for those were the days when gentlemen were officers (and vice versa), and officers were mounted. Only later was it realised that officers, especially subalterns, were 'first over the top' in trench warfare, and least likely to survive for long.

The vicar, Thomas Heywood Masters, wasted no time in applying for a chaplain's commission, and, on being rejected through age, took a British Red Cross ambulance to France. By October 1915, his age was no longer a barrier, and he was 'sent home for a chaplain's commission', which took a remarkably short time, for he returned to France on 1 November. After two years with the 4th Army H.Q. (including the Somme battles of 1916) and further service near Dunkirk and in Flanders, he became Assistant Chaplain General, Etaples, was twice mentioned in despatches, and awarded a C.B.E. The war was the first in which women assumed a major role, and Majorie Gallup and Kate Masters, wives of the squire and vicar, left the village for Sherborne, where, for two years, they nursed at Greenhill Hospital as V.A.D.s. For good measure, the vicar's daughters also served as V.A.D.s and Y.M.C.A. workers in France. Major Reginald Nicholson, who was later to succeed Gallup as owner of Bereleigh, spent the war as an officer in the Hants Carbineers; Colonel Le Roy Lewis was Military Attaché in Paris, and his son, Henry, fought in France as a cavalry subaltern. To complete the picture of East Meon's gentry and professional men, Dr. Edward Jones served in Gallipoli and France for two years before returning to his practice.[1]

After their training at Larkhill, Gallup, Neil and Knight (still with the hunter) and another villager, blacksmith Walter Lambert, were despatched overseas to join the British and Indian forces in Mesopotamia who were protecting the Royal Navy's oil supplies. By December 1915 these East Meon men (other than Lambert, who was sick with dysentry) were with many others besieged by the Turks in the town of Kut-al-Amara, situated in a loop of the River Tigris, a fact noted in East Meon's parish magazine the following March:

> We are sorry to hear that Mark Neil and George Knight have been wounded. It appears that they, with Mr. Gallup, are besieged in Kut-al-Amara, but we are told that all is well with the garrison.

It was a blessing that those at home were spared knowledge of the garrison's true predicament, for, weakened by disease and malnutrition, and having even eaten their own horses, they were forced to capitulate after four and a half months. They numbered over 200 British, and a few less Indian officers, together with just under 13,000 rank and file. Of the latter, 2,592 were British, over 1,700 of whom were destined to die in Mesopotamia or Turkey. One of the first acts of the Turks after the capitulation was to separate officers from men, and as Gallup with other officers headed up the Tigris for prisoner-of-war captivity aboard a river boat, he caught a last glimpse of his gardener and chauffeur, part of a huge, pathetic, sick and half-starved rabble of men shambling on foot towards Turkey, hundreds of miles distant across barren and inhospitable country. They died in their hundreds from lack of food and from ill-treatment; that any survived at all is almost a miracle. On the journey the prisoners were treated like cattle and scourged from place to place by Arab guards, regardless of any human feelings.[2] Nothing is known of the ultimate fate of Neil and Knight. Though the officers faced great hardships, their treatment was less severe, and Gallup survived, though, after two and a half years in a Turkish prisoner-of-war camp, he was a changed man.

The issue of the parish magazine from which I have quoted, made other references to the war:

> We sympathize with Mr. and Mrs. Gilbert Kille and their family on the loss of Claude, who was killed in the trenches on January 26. Yet we are proud of him, as they are, for he has made the supreme sacrifice for us all and no man could do more. We are glad to hear that Bruce is recovering from his wound satisfactorily. The following have been called up in their groups and have joined the Colours: Albert George Blackman, Clifford Blackman and Herbert Lambert.It was a happy chance that the Vicar was able to marry Mr. Lambert to Miss Roach while he was at home. All good wishes to them!

Clara Fisher recalls events on 'the home front':

> Women got busy with their sewing machines and knitting-needles, making night-shirts and day shirts, and gloves, balaclava helmets, socks and seaboot stockings for sailors. Other women found disused plots of ground and grew potatoes, for enemy submarines threatened the country with starvation. Each Friday there was a house-to-house collection of vegetables which were taken to Lady Penthyn at West Meon, who packed and despatched them for the Navy. Young girls went off to train for the Women's Land Army, and returned to do manual work on local farms. News came that horses were getting killed, and several replacements were sent from the parish. Iron railings and gates were taken to be melted down and made into munitions; and several people left the village to work in weapon or munition factories. Families were continually having shocks as news came by telegram of menfolk killed, wounded or missing. Then we learnt that the Germans were using poison gas, which was terrifying, and we wondered whatever would they do next.

In 1916 Lloyd George became prime minister, and the slaughter continued, with particularly bloody battles waged at Verdun and on the Somme. Frank Collyer, aged 19, joined the Rifle Brigade, and, arriving in France, was pitched into battle. 'I went straight

over the top in the Battle of the Somme immediately I arrived there'. He survived the
battle and many others, and was awarded the Military Medal for outstanding bravery in
the field, a strange apprenticeship for a man destined to become the village sexton for
30 years. When at long last, hostilities ended with the 1918 armistice, signed at the
eleventh hour of the eleventh day of the eleventh month, those of the warring nations
who had fought for over four years were physically and economically exhausted. In
East Meon the announcement of the wonderful news was preceded by clarion calls from
a West Meon trumpeter, after which the church bells pealed, and everyone rejoiced
and felt a great weight had been lifted from their minds.

Some 140 men from the parish had served in the forces, of whom 21 lost their lives,
10 were taken prisoner, and very many others were wounded. Two Coopers, two
Pollards and two Titheridges were among the dead. Brothers Richard and Philip Berry
from Oxenbourne Farm had both served in the army, Philip surviving severe wounds,
and Richard dying on the way back from Gallipoli. Albert Luff, too, had been a soldier,
and, contracting tuberculosis, came home to die in 1916. Edwin Broadway was wounded,
brought back to Netley Hospital, near Southampton, patched up, and sent straight back
to the fighting line without so much as a day's leave, so desperate was the manpower
shortage. Twenty-year-old Albert George Blackman found himself like Frank Collyer in
the Battle of the Somme, where, after being badly wounded in the leg by a hand-grenade,
he spent 18 hours in a dug-out before enemy shelling eased sufficiently for removal
to a dressing station. Then followed, in succession, progress through a casualty clearing
station, a Channel crossing to Southampton, and a 17-hour train journey to a military
hospital in Aberdeen of all places. As the train passed through Wolverhampton he
managed to throw a letter on to the platform telling his mother of his survival and
whereabouts. It duly arrived, and she kept it for years. When repaired, he was luckier
than Edwin Broadway, having 10 days sick leave before being ordered back to France.
But his luck ran out at Arras, when during a night patrol a shellburst cost him his right
eye. George Cannings, enlisting as an 18-year-old in 1915, served three years in
Mesopotamia, missed the siege of Kut, but there were times when he 'would have
gladly paid £1 for a teaspoonful of water'. Wounded in the back by shrapnel, and
enduring malaria seven times, he survived and lived to a ripe old age.

Yet other men emerged unscathed, including professional soldier, John Macdonald,
who served in the Hampshire Regiment in Mesopotamia, the North-West Frontier of
of India, and eventually in Siberia. George Wilson Atkinson, elder son of the original
George Atkinson of South Farm, was 'posted missing' when taken prisoner in France
in March 1918. By a coincidence, Albert Smith was also captured in France a couple of
months later, and encountering Atkinson in a prisoners' reception camp, mentioned
the meeting in a message that got through to his family. When the news was passed
to the Atkinsons it was their first intimation that George was alive, much to their
relief after months of suspense. Another to come through 'without a scratch' was Royal
Marine John Applebee, who, at the time of his 1909 marriage to Lily Adams (daughter
of Alfred Adams) was described as 'Gunner H.M.S. *Inflexible*'. His ship's home base
was Portsmouth, whence he habitually walked to East Meon whenever a few days leave
was granted.

Some of the social and other repercussions of 'the war to end all wars' will be
referred to in a later chapter. Yet, even *before* the war ended, it was widely realised that
the old order had changed irrevocably, and few families could keep up the large,

well-staffed establishments that were part of the Victorian and Edwardian country scene. Thus it was not entirely coincidental that both Bereleigh and Westbury estates were offered for sale by auction in July 1918.

The scene now moves 21 years forward to 1939, when, on 1 September, a revived and re-armed Germany, led by the evil fascist dictator, Adolf Hitler, launched a brutal and devastating attack on her eastern neighbour, Poland. Britain and France were in no position to go directly to the rescue, but having guaranteed Poland against foreign aggression, they declared war against Germany. Sunday, 3 September was the day on which Neville Chamberlain, in a radio broadcast to the nation, made the grave but expected announcement, echoed at many a morning church service, including that of East Meon. For the first time, British civilians were 'in the front line'.

As East Meon had been designated a 'safe', or 'reception' area, householders were obliged to accommodate elderly people, mothers with babies, and, numerically greatest, children of school age. Billeting officers employed by the local authority had surveyed the area, and assessed the number of 'evacuees', as they were called, whom families must be prepared to take in. Even before the declaration of war, special trains and other transport were streaming out of London and other large towns, crammed with hundreds of thousands of confused and apprehensive human beings going into the unknown.

Mr. and Mrs. Herbert Goddard's spacious High Street house had been designated as suitable for lodging 10½ people! Following the arrival in the village of London double-decker buses full of evacuees, the Goddards found themselves hosts to one elderly lady who paced up and down her bedroom all night and insisted on returning to London the next day. Another Cockney family enquired, as soon as they arrived: 'Where's the fish and chip shop?' On being told none existed, they said they were going home, and did. The fact that Britain experienced virtually no enemy air attacks for eight or nine months understandably lulled people into a sense of false security, and vast numbers of evacuees trickled back to the homes, families and familiar surroundings they had missed.

The whole life and economy of the nation became geared to winning the war, and many basic freedoms were suspended. Food rationing, introduced in January 1940, became progressively more severe, until non-manual adult workers were limited to a few ounces of meat per week and one egg a fortnight, and 'luxuries' such as sweets, wines and spirits were virtually unobtainable. Yet the general standard of health, in spite of the traumatic circumstances, was good; and illnesses attributable to obesity became rare! Morley John Tosdevine, three of whose brothers perished in World War I, was a special constable and also treasurer of the village pig club, a permitted organisation that involved groups of villagers, each of which collectively owned a pig that was nourished on household food scraps and any other edible matter that could be found. The exciting climax came when porker was due to be slaughtered, and club members enjoyed the almost forgotten experience of tucking into roast pork; even the offal was not despised.

Prior to the outbreak of war, civilians had been encouraged to join part-time bodies that included Civil Defence (air-raid wardens, etc.), the Auxiliary Fire Service, and, as from May 1940, the Local Defence Volunteers (L.D.V. for short); and units of each were formed in East Meon. The first man to enlist in the L.D.V. was sexton/postman Frank Collyer. Initially, the vicar, the Rev. C. H. Mylne, commanded the platoon, and a photograph taken in front of the then vicarage shows 29 men in army uniform, a good sprinkling wearing N.C.O.s' stripes and medal ribbons earned over twenty years before. By the time of the photograph the title L.D.V. had been changed to Home Guard, and the village unit, though short of rifles, was a smart, disciplined and enthusiastic body far removed from the 'Dad's Army' television image. Farm workers who had been harvesting till eight o'clock would man look-out posts at Old Winchester Hill till six next morning, and then face another day's work almost without sleep. Later, Frank Collyer succeeded the vicar as platoon commander, becoming a company commander and earning an M.B.E. to add to his M.M.

One of the Home Guard recruits in 1940 was Edward Fitzroy Talbot-Ponsonby, a young man in his 20s, living at Langrish House, and working in the family's munition factory next door. After the collapse of France he received a devious and confidential approach to ascertain whether he would join a secret organisation involving danger, and possibly death preceded by torture. Characteristically, the prospect appealed to his adventurous nature; and whilst his Home Guard membership continued as a 'cover', he received secret training as a member of 'XII Corps Observation Unit', a body of 5,000 men who have been described as sort of stay-behind troops if the Germans invaded. 'Alone amongst the countries that opposed Germany . . . Britain had a complete Resistance organisation, trained, armed and waiting for invaders to arrive. By September 1940, long before the first threat of invasion had passed, it claimed an efficiency unparalleled by Britain's more conventional fighting units. Even the Gestapo knew nothing about it'.[3]

Resistance cells, each of six or seven men, typically included farmers, gamekeepers, poachers, burglars—men who knew the countryside and were used to moving about in darkness with only their eyes to guide them. Each cell had an underground hideout or base, stocked with arms, explosives and food. Weapon and explosive training was of a high standard, and 'the units were the first Britons to be armed with Thompson sub-machine guns, with sticky bombs, with the Piat anti-tank weapon, with phosphorus hand-grenades, and with the booby-trap device known as the stick pencil'.[4] Also every man was issued with a pistol, a rubber truncheon and a dagger.

Enormous quantities of explosives, including grenades, were stored at Langrish House, ready for distribution to the local hide-out deep in densely wooded Rookham Copse half-a-mile away. Soon Talbot-Ponsonby, promoted to the rank of lieutenant (ostensibly in the Home Guard), was commanding 28 men, split into four seven-man units in Buriton, Froxfield, Steep and East Meon; men who, if the area was overrun, would 'disappear', would not communicate with their families, and emerge only to commit sabotage and gather intelligence information. Captain J. Shields, ex-Guards officer and licensee of Petersfield's *Red Lion,* was the contact for radio messages. So great was the secrecy that married men were forbidden even to confide in their wives, until unexplained nocturnal outings caused such matrimonial stresses that the authorities had to allow wives into the secret. Talbot-Ponsonby speaks with pride of training exercises when his men undertook night-time activities without being seen or heard by people a few yards away, and in one such exercise a large, obsolete tank at Meonstoke was destroyed with plastic explosives. The local unit's only major disappointment was not being sent to the Isle of Wight before 'D Day' to face the anticipated German counter-attack there, which, in fact, never materialised.

The massive daylight air-raids endured particularly by southern England during the summer of 1940 had no sooner abated than night attacks, especially on London, grew in scale and frequency, the combination of high-explosive and incendiary bombs wreaking great destruction of buildings and inflicting awful civilian casualties, in spite of countless people seeking safety and a night's rest in underground tube stations. Many other towns, including Portsmouth and Southampton, were similarly blasted and burnt. In East Meon, Herbert Goddard was a member of the Auxiliary Fire Service eight-man unit:

> We had a Stolk motor-trailer pump, towed by a car and capable of delivering 180 gallons of water a minute. We went to Portsmouth and Southampton to help fight enormous fires. Once, we arrived at Southampton while a raid was in progress, and fought a fire at Edwin Jones's store for 16 hours before returning exhausted. Every man lost the next day's pay through being unfit for work!

On 21 November 1940 a German fighter-bomber, probably off course and lost, appeared through a break in the clouds over Petersfield. Passers-by witnessed it circle over the town at a height of 1,000 feet and then release its one bomb, which may have been aimed at the station or some other target. A direct hit on the workhouse demolished the entire front of the building, as well as the entrance hall, the porter's quarters, some stores and part of the Master's apartments, all of which were reduced to a huge heap of rubble.

The Master, Mr. W. Ixer, the porter, Mr. F. Weeks, and five inmates (four old men and 23-year-old Emily Rutter) were killed instantly, and the Master's wife died shortly after. Patients in the hospital block were severely shocked, and at the temporary reception centre set up in the Methodist church hall, old, dazed survivors, wrapped in blankets, and some hugging soft toys, were too shocked even to give their names.

Following repeated large-scale air attacks on Portsmouth, dispersal of naval establishments became imperative, and as 'Leydene', the East Meon mansion home of Countess Peel, appeared to fulfil the requirements of an independent Naval Signal School, it was requisitioned for that purpose in the summer of 1941. A story, possibly apocryphal, is told to the effect that in June a 'high-powered' deputation of senior naval officers visited 'Leydene' to discuss arrangements for taking over. They were ushered towards the huge drawing-room where Lady Peel awaited them, whereupon the butler, flinging open the double doors, announced: 'My Lady, the sailors have arrived'. The subsequent presence of H.M.S. *Mercury*, as the establishment was (and still is) known, may have been responsible for a night air-raid in June 1942, when 38 high-explosive bombs, five land-mines and an estimated 3,500 incendiary bombs were showered on East Meon; though an alternative explanation could have been use by defending forces of the technique known as 'bending the beam', which upset the navigation of enemy bombers, and resulted in loads intended for Portsmouth or Southampton falling in what was hopefully regarded as open countryside. The raid, starting about 9.30 p.m., luckily caused no casualties, apart from a pig killed at Frogmore. Most of the bombs fell on Park Hill or near Teglease Cross-roads, including one string of H.E.s that straddled Frogmore and came within 50 yards of scoring a direct hit on Forge Cottage, where I am now writing. Local Civil Defence workers did good work, in action until the following breakfast time, extinguishing incendiaries before buildings caught fire.

General descriptions of wars, even those profoundly affecting a nation's destiny, tend to be less colourful than personal stories—what the press likes to call 'eye-witness accounts'. Yet it would be both tedious and virtually impossible adequately to describe the war-time experiences of even a tenth of East Meon's people, for all were involved to some degree, hundreds directly so. In all, 14 servicemen lost their lives, and the first, in October 1940, was Stoker 1st Class William Allen, a World War I veteran and a bachelor of 40, who, rejoining the Navy, found himself aboard H.M.S. *Chasseur 07* as an instructor:

> ". . . two British-manned, former submarine chasers, Chausseur 06 and Chasseur 07, were on patrol off the Dorset coast on the night of 11/12 October 1940. Shortly after midnight they were attacked and overwhelmed by a force of German E boats.[5]

Both were sunk, and of *Chausseur 07's* personnel, eight were rescued and taken prisoner, but 13 drowned, including Allen, whose body was recovered at Portland nine days later.

Brothers Charles, Ernest and Leonard Blackman were all soldiers. Charles, a corporal in the R.A.C., was accidentally killed in a training exercise on Salisbury Plain in April 1942, aged 35, leaving a widow and daughter. Ernest, a lance-corporal in the D.L.I., fell at Arnhem in October 1944, in the same action that cost the life of Charles Bishop— the two comrades had managed to keep together and avoid harm for the previous four years. Leonard Blackman survived, ending up as a lieutenant. There were five Blackman brothers in all, and as one fought in the first war, and the fifth was in the Home Guard, they had as a family done more than their share. Young Sergeant Joseph Phillips, an exceptionally talented footballer, was air-gunner of a Wellington bomber, which, returning from a night raid over Germany in January 1944, crashed on landing at its base, killing all the crew, the cause almost certainly being 'pilot-error'. Phillips, aged 22, was to have married a W.A.A.F. who was on duty in the aerodrome's control tower when the crash occurred.

Many servicemen, with varying degrees of good fortune survived. Norman John ('Jack') Aburrow joined the D.C.L.I., received eight weeks' training, and went to France, where machine-gun wounds led to his evacuation by hospital ship from Le Havre, at the time of Dunkirk. Later, he served in North Africa with the Eighth Army and fought in the Battle of El Alamein; then, in a mobile battalion formed for invasion purposes, he participated in three successive landings, in Sicily and mainland Italy (the latter twice, including the Battle of Anzio), was subsequently wounded again, and ended up in Austria.

Fred Gibbs (the 14-year-old pipe-smoker encountered in Chapter Seven) was a gunner on the Reserve List when war broke out. He served in Crete, and, after eluding the Germans and escaping, served with the Eighth Army throughout the North Africa campaign, including El Alamein, coming through unscathed and with the rank of sergeant. John Macdonald was also a reservist (supplementary) in 1939, and was called up for home service duties in a battalion of old soldiers. In 1941 he was transferred to the Corps of Military Police, and was involved in the crossing of the Rhine in the 1944/5 winter as part of 21st Army Group. He had the distinction of serving throughout both world wars, and the luck to avoid harm.

Yet another survivor was Lynton White (also encountered in Chapter Seven). A gunner, captured by the Japanese in Hong Kong in late 1941, he, with three others, risked escaping from Shamshuipo Camp via a lengthy surface-water drainage pipe leading into Hong Kong harbour, and swam to enemy-occupied Kowloon; then, separated from his companions, and exhausted and disorientated, he walked the length of the main street without encountering a single Japanese, continued walking for five days through China, and eventually, with Chinese help, completed the escape, and continued his army service in the Far East and Australia. Had he remained a P.o.W., prospects of his survival would have been dubious.

As for civilians uprooted from the village and plunged into distant war factories, one such was Alfred Benjamin ('Ben') Aburrow, brother of Jack, who toiled as a metal worker in Vickers Armstrong's war-plane factory at Blackpool from 1939 till about 1946, before returning to the family business. Miss Lilian Luff (niece of former licensee William Luff, and also of Albert Luff who died of T.B. in 1916) worked in a Plessey factory at Ilford, making electrical equipment for planes. She is a reserved, modest and shy person, but the area in which she worked and lodged was on the receiving end of many bombing raids, as well as 'doodle bugs' and rockets, and she had several narrow escapes.

At last it was all over, V.E. Day ('Victory—European') was suitably celebrated, four months later V.J. Day ('Victory—Japanese') was the occasion for equal rejoicing, silent tears were shed on behalf of the dead and maimed, and the long, difficult task of rebuilding, literally and metaphorically, began.

Chapter Eleven

PEOPLE

PREHISTORIC EARTHWORKS and artefacts, ancient buildings, Anglo-Saxon charters, and countless other old documents are interesting, many fascinating. Yet most of us find a study of human beings, each with a complex, sometimes unpredictable, physical and mental make-up, even more rewarding. East Meon parish has housed a generous share of notable, colourful or downright eccentric individual characters and families, some of whom have already been noticed. Innumerable others, having failed so far to fit into my story, ought not to be ignored, though the task of selecting a small handful from all those who have made their mark is formidable. For example, internationally renowned playwright, William Douglas Home, who has lived at Drayton since 1953, endured being cashiered from the army, followed by a year's imprisonment, rather than take part in the 1944 bombardment of Le Havre, on the ground that French civilians were likely to be unnecessarily killed. Brother of the former prime minister, he himself stood for parliament at different times—as a Liberal, a Tory, and an Independent. His autobiography[1] makes very, very good reading.

For those attracted by the improbable, Cyril Coles, nephew of village builder Henry Coles, deserves a chapter to himself. Educated at Churcher's College, Petersfield, and apprenticed to Thorneycrofts, the Southampton shipbuilders, when World War I broke out 'he fled to join the Hampshire Regiment under an assumed name and an optimistic estimate of his age'.[2] After serving in France with the 29th Division, 'his gift for languages and an uncanny knack of emerging unscathed from incursions into German lines came to the notice of the authorities and he was transferred to British Intelligence'.[3] Incredibly, he spent the rest of the war living in Germany, well knowing that detection would result in his being shot as a spy. With the war over, and finding life back in East Meon understandably dull, world-wide travel followed, including a spell in Australia where his volume of short stories, *The Islands of the Sea,* was published. Returning again to East Meon, Coles found Fate had a completely unforseen quirk in store for him—the arrival next door of aviation pioneer William Manning, with his crippled sister Adelaide. She, too, had literary aspirations, and had written a novel which, in spite of 'an excellent press', did not do well.

In true story-book style, Coles confided to his new neighbour that there was a tale of war-time British Intelligence 'in his head', waiting to be written; whereupon the two, under the name of 'Manning Coles', wrote *Drink to Yesterday,* published by Hodder and Stoughton in 1940. It succeeded, and was followed, between 1940 and 1954, by a further 30 full-length thrillers, several described as 'classic spy stories'.

As for *families,* rather than specific individuals, the Killes have been around for 400 years, supplying the village with many a skilled tradesman and artisan, especially bricklayers, carpenters, plasterers, glaziers and painters; and, as we know, Samuel Kille was a master-builder in quite a big way. The name was formerly often spent *Kiln,* possibly indicating an association, in the distant past, with pottery, then bricks and tiles. Successive generations of Killes have, in their practical way, contributed a valuable share towards today's 'streetscape', and many, fanning-out over the country, and beyond, have taken their skills elsewhere. Only retired George Kille remains, and, needless to say, he was formerly a builder and undertaker.

Surnames of other families with long parochial associations run through the village's history like threads of tapestry. Names such as Collins, Hobbs, Langrish, Lock, Pink, Steel, Tyrell, Witcomb, and Vinn reappear in the church registers for hundreds of years, though none survives today. But the Aburrow family, who lived in the village and its neighbourhood for 500 years, probably longer, takes first prize for longevity. The name suggests a possible French origin, subsequently anglicised; or its origin may have been far more local, such as *Atte Burrow* (or *Barrow*), later contracted to *ABurrow,* which was, in fact, the way it was frequently written as recently as the last century. What we do know is that local members of the family were never famous, nor, with one possible exception, infamous; yet, successive generations were honest, expert craftsmen, the very lifeblood of the community.

Early in the 16th century, an innkeeper, one Henry Aburrow, was the first recorded mayor of Petersfield, and therefore a man of standing. He must have been born well back in the 15th century, for his wife, Maude, was a widow and mother of four children when she made her will in 1517.[4] She bequeathed her 'grett potte' to her son, Giles, who later became a prosperous (but apparently childless) yeoman, and by his 1558 will[5] benefited John Strowder, nephew of the East Meon testator of that name referred to in Chapter Three. That does not *prove* that the Petersfield and East Meon·Aburrows were the same family, but moving on to 1563, one of the years when plague struck East Meon, the baptismal register records at least two Aburrow households in the parish:

Feb. 20th. Anne daughter of John Aburrowe
July 2nd. Joane daughter of George Aburrowe

Four years before the Spanish Armada another two East Meon Aburrow families were each blessed with the birth of sons within a couple of days, when in 1584 Edward, the son of Rolfe Aburrow, and Henry, son of Richard Aburrow, were baptized; and in 1586 John Aborroughe of Riplington appeared in the Lay Subsidy Roll with goods assessed at three pounds. That year Anthonie Aburrow married Margaret Yalden, whilst in 1594, Edward, the son of Edward Aburrow, was baptized. So by then the family had numerous local branches. Rolfe was probably the beadle named in the 1607 Court Baron:[6] 'Wee presente that Ralphe [*sic*] Aburrow, being a beedle, came to a distringas on the goods of John Houghton at Langrish and was there resisted by the said Houghton'.

Copyhold tenants in 1647[7] included Anthony Aburrow (son of another Anthony—the family's favourite Christian name) and John Aburrow, whose land was in Oxenbourne tithing; and the 1662 Hearth Tax Return listed 'Widow Aburrow' as occupant of an Oxenbourne house with three hearths. We are already aware of John Aburrow, the tailor who took an apprentice in 1678, this being the family's earliest specific occupational mention, apart from that of Henry the innkeeper and Giles the yeoman. The tailoring business remained with that branch of the family for some time, since the 1753 will[8] of another John (called 'the Elder', and probably a grandson, John, who took the apprentice) described him as a tailor. He was reasonably well-to-do, owning freehold and copyhold property which he gave to his son, Stephen, whilst another son, John, received 'one featherbed with the bedstead curtains and valliants upon which I now lye, one rugg and two blanketts . . . one chest of drawers six pewter plaits six pewter dishes one bell mettal skillett and one deal screen'.

So much for the tailors. However, three 1728 entries in the East Meon Workhouse account book point to another trade:

Sept. 7th. Paid to Anthony Bourow for Peter Stigants using of his tooles ..	4s. 3d.
Sept. 28th. Paid to Anthony Burrow for the use of his tooles	1s. 0d.
Oct. 8th. Paid to Anthony Aburrow for the use of his tools	2d.

Doubtless the tools enabled repairs or maintenance work to be undertaken at the workhouse on a do-it-yourself basis; and as Peter Stigants was a skilled carpenter, it follows that Anthony's trade was also carpentry.

Stark tragedy struck the West Meon branch of the family in 1749, when a Henry Aburrow was hanged at Winchester, following conviction for a capital offence at the Winchester Assizes held in July. What awful crime could have resulted in this terrible punishment? In fact, he was tried 'for maliciously and feloniously cutting down the head and mount of a fish pond belonging to Ellen Foxcroft widow'.[9] He pleaded not guilty, but was found guilty of felony, the value of the damage committed being 2s. 6d., and was sentenced to death. The 'head' of the pond would have been the bank or dam maintaining the head of water, and the 'mount'—perhaps for 'mound'—the surrounding embankment. Since 1733, causing flooding by breaking a river-bank had been a capital offence, as were nearly 200 other crimes in the 18th century. (Almost unbelievably, in those days a boy of 10 was hanged for stealing a penknife, and a girl of 14 for taking a handkerchief.[10]) As for Ellen Foxcroft—properly Eleanor Foxcroft—she was the widow of Henry Foxcroft of Hall Place, West Meon, a J.P., and man of importance. Assuming poor Henry did commit the comparatively trivial offence that cost him his life, no motive is known, but, as his body was buried at West Meon in consecrated ground, the rector must have thought him forgiveable.

Between 1753-55 three Aburrows were assessed for the East Meon Church Rate: John (not John the tailor, who died in 1755) in respect of several properties that included 'the Old Queen's Head'; Stephen for 'Cumbers' in Oxenbourne tithing; and Joseph for 'late Jarmans'.[11] This John, and a Joseph (probably father and son) were also carpenters, and apparently partners, since the churchwardens paid £3 3s. 10d. to them jointly in 1756-57; but for the next 35 years Joseph alone received periodic payments for church repairs, sometimes between £16 and £30, and he was expressly described as a carpenter. In 1792, separate payments were made to 'Joseph Aburrow Senr.' and to 'Joseph Aburrow', so by then the carpentry tradition had been extended to a further generation.

Although the family produced skilled tradesmen and artisans, one member found time for cricket, and must have been an outstanding player. He was Edward, who lived at nearby Hambledon, played for that most famous of all village clubs, and in 1777 participated in their glorious victory when they overwhelmed All England by an innings and 168 runs! That match was one of 39 encounters against All England between 1772-96, of which Hambledon won 23; and numbers of spectators at the home ground, Broadhalfpenny Down, reputedly reached 20,000. Even if we discount that figure by 50 per cent., it still remains eloquent testimony of cricketing enthusiasm for matches played in the 'backwoods' of Hampshire's countryside when communications and transport were limited, to say the least. Edward Aburrow (allegedly nicknamed 'Curry' because of his prowess with the girls, rather than cricketing skill) was one of only two members of the 1777 team actually born in Hambledon.[12]

Joseph Aburrow, who in 1792 was succeeding his father as church repairer, emerges again in 1818. This time, his account against the Overseers (among those displayed at *The George*) shows he was still a carpenter, and also an acknowledged coffin-maker:

				£	s.	d.
1818	Nov.	20th.	Joseph Aburrows Bill to the Overseers of Eastmeon Workhouse			
		20th.	To 100 of 10d. nails	0	0	10
		29th.	To a coffin for William Phillips	0	12	0
	Dec.	3rd.	To 100 of 10d. nails	0	0	10
		3rd.	To 1 gimblett	0	0	3
		3rd.	To 1 pad lock	0	1	8
		21st.	To whetting a handsaw	0	0	6
				£0	16	1
			Remains due to me for making Mrs. Smiths coffin and Miles wifes coffin, from 10 shillings to 12 shillings remain due to me		4	0
				£1	0	1

Joseph ABurrow.

Another James Aburrow, born in East Meon in 1809, was working as a cordwainer in Buriton in 1851.[13] His younger son, Alfred, born in 1841, became a wheelwright, married Ellen Porter, and returned to East Meon to live and work at 'Drayton Mill and Cottage', probably one of the seven mills mentioned in the Domesday Survey, and certainly the Shutt Mill of the 1747 Parliamentary Survey, which he rented from the Westbury Estate for £9 per annum. The water-mill still ground corn, though probably on a diminishing scale, but the premises included ample space for what developed into the multiple business of timber-yard, sawyers, wheelwrights and blacksmiths. The highly specialised trade of wheelwright, formerly of great importance when all wheeled road vehicles depended on the wheelwrights' skill, called for great expertise on the part of woodworker and blacksmith, who combined to produce the finished article; and, of course, wheelwrights did more than make wheels—they built complete wagons, carts and other vehicles.

Alfred and Ellen had four surviving children, all of whom spent their lives in the family business. Alfred, the eldest, like his father, was a wheelwright, carpenter and sawyer; Harry became blacksmith, Stephen another wheelwright, and Nellie the book-keeper. As both family and business expanded, father Alfred opened a branch in East Meon village, building a wheelwrights' and blacksmiths' shop fronting The Square (where East Meon Stores now stands), the premises extending across the stream to the back of *The George,* and including the old village pound. Thereafter Stephen and Harry, married men, lived in the village and worked as wheelwrights; whilst Alfred and Nellie, both single, remained at Drayton, and, after their father's death in 1894, and their mother's subsequently, ran the timber-yard and sawyers, motive power being supplied by one or more steam traction engines. Meanwhile, Hampshire wagons and carts were built by Stephen and Harry, using techniques handed down by their forefathers, reaching standards of craftsmanship appreciated far and wide; and more than one East Meon man, enduring the horrors of World War I in Flanders, was cheered by the sight of horse-drawn wagons bearing the familiar name-plate of 'E. Aburrow and Sons'.

After that war, replacement of horses and wagons by tractors and trailers spelt the demise of the wheelwright, whose craft could not adapt to the agricultural revolution. The Drayton timber-yard was given up about 1947, following the deaths of Harry, Alfred and Nellie. Harry's sons, Jack and Ben (whom we met in the last chapter) took over the other branch on their uncle Stephen's retirement. But the writing was on the wall, Ben soon retired from the partnership, and Jack, after 'diversifying' with a taxi side to the business, eventually also retired, and, in 1965, emigrated to Victoria, Australia, having donated his wheelwrights' tools to the Curtis Museum at Alton. 'With the passing of the farm wagon there has gone a race of men who were artists to the tip of their very sensitive fingers'.[14] Equally sadly, for the first time in 500 or more years, East Meon and its neighbourhood was without an Aburrow.

Notwithstanding comments about deeply-rooted village families, there have, of course, been individuals whose comparatively short residence has been noteworthy. Two such people, Lady Peel and Morley Horder, in no way connected, came on the scene in 1913 and 1926 respectively; and, ignoring chronology for once, I propose first to say something of the latter, and then to discuss the countess at greater length.

In 1926 the Court House and Hall, the latter having survived from the 14th century, were in a sorry state. The splendid hall itself housed farm workers and their families, following its crude conversion into uncomfortable and unattractive 'flats'. Surrounding buildings consisted of cowsheds, implement and other sheds, and the scene was completed by a dirty pond and a midden, as described by John Macdonald 20 years previously. The ancient and prestigious building, for over five centuries a symbol of authority, had deteriorated into a shabby farmhouse sited among equally shabby (and smelly) surroundings.

Then, providentially, came a man determined to restore it to its former status, not with a speculator's eye, but as a home for his family. He was Percy Richard Morley Horder, an eminent architect with a specialised aptitude for restoring old properties. Under his experienced direction, both buildings and grounds underwent sympathetic reconstruction and modernisation. To use the words of a subsequent owner. 'he had fallen under the spell of the Court House, and made it his home till he died in 1944. His painstaking restoration of the old fabric, and conversion of the farmyard into an attractive terraced garden, would have been hard to better'.[15]

Not content with these achievements, Horder purchased and restored a number of village cottages, most dating back to Tudor or earlier days, all thatched, and suffering from neglect. These were 'Kews Cottages' in Workhouse Lane, Nos. 1 and 2 High Street (now 'Hockley Cottage'), Nos. 1 and 2 'Brook Cottages', 'Bottle Ale Cottages' and 'Frogmore Cottage'. Every restoration was undertaken with characteristic thoroughness and good taste and, following Horder's death, his widow conveyed all except 'Hockley Cottage' to the local authority, who still own them.

What sort of a man was Horder? His chauffeur for several years in the 1930s, Herbert Goddard, grew to know him pretty well: 'He was one of the leading architects in the country, and I drove and looked after his 4-litre Bentley and Morris Oxford. He had an abrupt manner, but a clever brain, and, in his professional capacity was a perfectionist. I am sure all the restoration work he carried out in the village was due to dedication—

never a money-making exercise. At the time he was in his sixties (born 1870), and slightly eccentric in some ways. He held strong views on eating wholesome food—would never eat tinned foods, and insisted on wholemeal bread baked in the village'.

Apart from becoming a member of the parish council in 1931 (and resigning the following year), Horder took little part in local affairs, possibly being more interested in buildings than people, and today his name is almost forgotten. Yet, from altruistic motives, he did more than any other to preserve and restore buildings of historic and architectural interest. The 1930s was a time when old cottages were pulled down simply because they were out of repair, and without Horder's activities the village may well have been irrevocably mutilated.

Any attempt to understand the unusual character of Eleanor Countess Peel, who made herself this century's biggest local landowner, demands knowledge of her background and, to a lesser extent, that of her husband. Her father, James Williamson, son of a Lancaster linoleum manufacturer, was born in 1842, and brought up in the family business which he developed and expanded with depots and factories abroad. Meanwhile, he subscribed generously to charities, but displayed more than a normal share of eccentricities. In 1885 he gave a breakfast in Lancaster, when 10,000 people sat down to his bacon and eggs, bread, marmalade, butter and tea. Having been elected a Liberal M.P. in 1886, he retired from parliament in his early 50s and was created Lord Ashton, only to be confronted with political attacks alleging he had 'bought' his peerage.

Stung by such hostility during the first 1910 election, he publicly threatened to withdraw from every charity and organisation to which he had hitherto subscribed; a threat carried out to the full when the attacks were repeated at the following year's municipal elections. He had previously showered the City of Lancaster with gifts totalling over half a million pounds, yet refused to subscribe another penny to any local charity, though he later gave away thousands of pounds in London's East End.

Having quarrelled violently with Lancaster town council, matters were patched up and he generously built a magnificent new town hall. But prior to its completion, the council annoyed him, and he not only declined to attend the opening ceremony, but ever after refused even to look at the building, drawing his carriage blinds when passing by. He seldom used his magnificent London house, preferring when in London to stay at a hotel near Euston Station 'because they made such a good apple-pie'. Ashton died in 1930 aged 87, leaving the then tremendous fortune of £10,000,000, but no will. So, after payment of death duties, his only child, Eleanor, became immediately entitled to half the residue of his estate, plus a reversionary interest in the other half, expectant on the death of the widow (his third wife).

Eleanor, born in 1872, was married in 1899 to William Robert Wellesly Peel, grandson of the famous Sir Robert, and son of the first Viscount, Speaker of the House of Commons. Her father's main wedding gift was a settlement of £800,000, probably an ingredient in an 'arranged' marriage, rather than a love-match. Peel sat as Liberal Unionist M.P. for a Manchester Division (1900–06), and for Taunton (1909–12), in which latter year he inherited the viscountcy. After service as Colonel of the Bedfordshire Yeomanry, he became Joint Parliamentary Secretary to the National Service Department in 1917, Under Secretary for War in 1919, Chancellor of the Duchy of Lancaster in 1921, as well as unpaid Minister of Transport, and Secretary of State for India in 1922 and again in 1928. In 1929 he was created the first earl and ultimately became chairman of the Royal Commission on Palestine.

Being so affluent from the commencement of their marriage, it was understandable that prior to World War I the Peels decided to build a splendid country house, regardless of cost. In 1913, after much searching, they found the perfect place near the summit of Hyden Hill in East Meon parish, two miles south of the village, 700 feet above sea level and within yards of the South Hampshire Ridgeway. The elevated position commanded extensive views across gentle slopes to the south, with the Solent glittering beyond, and the Isle of Wight's distant rolling hills on the horizon.

The air was considered clean and invigorating, and the site, just below the crest of Hyden Hill, was sheltered from the north winds, whilst woods gave protection from the east. Accessibility to London, vital to a politician, was no problem, with cars rapidly coming into general use; and finally, an unlimited supply of pure spring water was at hand. The Peel's head chauffeur, Lewis Tyrode, a practical man not given to flights of fancy, described what he saw on a midsummer's day in 1913: 'The first impression was one of complete peace. The sloping downland was thick with wild strawberries, a number of grazing sheep, and a variety of wild flora and fauna'.

The site, and the major part of the estate of which it formed part, was purchased from Lord Hotham's trustees. Lady Peel had previously had dealings with Hooydonk Brothers, who, as 'Decorative Artists', prepared and executed elaborate interior schemes for homes of the 'moneyed classes'. She turned to this firm to design a country mansion, complete with decorations and furnishings, though Hooydonk Brothers called in London architects to prepare architectural drawings of the shell of the building. In the spring of 1914 work of levelling and digging foundations began, with direct labour, mostly local. The Peels, in order to watch and supervise building activity, adapted and took up temporary residence in a nearby farmhouse, Coombe Cross. Tyrode continues the story:

> Alas, in August 1914, war began, building work ceased, and the house at Coombe Cross had to do for the next 10 years, for it was not until the Summer of 1919 that building recommenced. Work then proceeded apace, with a large body of artisans and labourers, steam tractors and lorries moving chalk and fetching materials. Bricks were specially made at Rowlands Castle brickworks, limestone, imported from Belgium, was landed at Littlehampton, taken by train to Havant, and finally completed its journey by lorry. The main staircase was made by a Gosport firm. By the Autumn of 1924 the house, christened 'Leydene', after the hollow immediately to the south called Leydene Bottom, was sufficiently advanced for the owners to move in, though not completed till early 1925. Garages and cottages were finished by Easter 1925, after which the sunken rose garden, hard tennis court, main fruit and vegetable gardens, drives and walks followed.

The house was magnificent, with its huge and lofty entrance hall, backed by a handsome wooden staircase of unique design, and spacious, elegant reception rooms. These rooms, and indeed all other main rooms, had beautifully moulded 'Georgian style' ceilings and throughout the building the impression was of elegance without vulgarity. Hooydonk Brothers more than justified the faith placed in them by a demanding employer, though Auguste van Hooydonk, on his frequent visits, was invariably faced with luncheon of cold pheasant—not his favourite food—because, according to her ladyship, the pheasants were shot on the estate and she could not afford butchers' prices. Nevertheless, Hooydonk and Eleanor Peel struck up a real and lasting friendship.

As for the gardens and pleasure grounds, George Cannings (who, in Mesopotamia, 'would have gladly paid £1 for a teaspoon of water') worked there for 17 years:

To start with there were 14 gardeners, including a man who looked after and worked the horse used for haulage. A donkey pulled the lawn mower. I was in the kitchen garden nearly all the time, but also carted large quantities of coke from West Meon railway station for greenhouse fuel. The kitchen garden comprised seven acres, plus an orchard and extensive greenhouses, where grapes, peaches, nectarines, tomatoes, cucumbers and potted plants were grown. I was always well treated and content with my 30s. a week wage and rent-free cottage and free firewood.

From 1927 onwards the summers saw brilliant weekend parties, the guests once including Mr. Winston Churchill (as he then was) whom Lady Peel subsequently described as 'a very rude man'. In winter, pheasant shooting was organised by the head of three gamekeepers, Harry Dean, tall and heavily built, with rosy cheeks and a genial disposition, and invariably dressed in a traditional heavy tweed knickerbocker suit. Beaters included estate employees, other local men and schoolboys. Jack Aburrow vividly recalls such days when, as a boy of 12, and wearing short trousers, he endured painful bramble scratches on his bare legs to earn 5s. a day plus bread, cheese and beer for lunch, and, if lucky, a rabbit worth 8d. to take home at dusk. The shooting party usually lunched in a rustic timber 'lodge' in Hyden Wood, which was accidentally burnt down through the excessive enthusiasm of a footman sent there on a shooting day to ensure a warm lunch-time fire for Lord Peel and his guests.

As for the lifestyle and characters of the couple who created what is thought to be the last 'purpose-built' English mansion, East Meon people (apart from employees) saw little of Lord Peel. His distinguished political career necessitated having a London home, No. 34 Holland Park, W.1, where he mostly lived except for weekends and parliamentary vacations. His personal chauffeur, Clement Allman, until recently farming 190 acres near 'Leydene', describes him as a considerate employer, though strict about good time-keeping. When his lordship was driven to other parts of the country in his 5½-litre Daimler, staying overnight in the best hotels, Allman was similarly accommodated, and when in London Allman had his own flat at 34 Holland Park.

A picture emerges of an essentially serious-minded individual, probably too fully occupied with affairs of state to regard 'Leydene' as more than a magnificent 'country retreat'. Certainly he was a keen game shot, not only at 'Leydene', but annually on Scottish grouse moors near Beaufort Castle, and Allman remembers Peel's regular visits to the shooting grounds of an Inverness gunsmith for a 'warm-up' at clay pigeons to get his eye in before tackling grouse. Yet even shooting parties were apparently a means to an end, affording opportunities for diplomatic entertainment of British and other political personalities.

Eleanor Peel had inherited from her father an active brain, outstanding financial acumen, a pronounced antipathy towards local authorities, and (in old age at least) an urge to benefit certain charitable causes. Puzzling though was an extreme reserve almost amounting to pathological shyness. She abhorred London, was a fresh air fanatic, habitually 'dressed like a tramp' in ankle-length shabby black clothes, but found some degree of contentment at 'Leydene', though preferring the even greater isolation available in Scotland. Mother of a son and daughter, she had no liking for children, either her own or other people's. By 1928 she was at war with the then local authority, Petersfield R.D.C., whom she sued for £7 17s. 7d., being 'estimated cost of keeping six visitors for four days in excess of their invitation' through the council's failure to clear snowbound roads!

For her, life at 'Leydene' tended to be quiet, perhaps lonely. Apart from a friendship with Lady and Miss Du Boulay, her tenants at what was then Upper House, Oxenbourne (now Oxenbourne House), she seemed without local friends. On a typical non-entertaining day she would appear outside the mansion about mid-morning, carrying a large basket filled with bread and toast. After inspecting the rainfall gauge and weather chart she invariably met and spoke, often at length, with Tyrode, now the head of three chauffeurs (excluding Allman, his lordship's chauffeur, usually in London). Next came a shorter conversation with the head gardener, who always had 11 or more other gardeners under him. But the climax of the morning was a visit to her herd of pedigree Saddleback pigs— each of whom had its own name—the recipients of the bread and toast.

Leonard Cannings, cousin of George Cannings and living at Coombe Cross Cottages, was one of the gardeners from about 1922 till 1939, working in the glasshouses, then in the kitchen garden, and also tending pigs:

> Her Ladyship was very fond of her pigs, and when a sow had to be taken by lorry to be mated with a prize boar, she would travel with it to ensure all went according to plan. I also remember an occasion when I was trimming the grass edges of small circles cut in the lawn where trees and shrubs were planted, when I realised her ladyship, watch in hand, was standing beside me. I must have looked startled, because she said she was timing each trimming operation so as to calculate how long it would take to trim all the circles. Another peculiar arrangement affecting my job arose when the grounds were opened to the public, and we gardeners, having had to put in overtime beforehand, were each paid an extra 5s. in cash with the balance of our wage entitlement in kind—tomatoes!'

Len Cannings' wife, Edith, employed as a kitchen maid at 'Leydene' from 1926 to 1930, provides a glimpse of life completely in the 'upstairs, downstairs' tradition:

> The cook had her own sitting room, and I think the lady's maid had hers too. In the servants' hall the butler presided over two footmen, four housemaids, and the hall boy, but I and the scullery maid were the lowest of the low and not allowed to use the servants' hall. Our only sitting room was the kitchen. When Lady Peel was alone at 'Leydene' she often knitted, read, and listened to the wireless all at the same time, and frequently had nothing but a bowl of soup for lunch, usually served on an outdoor verandah, irrespective of the weather. Sometimes I was taken by road to 34 Holland Park for a few days, with a housemaid, a footman and the lady's maid. Mr. Tyrode drove an open car, Lady Peel sat in the front seat beside him doing a crossword puzzle, and the rest of us in the back were almost frozen to death. In the four years I was in her employ I cannot remember Lady Peel ever speaking directly to me.

After buying the estate on which 'Leydene' was built, Eleanor Peel acquired numerous adjacent farms and estates until her land empire comprised over 10,300 acres. Taking a practical interest in its management, she frequently accompanied a partner of her agents, Hewitt and Lee, when matters such as repairs, improvements and rent adjustments necessitated farm inspections. Though habitually striking a hard bargain, and rightly described as 'close with her money', she was a good landlord in the sense that repairs or improvements which were her responsibility were always carried out to a high standard. But contact with tenants on a personal level was, with one exception, virtually non-existent. Indeed, she would go out of her way to avoid casual meetings with everyone, whether they were staff, tenants or other country folk. The exception was Cecil Kille, tenant of Stoneylands Farm, who supplied dairy produce to 'Leydene'. He was widely regarded as her 'favourite', but his daughter (now Mrs. Joan Walther), who as a child rode her pony to the big house with urgent deliveries of cream or whatever was needed at short notice, thinks Lady Peel simply respected her father's hard-working and thrifty character.

Each summer the Peels and most domestic staff from 'Leydene' and 34 Holland Park headed north for a prolonged stay in Scotland, usually at Beaufort Castle, Inverness-shire. Staff travelled by night train, and on arrival had a day off duty to recover, and then worked for 11 weeks without a break, occasionally till midnight, until rewarded with another day off before returning to London. The Peels travelled by car, sometimes calling at Lancaster en route for business conferences relating to the linoleum business. Following Lord Ashton's death, Eleanor satisfied her father's wish and her own business ability by becoming governing director of the company, with her husband as chairman. The business continued to prosper.

In Scotland when Peel was leading grouse-shooting parties on the moors, Eleanor never joined these expeditions, going salmon fishing instead with Tyrode, whose position in the household became increasing important: 'Officially I was chauffeur, but it might be more correct to describe my job as the buffer between Lady Peel and the social world she didn't care a lot for'. So perhaps it was unsurprising that Tyrode, too, became a salmon fisherman, sharing the sport with his employer, and also making a second fishing trip to Scotland with her each spring.

In 1937, Lord Peel died at 'Leydene', aged 70, and was buried in East Meon churchyard, having shown virtually no interest in local affairs. Two years later Eleanor bought Hendersyde, a famous 1,600-acre estate in southern Scotland. Disliking the existing mansion, she promptly pulled it down and built a more modern residence; but, reluctant to miss the Tweed's salmon-fishing season during the rebuilding, stayed in a cottage by the river, the home of elderly Mr. and Mrs. A. Brown, where 'she lived in the most simple fashion, just like any of the village folk'.

Eleanor, Dowager Countess Peel, died at 'Hendersyde Park' on 9 November 1949, aged 77, survived by her son, the second earl, and her daughter, Lady Doris Blacker, and, like her husband, she was buried at East Meon. Her estate, estimated at over four million pounds, was cut by death duties to just under one million, which, after payment of modest legacies and annuities, became a trust fund, the income from which was particularly to benefit 'old people and needy cases where people have fallen on evil days through no fault of their own'. Significantly, her will precluded grants to 'charitable bodies primarily devoted to children, or which are under the control of the central or any local government'. The capital value of the trust fund has since risen to over two million pounds, and income for 1982 comfortably exceeded £200,000. 'Leydene' and 100 acres had been bought by the Admiralty in 1949, and in May 1953, the remainder of the estate was sold by auction in 51 lots, many of which were gratefully acquired by sitting tenant farmers. An era had ended.

Lewis Tyrode, the grocer's boy who for 44 years worked as trusted chauffeur, friend and right-hand man, and perhaps knew and understood Lady Peel better than any other living person, was rewarded by his multi-millionairess employer with an annuity of £5 a week. Ethel Loasby, her maid for 20 years, received a £400 legacy, and Mrs. H. Brown, widow of her boatman, had an annuity of £2 a week. Almost the last word came from the High Court which, in the person of Mr. Justice Barnard, decreed that certain passages in the will which would cause 'pain and embarrassment' should be omitted when probate was granted and the will's contents made public.

As for her dislike of children and local authorities, predictably the pendulum swung the other way with her progeny. Her son, Arthur, who succeeded to the viscountcy, became Lord Lieutenant and an Honorary Freeman of Lancaster, and President of the Lancashire Association of Boys' Clubs for 35 years, also holding many other public offices. Her daughter, Lady Doris Blacker, travelled extensively with her father as his unofficial personal assistant, and undoubtedly inherited or acquired many of his characteristics. In turn, she became a London County Councillor, Mayoress of Westminster, and a Hampshire County Councillor from 1952-74; as well as being a magistrate, first in London and later at Midhurst. Her involvement in these and other public activities was marked by a special concern for the welfare of children; and, continuing the family saga, her twin sons are both county councillors, David in West Sussex and Brian in Hampshire.

Chapter Twelve

'...NEVER HAD IT SO GOOD'

AFTER WORLD WAR I, life in East Meon gradually returned to normal as demobilisation got under way. Changes in the way of life were slow to appear. Indeed, on the very day following the longed-for armistice, the parish council's meeting was largely devoted to the formation of another Rat and Sparrow Club (1d. per rat tail, and 3d. for a dozen sparrow heads). And a few months later the council solemnly agreed to pay an allotment holder 10s. for unexhausted manurial value when his tenancy ended. Isaac Wren, in his 16th year as chairman of the council, may well have wondered whether four years of world-shattering catastrophe had really just concluded.

Agriculture and its ancillary trades still dominated village life, with saddlers, blacksmiths, thatchers, wheelwrights and millers part of the scene. Horses provided most motive power on the land and for road transport, though cars were increasing. Their proud owners now included not only Colonel Le Roy Lewis, but also Dr. Jones and Major Reginald Nicholson, the new owner of Bereleigh, who had a Napier; whilst on a more modest plane, Bill Luff's vehicles available for hire—a wagonette and dogcart—were supplemented by a grey 'T'-model Ford, and Savage and Parsons' new delivery van, the first in the village, was a Ford, too. *Kelly's 1923 Directory* listed David Coles and Son as 'motor engineers', yet neither electricity nor main drainage had arrived, mains water was only available at scattered standpipes, and the perennial problem of flooding constituted a recurrent nightmare.

Occasionally some local sensation became a great talking point, as when Sam Hardy and George Silk crossed swords in 1919. The former, living and farming at Lower Farm, was Master of the Hambledon Hunt, owned and drove a four-in-hand coach—a colourful and slightly unpredictable character. George Silk of Frogmore Mill, a half-mile downstream from Lower Farm, claimed to be entitled, by virtue of his mill ownership, to control the flow of water throughout a stretch of the river extending to Lower Farm, where Hardy had recently constructed a pond. When repeated requests by Silk for Hardy to open certain hatches were ignored, Silk went personally to Lower Farm to assert his rights by opening the hatches himself.

Hardy's tactless reaction was to send his gardener to forbid this step, whereupon Silk promptly threw the luckless man into the pond. This was good, robust stuff, but resulted in Silk being prosecuted before the magistrates, and convicted of assault and battery. But matters were not to rest there, for Silk next issued a High Court writ against Hardy, claiming damages, a declaration of his rights, and an injunction to restrain future interference; and when the case was heard at Winchester Assizes, judgment went entirely in favour of the plaintiff, together with an order for substantial costs.

The churches still played an important, though lessening, part in local life, and in 1918 young Elizabeth Parsons was appointed organist at All Saints' church, her salary of

£10 per annum being far more than that paid to the clerk of the parish council. Though Edwardian living standards in the more affluent households were destined to fade, the process was slow, partly because employment prospects for village girls continued to be mainly domestic.

Retired bank manager Thornton Hassell, living with his invalid wife at Upper House, Oxenbourne, was far from being a member of the landed gentry, yet his domestic set-up was considered normal for a man of his status: employing a resident cook and house parlour-maid, a gardener and garden-boy; and keeping a cow to provide household milk, cream and butter. In 1924, Ellen ('Nellie') Christmas, a village girl then barely 15, 'went into service' there as house parlour-maid; and for the next five years her weekly off-duty time consisted of a half-day, usually commencing about 3.30 and ending at nine. Expected to attend church every Sunday—alternatively morning and evening services, her final duty at night was carrying the family silver to the master's bedroom and placing it beside his bed, where he kept a weighted cudgel to protect it.

Nellie made her own morning and afternoon uniforms, her employers' annual Christmas present being the material needed for that purpose! When Mrs. Hassell's rheumatic illness became increasingly severe, professional round-the-clock nursing was really essential. However, that work was added to the parlour-maid's duties, who became her mistress's day and night nurse, even sleeping in her bedroom, until Mrs. Hassell died in 1929; Nellie's wage having been increased by then to £24 a year. When, following the death she told the master she wished to leave to see something of the outside world, she forfeited her annual holiday.

A year after Nellie's arrival at Upper House, a 16-year-old fatherless boy, Herbert (Herbie) Goddard, became employed by farmer Philip Berry, also at Oxenbourne. Responsible for two horses, Prince and Diamond, he had to arrive at the stables at 5 a.m., and to be out in the fields at seven, when the head carter had received daily orders from the farmhouse. Herbie's starting wage was 24s. a week, progressing to 32s. after four years. Then in 1929, he too sought a change of scene and a completely different job—industrial engineering near Manchester; returning to East Meon two years later, where we have already encountered him as Morley Horder's chauffeur. Meanwhile, Nellie was working, still as a house parlour-maid, in Cheshire, at St John's Wood and at Mill Hill School before also coming back to East Meon and marrying Herbie in 1933.

In the late 1920s and early 1930s the worldwide economic slump and agricultural depression brought unemployment in its wake, alleviated in East Meon by the many jobs created at 'Leydene', where most of the army of gardeners, chauffeurs, gamekeepers and domestic staff were recruited locally. Poverty still existed, and times were hard and drab for many. Indeed, between 1926–31 nine villagers died in the Petersfield Workhouse, euphemistically labelled '1 Ramshill, Petersfield' in the parish burial register. Yet small incidents still caught the imagination, as when, in 1930, the church weather-cock was being re-gilded by steeple-jacks, during whose lunchtime absence cousins Stephanie and Alfreyda Aburrow climbed the dizzy heights before pausing and loudly announcing their achievement as the village streets filled with incredulous and apprehensive spectators.

World War II came, dragged on for nearly six years, and ended less than forty years ago; since when village life, in step with farming, has perhaps changed more fundamentally than in the preceding millenium. Vastly accelerated mechanisation in the broadest sense—of transport, household equipment, even entertainment in the home—has led to job mobility, working wives being the norm, and television largely dominating leisure hours. Thankfully, 'the welfare state', born in 1948, has, for all its limitations, almost outlawed poverty, while secondary and higher education have opened up new horizons for all. As for housing, there is now a 'good mix' of owner-occupied, local authority rented, and privately-owned rented accommodation, the proportion of the last category inevitably diminishing. Successive local authorities have made a vital impact on the situation, doing much to counter the widespread cry of rural housing shortages being aggravated by outsiders paying high prices for country dwellings as retirement homes or weekend cottages. Certainly a number of old, formerly tenanted properties which fell vacant, mainly in the 1950s and 1960s, were bought and refurbished by newcomers; and an annual average of one or two houses are built, either where 'infilling' is permitted or modern farm workers' cottages are provided.

East Hampshire District Council still owns the nine ancient thatched cottages restored by Morley Horder—distinctly unusual 'council houses'—as well as three conventional purpose-built housing estates. In 1980 the council completed a block of 16 flats for the elderly right in the centre of the village, and erection of yet another 21 council houses is currently under way. Fortunately, no one housing category at present 'swamps' the others, nor obtrudes too markedly upon the village's outstanding historic and architectural features. At the same time a significant proportion of council house tenants are exercising their right to purchase at a discount based on length of prior occupation. Disregarding political implications, it cannot be a bad thing for owner-occupied and rented housing to be intermixed rather than grouped in separate socially divisive enclaves.

Consistent with national trends, the parish church, once the hub of village life, is no longer such, though its influence is disproportionate to the number of its regular worshippers; nor are we—the villagers—a largely self-contained social and economic unit. Electricity and main drainage eventually arrived, flooding was overcome, and more recently a new school and village hall erected—all major contributions towards civilised existence. Much of the village, including Frogmore, is designated a conservation area, which does *not* mean it is moribund. Shops are few, but include an efficient privately-owned 'supermarket-style' store, and we continue to have our own policeman, motor garage, post office, two pubs, and mobile library. Judged by material standards, life for most is *comparatively* easy, and certainly far more comfortable than ever before. Sadly, some unemployment exists, particularly among school-leavers, petty vandalism is not unknown, and age-old links with the past were severed with the departure of the surviving members of the Hobbs and Aburrow families.

So what sort of community is left? A partial answer, expressed negatively, is that the village is *not* a 'commuter dormitory' within the usual and rather unattractive meaning of that expression, still less an 'overspill area'.

Of persons employed within the parish, farm workers still constitute the largest occupational group, and those self-employed include shopkeepers, a builder, electrician, heating engineer, and baker (the latter also owning the part-time fish and chip shop). Most wage-earners travel daily, usually moderate distances, to employment outside the village in the service of local authorities, public utility and transport undertakings, hospitals, educational establishments, shops, offices, surgeries, and building contractors. Likewise, members of the professions, of the armed forces, and of the merchant navy obtain their livelihood beyond the parish.

To quote statistics just once more, the parish population at the 1981 census, subject to deducting approximately 450 'resident personnel' at H.M.S. *Mercury,* was almost exactly 1,000, very slightly less than that of 1901; and this lack of population growth may well be an important factor in the village having retained its identity and character, why it remains a *community.* Newcomers, since the last war have, generally speaking, become well integrated, and often enriched, without dominating village life. Football, cricket and badminton are played enthusiastically; the British Legion (Women's Section), and Horticultural Society all hold regular meetings; volunteers ensure that 'meals-on-wheels' and a well-supported luncheon club function efficiently. For the young, a youth club and Scouts Group are very much alive, and the school's continual existence is not threatened. But perhaps today's most unifying local activity is fund-raising, often, but not necessarily, for charities. Whether finance has been needed for the new village hall, the Queen's 25th jubilee celebrations, sporting organisations, the Scouts Group, a send-off for a recently retired policeman, or national or local charities, achievements have been quite staggering. One family alone, led and inspired by an elderly widow, has organised the raising of funds probably totalling over £10,000 during recent years, cogent evidence of a 'caring society'.

As a valediction, I intend to finish on a personal note, not personal to me, but to two people who would never regard themselves as other than 'ordinary' village folk—none other than Herbie and Nellie Goddard. We already know something of their early days in Oxenbourne, which were followed by a brief spreading of wings, return to the village and marriage in 1933, the receiving of London evacuees in 1939, and Herbie's fire-fighting during 'the blitz'. Their story continues.

By 1943 Herbie was serving with a British army R.E.M.E. unit in North Africa and Italy. 'During that time I said to myself if ever I get out of this alive and return home I'll try to do something for East Meon. So when I did get back and Colonel 'Jock' Swayne said new parish councillors were needed, I put my name forward and was elected'. That was in 1947, after which Herbie served as a councillor for the next 37 years, including 16 consecutive years as chairman. Living and working at the time in the centre of the village (first as manager, then owner of the garage business), escape from constant involvement in local affairs was impossible; and then, in 1968, he also became chairman of the Village Hall Management Committee.

A move developed for replacement of the old wooden and corrugated-iron Village Institute (originally the 'East Meon Reading Room, Library and Coffee House' opened in 1881) by a modern hall; a project supported by the vast majority of parishioners, except those who understandably resented its being sited near their homes, and therefore tenaciously opposed it. Innumerable committee and public meetings, conferences with site owners, lawyers, surveyors, planners and architects, not to mention many a fund-raising exercise, followed. Yet, over the years, Herbie led a dedicated Hall Committee who eventually overcame daunting obstacles to be rewarded with the creation of arguably the finest village hall in the county. At times he was lobbied as chairman of one or other of the local bodies primarily concerned, almost hourly, for feelings can run as high in parish government as at national level.

Dogged determination, patience, sheer persistence, unselfishness and complete integrity elevated Herbie to the roll of mayor of the village in everything but name—a combination of father figure, wise man, respected leader and solver of problems. More than half a lifetime of service to the community has matched or exceeded that of any one person. Meanwhile, Nellie, his loyal and staunch supporter for 50 years, has found time to be founder-member, then chairman, and still committee member of the Women's Section of the British Legion, Parochial Church Councillor for 40 years till recently, and chairman of the Over 60s Club throughout its 19-year existence. East Meon is blessed with a tremendous natural and unforced community spirit; and though its future is unknown, the outlook must surely be hopeful if a kindly Providence will very, very occasionally produce a Herbie and Nellie Goddard.

GLOSSARY

Chapter One

Charter: a formal document evidencing a grant of (*inter alia*) land.

Currency bars: iron bars, sword-shaped and 30–35 inches long, used as currency before coinage came into use.

Hide: originally a land unit capable of being ploughed annually by one plough, and sufficient to support one family; often amounting to 120 acres, though, especially in the case of poor quality land, sometimes a larger area. Also called a *carucate*.

Hundred: a sub-division of a county, having its own court. Originally perhaps 100 hides in extent, being a district that furnished 100 warriors.

Pipe Rolls: written financial records of income and expenditure; at the highest level, sheriffs' accounts to the Exchequer; on a more local level, relating to a manor. The name originated from the parchments being wrapped round a rod or pipe.

Tithing: a sub-division of a hundred, of obscure origin, but perhaps a district containing 10 households, each responsible for the others.

Tithe terrier: a register or roll, used in conjunction with a tithe map, specifying details of each numbered unit.

Turnpike trust: a body authorised by Act of Parliament to collect tolls in consideration of providing and maintaining a road.

Virgate: a land measure, commonly a quarter of a hide, and therefore usually 30 acres, but variable.

Chapter Two

Assart: a forest clearing or enclosure.

Assize of bread and ale: a royal declaration made by Henry III in 1266–67, specifying permitted prices for sale of bread and ale, based, from time to time, on current prices of corn and malt.

Beadle: a petty officer of a parish, with power to punish minor offenders; also an under bailiff, one who makes a proclamation, and one who executes the mandates of an authority.

Corrody: allowance of food, or maintenance.

Churchetts: a fine payable in hens or corn. (*See fine*).

Coffer: a wooden chest for storing clothes, money and other valuables.

Crib: a manger or fodder receptacle.

Fine: fines, in a manorial context, were payments due to the lord, usually monetary, but sometimes in kind. When of an annual nature they approximated to groundrents, but included larger payments on the admission of each new tenant, payments called *merchets* on the marriage of a tenant's daughter, and a *heriot* on a tenant's death. (*See heriot*).

Grange: a granary or tithe-barn, a large barn for storing corn in the sheaf, and also a farmhouse and ancillary buildings.

Hayward: the manorial officer responsible for maintenance of fences and enclosures, especially to prevent cattle straying from the common into enclosed fields.

Heriot: a lord's right to seize the best beast (occasionally best chattel) belonging to a deceased tenant. In time, most heriots were commuted into cash sums.

Hogget or hoggett: a yearling sheep not yet shorn.

In lordship: land farmed or occupied by the lord, as distinct from being tenanted by copyholders; otherwise 'in demesne'.

Mortuary: the right of the Church to the second-best beast or chattel of a deceased copyhold tenant.

Pannage: the right to pasture swine in woodland. Also the payment due for exercising such right.

Pell: a skin or hide.

Pinder: the parish officer in charge of the pound.

Quarter: as a capacity of grain, etc., the British Imperial Quarter, equivalent to eight bushels or 64 gallons.

Sester: a sixth part of a *modius*—about a peck.

Slave: in Saxon society, just a slave, almost devoid of rights, though after the Conquest likely to be promoted into a smallholder.

Smallholder: a *bordar, cottar* or *cottager*, being a manorial tenant of lower status than a villager, cultivating five to eight acres.

Stoup: a bucket or drinking vessel.

Tithing-pence: payment by a tithing of a monetary sum at the holding of a manorial court in lieu of the roll of suitors being read.

Toll: a payment in cash or kind extracted by a national or local ruler, including, specifically, a proportion of grain or flour taken by a miller in payment for grinding.

Twibill: a double-headed axe.

Tun: a liquid measure, 252 gallons of wine, 216 gallons of ale.

Villager: in the Domesday Survey context, a villein—i.e. an unfree manorial tenant, usually cultivating about 30 acres.

Chapter Three

Amour or armour ryvetts (a peyer of): armour plates to protect the breast and back.

Andyern or andiron: a fire-dog with hooks at variable levels from which cooking spits were supported.

Armar: armour.

Banker: a cloth or tapestry covering for a form, bench or seat.

Brosh or Bruch: a brush.

Bushel: a measure of capacity used for corn, etc. The Winchester bushel, much used from Henry VIII's time contained 77.627lbs.

Byll: a kind of hatchet with a long blade and wooden handle in the same line with it; also a concave battle-axe.

Caliver: a light musket.

Carpet or carpette: a table-cloth.

Catels or cattells: chattels.

Cawdron: a cauldron, being a large kettle or other vessel for heating liquids.

Chafynge dyshe: a dish or saucepan for heating above a portable brazier.

Chawncell: a chancel.

Coborde or Cobbard: either a sideboard consisting of a long table for displaying plate, or a hanging cupboard fixed to a wall for use as a wardrobe.

Coffer or cofer: a chest, especially for money or treasure.

Commissary: an officer exercising spiritual or ecclesiastical jurisdiction as representative of the bishop in parts of his diocese; or one entrusted with the performance of an absent bishop's duties.

Curat or curate: properly a clergyman having the charge (*cure*) of a parish. The incumbent, though the word is now used to denote an assistant.

Dyaper: a rich figured cloth; also a kind of printed linen.

El or ell: a measure of cloth equal to 1¼ yards.

Flockbedde: a bed stuffed with wool, or pieces of cloth.

Good children: godchildren.

Grote: a groat, i.e. a silver coin worth 4d., after 1662 minted only as Maundy money.

Guild: primarily an association of medieval origin. Religious guilds provided masses for the dead.

Hennys: hens.

Heyfer: an heifer.

Hoggs and pyggs: hog formerly referred to the castrated male, and pig to the young of swine.

Honest apparell: decent clothing.

Irebound: ironbound; descriptive, for example, of cartwheels.

Kercheve: a square piece of cloth worn to cover the head and neck.

Keve: a fermenting vat for beer.

Kever: a shallow wooden tub.

Kyen or kine: the archaic plural of cow.

Lytte: a burial enclosure, a word still in use, with its spelling altered to liten or litten, as late as 1816.

Mark: not a coin in England, but a unit in accountancy valued at twenty silver pennies, namely 13s. 4d.

Masar or mazar: a cup of maple wood or other similar material.

Monethes mynd: the Requiem Mass celebrated on the 30th day after death or burial.

Moo: archaic form of 'more'.

Nuncupative will: an oral will.

Oon or on: one.

Paine: a penalty.

Panys or pannys: pans.

Pesys or pceses: pieces.

Platter or plater: a large, flat plate or dish.

Posnet: a small cooking pot with feet and handle.

Potynger: a pot-hanger or porridge bowl.

Preysyd indyfferently: valued impartially.

Pteynyng: pertaining.

Raile: a garment of fine linen formerly worn by women round the neck.

Rother beastes or bestes: black oxen used for ploughing, etc.

Ryvetts or rivets: *see under* amour ryvetts.

Shettes or shetes or shetis: sheets.

Sheyff (of arrows): a bundle of 24 arrows.

Stalle beysse or beys: a hive or skep of bees.

Stere: a steer.

Tegg: a sheep in its second year.

Tester: a bed canopy.

Tode of Wulle: a tod of wool (weighing about 28lbs.).

Vyinshete: a winnowing sheet.

Wether: a castrated male sheep.

Wulle or woll: wool.

Yewys or yowys: ewes, i.e. female sheep.

Yowtynge vat or vate: a vat for soaking barley.

Chapter Four

Bandlere: a bandoleer, being a shoulder belt for ammunition.

Cartboote: the right of a tenant to use his landlord's wood for repairing carts.

Churgion: a surgeon.

Coslett: a corslet or curass, being a defensive breastplate and backplate fastened together.

Fireboote: the right of a tenant to his landlord's wood for fuel.

Foulling peese: a fowling piece, i.e. a shotgun.

House boote, post boote, pale boote and rail boote: the right of a tenant to use his landlord's wood for repairing respectively his house, posts, pales and rails.

Kill: a kiln (in the case of the 1647 Survey, for drying hops).

Multon: a castrated male sheep.

Musket or muskett: from about 1588, an infantryman's handgun, with a 4½ft. barrel, its weight necessitating use of a forked rest.

Pike: an infantry weapon with a long, 16ft.–18ft. shaft and a sharp head like a spear.

Tithing-man: probably a term originally used to describe a tithing's elected representative, but, after the Conquest, a constable or his deputy.

Wattle: interwoven rods forming a hurdle, or used as building material when plastered with mud (wattle and daub).

Woodard: a woodward, being an officer to guard woods.

Chapter Seven

Couched: cleaned (or, more usually, partially cleaned) of couch-grass, a troublesome weed.

Steam ploughing: ploughing by means of a multiple-furrow metal plough drawn across a field by a cable attached to a winding drum on a stationary steam traction engine. The plough's return journey was achieved either by using a second engine on the other side of the field, or alternatively, with a moveable 'anchor' at one end of the run, in which case a reversible 'balance plough' was used.

Bavins: the same as bunts.

Brucellosis: contagious abortion.

Followers: heifers and other young female cattle destined, when older, to join a dairy herd.

Chapter Ten

V.A.D.: Voluntary Aid Detachment.

H.E.: high explosive.

'D' Day: the day on which the invasion of Europe was launched.

R.A.C.: Royal Armoured Corps.

D.L.I.: Durham Light Infantry.

D.C.L.I.: Duke of Cornwall's Light Infantry.

'Doodlebug': slang for a flying bomb, otherwise known as a 'V.I.'.

REFERENCES

ABBREVIATIONS

H.R.O.   Hampshire Record Office
P.R.O.   Public Record Office
V.C.H.   *Victoria County History of Hampshire*

Chapter One

1. H. W. Timperley and Edith Brill, *Ancient Trackways of Wessex* (1965).
2. Arthur Bryant, *The Medieval Foundation* (1966).
3. Barry Cunliffe, *The Regni* (1973).
4. E. Lewis and G. Walker, 'A Middle Bronze Age Settlement Site at Westbury, West Meon', *Proceedings Hants Field Club Archaeol. Soc.* 33, 1977, 33–43.
5. A. H. A. Hogg, *Hill-Forts of Britain* (1975).
6. Peter J. Reynolds, *Iron-Age Farm, The Butser Experiment* (1979).
7. Robert Downey, Anthony King and Grahame Soffe, 'The Hayling Island Temple and Religious Connections Across the Channel' in *Temples, Churches and Religion: Recent Research in Roman Britain,* edited by W. Rodwell (British Archaeological Reports, British Series 77 [i and ii] 1980).
8. Barry Cunliffe, *Iron Age Communities in Britain* (1974).
9. Ibid.
10. S. Sheppard Frere, *Britannia, A History of Roman Britain* (1967).
11. A. Moray Williams, 'The Roman–British Establishment at Stroud, near Petersfield, Hants', *Archaeological Journal,* vol. 65, 66 (1908–9).
12. Richard Whinney and George Walker, 'Salvage Excavations at Old Down Farm, East Meon', *Proceedings Hants Field Club Archaeol. Soc.* 36, 1980, 153–160.
13. K. S. Painter, 'Roman Sculpture from Hampshire, Somerset, Wiltshire, and Sussex', *British Museum Quarterly,* vol. 36 (1971–72).
14. J. E. Gover, 'Hampshire Place Names' (unpublished work, 1961, a copy deposited in The Library, University of Southampton).
15. R. W. Hooley, *Antiquaries Journal,* vol. 17, pt. 2 (1937).
16. Cunliffe, *The Regni* (1973).
17. S. C. Carpenter, *The Church in England 597-1688* (1954).
18. G. B. Grundy, 'Saxon Land Charters', *Archaeological Journal,* vols. 78, 83 (1921–28).
19. J. M. Kemble, *Codex Diplom. 1243.*
20. P. H. Hase, 'The Parish in Hampshire' (unpublished work, 1975, deposited in H.R.O.).
21. John Morris (gen. ed.), *Domesday Book—Hampshire* (1982; county editor, Julian Munby).

Chapter Two

1. Hase, op. cit.
2. *Domesday Book—Hampshire* (1982), op. cit.
3. Hase, op. cit.
4. Pat. 7 Edw. 1, m. 5d.
5. H.R.O. Pipe Roll 159270.
6. H.R.O. Pipe Roll 159270A.
7. H.R.O. Pipe Roll 159306.
8. H.R.O. Pipe Roll 159307.

9.   H.R.O. Pipe Roll 159308.
10.   H.R.O. Pipe Roll 159311.
11.   H.R.O. Pipe Roll 159317.
12.   H.R.O. Pipe Roll 159308.
13.   H.R.O. Pipe Roll 159317.
14.   H.R.O. Pipe Roll 159321.
15.   H.R.O. Pipe Roll 159322.
16.   H.R.O. microfilm of document at P.R.O.
17.   H.R.O. Pipe Roll 159361.
18.   Leslie Bradley, 'Some Medical Aspects of Plague', in *The Plague Reconsidered* (Local Population Studies supplement, 1977).
19.   Christopher Morris, 'Plague in Britain', in *The Plague Reconsidered,* op. cit.
20.   H.R.O. Pipe Roll 159358.
21.   E. Lipson, *The Economic History of England, Vol. 1* (1966).
22.   H.R.O. 80/9.
23.   H.R.O. 80/10.
24.   H.R.O. 80/13.
25.   Parl. R. (Rec. Com.), v, 475–476.

Chapter Three

1.   H.R.O. Consistory Court will dated 6 June 1522.
2.   H.R.O. Archdeaconry Court will dated 22 October 1538.
3.   H.R.O. Consistory Court will dated 18 April 1548, and undated inventory.
4.   H.R.O. 'Unclassified' Court will dated 10 September 1550, and undated inventory.
5.   H.R.O. Consistory Court will dated 14 August 1558, and inventory dated 16 November 1558.
6.   H.R.O. 'Unclassified' Court will dated 13 November 1558.
7.   Christopher Morris, 'Plague in Britain', in *The Plague Reconsidered,* op. cit.
8.   E. M. Yates, *Petersfield in Tudor Times* (1979).
9.   Parish Register.
10.   H.R.O. Consistory Court will dated 30 March 1566, and inventory dated 2 April 1566.
11.   H.R.O. Peculiar Court will dated 9 May 1569.
12.   H.R.O. Peculiar Court will dated 5 November 1569.
13.   H.R.O. Consistory Court will dated 1 September 1570, and inventory dated 16 March 1571.
14.   H.R.O. Consistory Court will dated 24 September 1571, and inventory dated 22 October 1571.
15.   Lindsay Boynton, *The Elizabethan Militia 1558-1638* (1967).
16.   Ibid.
17.   H.R.O. Pipe Roll 1558 51.
18.   H.R.O. Pipe Roll 1558 66.
19.   H.R.O. Pipe Roll 1558 89.
20.   H.R.O. Eccles. Court Roll 79/25.
21.   Ibid.
22.   Herriard Collection, deposited at H.R.O.—44 M 69.
23.   Boynton, op. cit.
24.   H.R.O. Consistory Court will dated 30 May 1598.
25.   Eccls. Court Rolls 1/144 f. 32.
26.   Eccls. Court Rolls 1/145 Roll 1 f. 4.
27.   Eccls. Court Rolls 1/145 Roll 2 f. 22.
28.   Eccls. Court Rolls 144 Roll 5 f. 18.

Chapter Four

1.   H.R.O. Consistory Court will dated 11 March 1605 and inventory dated 9 July 1607.
2.   Note in Parish Register at H.R.O.
3.   Parish Register.

4. Eccls. Court Rolls (fine book) 119/3.
5. Eccls. Court Rolls 151/1.
6. P.R.O. probate records, will of John Terrill, dated 20 Feb. 1626.
7. S. C. Carpenter, *The Church in England, 597-1688* (1954).
8. Ibid.
9. A. French, *Charles I and the Puritan Upheaval* (1955).
10. Herriard Collection, deposited at H.R.O.—44 M 69 XXV 7.
11. Herriard Collection, deposited at H.R.O.—44 M 69 XXVII 6.
12. John Adair, *Cheriton 1644; The Campaign and the Battle* (1973).
13. H. D. Gordon, *A History of Harting* (1877).
14. John Goldsmith, *Hambledon* (1971).
15. H.R.O. Consistory Court will dated 22 July 1643 and inventory dated 31 July 1643.
16. H.R.O. Consistory Court will dated 16 Nov. 1643 and inventory dated 28 Nov. 1643.
17. Gordon, op. cit.
18. Note dated Sept. 1912 written by Rev. T. H. Masters, former vicar of East Meon.
19. Kent Record Office, Military Papers, 1644.
20. Copy Parliamentary Survey of the Manor of East Meon, 1647, at H.R.O.
21. *V.C.H., Hampshire*, vol. III, p. 65, quoting court rolls.
22. Eccls. Court Rolls 158/3 f. 138.
23. P.R.O. Hearth Tax Assessment for East Meon Hundred, 1662.
24. W. G. Bell, *The Great Plague of London* (1924).
25. G. C. Williamson, *Trade Tokens Issued in the Seventeenth Century* (reprinted 1967).
26. James H. Thomas, *Petersfield under the Later Stuarts* (1980).
27. J. P. Kenyon, *Stuart England* (1978).

Chapter Five

1. N. L. Fyson, *Growing up in the 18th Century* (1977).
2. E. G. Thomas, 'The Old Poor Law and Medicine', *Medical History, Vol. 24, No. 1* (1980).
3. Ibid.
4. W. G. Hoskins, *The Making of the English Landscape* (1955).
5. H.R.O. 46 M 68—13.
6. H.R.O. 46 M 68—14.
7. W. W. Capes, *Scenes of Rural Life in Hampshire among the Manors of Bramshott* (1901).
8. Frances Collins, 'Westbury', in *West Meon, Hampshire—Some Chapters of its History* (1972).
9. Ibid.
10. East Sussex Record Office, SAS. G/HA 66/2.
11. Collins, op. cit.
12. Ibid.
13. East Sussex Record Office, SAS. G/HA 66/20.
14. *V.C.H., Hampshire*, vol. III.
15. Ibid.
16. East Meon Church Rate Book, H.R.O. 46 M 68—11.
17. Hugh Braun, *A Short History of English Architecture* (1950).

Chapter Six

1. N. L. Fyson, op. cit.
2. S. J. Curtis and M. E. A. Boultwood, *An Introductory History of English Education Since 1800* (1960).
3. H. C. Barnard, *A History of English Education from 1760* (1947).
4. Barnard, op. cit.
5. Edward Walford, *Old and New London* (c. 1875).
6. John Timbs, *Curiosities of London* (1867).
7. *White's History, Gazeteer and Directory of Hampshire* (1878).

8. *Post Office Directory of Hampshire* (1847).
9. *Minute Book of East Meon School Committee, 1848–1878.*
10. *East Meon School Treasurer's Accounts, 1846–78.*
11. S. J. Curtis and M. E. A. Boultwood, op. cit.
12. *Minute Book of East Meon School Committee, 1879–1900.*

Chapter Seven

1. T. Hennell, *Change in the Farm* (1934).
2. E. J. T. Collins, *Sickle to Combine* (1969).
3. Collins, op. cit.
4. *A Century of Agricultural Statistics—Great Britain, 1866-1966*, H.M.S.O., 1968.
5. Advice to author from the Chairman of The British Farm Produce Council.
6. ditto.
7. Milk Marketing Board records.
8. *The Times*, 1 January 1866.
9. Advice to author from Ministry of Agriculture (Animal Health Division).
10. Advice to author from the Chairman of the British Farm Produce Council.
11. ditto.

Chapter Eight

1. *V.C.H.*, vol. III.
2. Parish Register at H.R.O.
3. *Oxford English Dictionary.*
4. H.R.O. microfilm of 1851 Census at P.R.O.
5. *Kelly's Directory of Hampshire*, 1855.
6. East Meon Tithe Award, 1851, at H.R.O.
7. ditto.
8. *Kelly's Directory of Hampshire*, 1855.
9. J. G. Harrod and Co.'s *Directory of Hampshire*, 1865.
10. J. G. Ruffer, *The Big Shots* (1977).
11. J. Hurst, *Corhampton and Exton, Hampshire—some chapters of Their History* (1980).
12. *V.C.H.*, vol. V.
13. *Kelly's Directory of Hampshire*, 1875.
14. ditto, 1895.
15. Parish Council Minutes.
16. Parish Register in custody of the vicar.

Chapter Ten

1. Note by the Rev. T. H. Masters in East Meon Church Burial Register.
2. A. J. Barker, *The Neglected War* (1967).
3. David Lampe, *The Last Ditch* (1968).
4. Ibid.
5. Advice to the author from The Ministry of Defence, Naval Historical Branch.

Chapter Eleven

1. William Douglas Home, *Mr. Home Pronounced Hume* (1979).
2. J. Kunitz (ed.), *Twentieth Century Authors* (1955).
3. Ibid.
4. H.R.O. Consistory Court will dated 17 August 1517.
5. H.R.O. Archdeaconry Court will dated 12 February 1558.

6.   Eccls. Court Rolls 1/145 Roll 2 f. 22.
7.   Copy Parliamentary Survey of the Manor of East Meon, 1647, at P.R.O.
8.   H.R.O. Consistory Court will dated 8 September 1753.
9.   P.R.O. Assizes Gaol Book. ASSI 23/6.
10. N. L. Fyson, op. cit.
11. East Meon Church Rate Book, H.R.O. 46 M 68—11.
12. John Goldsmith, *Hambledon* (1971).
13. H.R.O. microfilm of 1851 Census at P.R.O.
14. James Arnold, *The Shell Book of Country Crafts* (1968).
15. Arthur Gill, *The Court House, East Meon*.

INDEX

LIST OF SUBSCRIBERS

Joan Aburrow
Nina Joyce Aburrow
Norman John Aburrow
Stephan John Aburrow
C. J. Allman
John Aston
M. J. Atkinson
E. W. Baigent
Lilian Mary Baker
A. W. Banham
Hazel Barber
Marie Barber
Annabel I. Barnes
Caroline Beatham
Deborah Beatham
Michael Beckett
Mrs. E. O. Bending
B. M. Biddlecombe
Brian Latham Peel Blacker
Alan Blackman
Freda & George Blackman
Michael & Tricia Blakstad
David Blowers
Peter E. Brain
Sir Basil Brickwood Bt.
Elizabeth Rose Broadway
C. J. & S. A. Brough
T. C. & B. J. Brough
Mr. & Mrs. A. A. Bull
Mr. & Mrs. Richard Burley
C. & D. Burridge
Surgeon Commander S. N. Bussell
D. J. Butler
E. R. Butler
John B. Butler
P. D. Butler
Mrs. E. M. Caines
M. Caines
The Captain, H.M.S. *Mercury*
Sir Richard Cave
Robert Cecil
James S. Challen
Derek A. Clarke
Alan & Stella Clifton
Daughne Stracey Clitherow
Christopher & Sara Cobley
Diana K. Coldicott
A. M. Collins
Albert John Cook
Jeanette & Malcolm Cooper
F. & B. Cutbush
Mr. & Mrs. C. H. Darby
Mr. & Mrs. B. H. Dicker
Winifred Dixon
C. Dowlen

Caroline Jane Dowlen
B. Dudman
Bill Dye
East Meon Primary School
J. Emptage
M. I. H. Ewing
Janet Fairbanks
J. L. Faithful
Mrs. G. E. Farmer
P. A. Fielder
T. V. Fielder
Reginald Files
C. & D. Fisher
Mrs. E. F. Fisher
The late Miss J. Fosberry
Neville Freeston
A. L. Fry
Hilary & Suzanne Fry
P. W. Gallup
Mr. & Mrs. R. A. Gard
David George Gibbs
C. H. J. Goatly
Herbert & Ellen Goddard
Dorothy & Edward Grainger
C. P. Gravett
Gay Gravett
Guy Gravett
Patricia Norma Green
Peter S. Groom
Cicely Winifred Gunn
Maureen Joan Gunn
E. Hammond
Hampshire Genealogical Society
C. & P. G. Harfield (nee Lambert)
A. Leslie Harris
Air Commodore W. N. Hibbert,
    R.A.F. (retired)
E. Hickox
H. L. Hiscock
David Hitchings
Gerald A. Hoare
Leslie C. G. Holden
Mr. & Mrs. John Holmes
Jeremy R. Hooker
Tim Hooker
V. R. Van Hooydonk
H. Mary Horn
Mr. & Mrs. David Hull
Anne M. Hunter
Rev. J. Hurst
The Hutchings family
Peter Hutchins
Hilary James
J. & M. Jeffreys
M. L. Jenkins

Peter Jenkins
William & Mary Johnstone
Rhona E. Jones
Stanley E. Jones
Audrey D. Kenny
George Kille
K. E. Kitcher
Sylvia P. Lake
Bridget J. L. Lambert
Douglas C. Lambert
Gwendoline Olive Lambert
Miss M. E. Lambert
Winnifred Kate Lambert
Doreen Lanham
Mrs. David Larke
Captain & Mrs. Geoffrey Lloyd
George Long
R. C. Low
Lilian R. Luff
Marjorie Lunt
John MacDonald
Rachel & John Mackinlay
D. O. Manning
Mrs. W. O. Manning
J. D. J. Marks
E. M. May
D. McGinn
Jacques Meon
T. J. Mercer
Mr. & Mrs. J. D. Mills
John Frewen Moor
G. W. Moorman
D. G. Mustchin
Sqn. Ldr. C. H. Newbury R.A.F.
    (retired)
Lt. Com. R. W. Paige, MBE, RN
Mr. & Mrs. D. G. Paine
Roger A. Parker
Cdr. & Mrs. Roger Parkes
Maud Parsons
I. M. Patrick
R. Patrick
Mr. & Mrs. A. V. Pelly
Ian Penney
Margaret Penney
Petersfield School
John S. Pile, BA
Michael D. Poland
David Porch
A. P. Powney
Christopher Powney, MBKS
Cdr. & Mrs. R. A. Preece
Jill Preston
S. L. Pritchard
M. C. & S. F. Purdue

Mary Ray
Eric Reed
Professor C. W. Rees
Juliet Rigden
Tora Robbins
E. Roberts
Lt. Col. K. A. B. Roberts
John S. Robottom
Joan & Keith Rockett
M. P. Roper
Mrs. L. F. Ross
O. W. Rowsell
R. E. Rowsell
John Rutter
Maureen Rutter
D. J. H. Ryder
A. E. Salwey
Isabel Sanderson

Terry & Janette Searle
R. Scivier
Pauline M. Shacklock
F. R. & D. G. Shillitoe
Peter Silk
Les & Wendy Sims
Joyce Smith
G. J. Spence, MA
Lt. Com. P. J. Stembridge, R.N.,
    H.M.S. *Mercury*
Jacqueline Stone
R. A. Stone
J. A. P. Street
S. J. Symes
A. M. Tabb
Anja Talbot-Ponsonby
Nigel E. C. Talbot-Ponsonby
Daniel Thomas

Rev. & Mrs J. N. Thomas
J. G. Tindell
The Tout family
D. T. A. Tucker, MASEE
Mr. & Mrs. E. B. Tyler
John E. Tyrrell, FRIBA
Mary Nonah Barclay Tyrrell
Francis Tyrwhitt-Drake
C. W. Veness
Nora Ventham
George P. Walker
Kurt & Joan Walther
Bob Warner
Mr. & Mrs. L. S. White & family
David & Lorelei Wilmot-Smith
C. H. Wood
C. E. Wren
Leal Wyatt

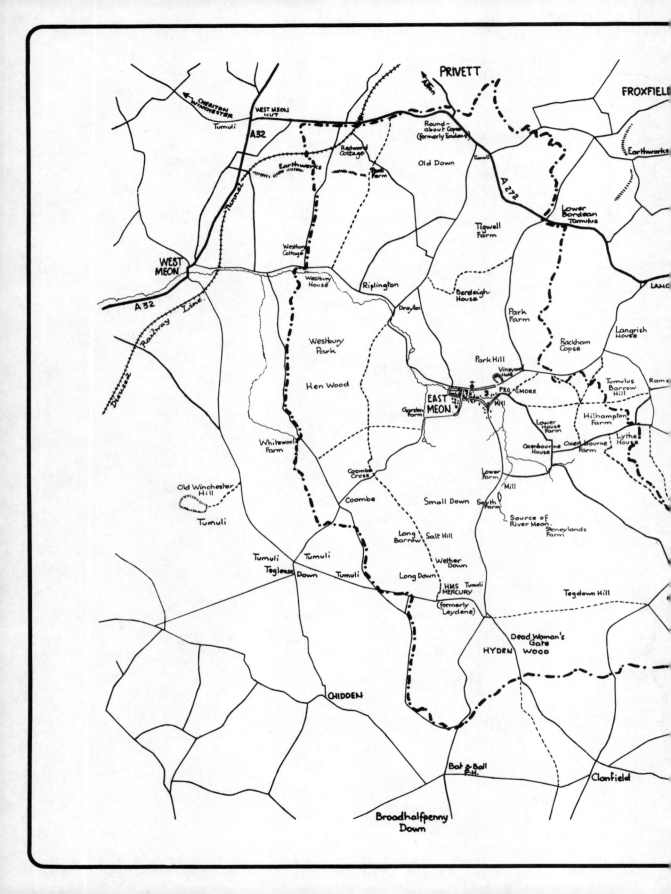